THOMAS BERRY IN ITALY
REFLECTIONS ON SPIRITUALITY & SUSTAINABILITY

Elisabeth M. Ferrero

Editor

PACEM IN TERRIS PRESS

www.paceminterrispress.com

Copyright © 2016 Elisabeth M. Ferrero

All rights reserved, except where otherwise noted.

ISBN-10: 0692616659
ISBN-13: 978-0692616559

Quotations from Thomas Berry's THE GREAT WORK
reprinted with kind permission from Random House

*Photographs by Elisabeth and Eugenia Ferrero
and Roberto Tagliaferri*

A peer-reviewed publication

*Opinions or claims expressed in publications
from Pacem in Terris Press represent the opinions and claims of the authors
and do not necessarily represent the official position of Pacem in Terris Press,
its sponsor, or of any officials of the Press or its sponsor.*

*Pacem in Terris Press
is the publishing service of the
Pacem in Terris Global Leadership Ecumenical Initiative
which is a project of*

PAX ROMANA / CMICA-USA
1025 Connecticut Avenue NW, Suite 1000
Washington DC 20036

*"In the immense story of the universe,
that so many of these dangerous moments
have been navigated successfully
is some indication that
the universe is for us rather than against us.
We need only summon those forces for our support
in order to succeed."*

THOMAS BERRY

"Opening Remarks"
Spirituality and Sustainability Conference
Assisi, 1991

TABLE OF CONTENTS

Acknowledgements   1

Introductions

1. Nature   5
   RASHMI MAYUR

2. Introducing Thomas Berry   7
   BRIAN SWIMME

3. Thomas Berry as Teacher, Scholar, & Mentor   11
   MARY EVELYN TUCKER

4. Remembering Thomas Berry   19
   ELISABETH M. FERRERO

5. An Ecologically Sensitive Spirituality   25
   THOMAS BERRY

Part I
Opening Reflections

6. Thomas Berry & Saint Thomas University   41
   FRANKLYN M. CASALE

7. Thomas Berry in Italy: Emergence of a Mythic Vision   43
   MIRIAM MacGILLIS

8. Thomas Berry in Italy: Relationship, Place, & Story   49
   GARY N. McCLOSKEY

9. Reflecting on Thomas' Legacy, the Assisi Experience,   55
   & the Way Forward
   RICHARD CLUGSTON

Part II
The Universe & the University

10. Thomas Berry to Higher Education: 61
    Lead Us on a Healthy, Just, & Sustainable Path Now
    ANTHONY CORTESE

11. Prescriptions from the Classroom   75
    ELISABETH M. FERRERO

12. Knowing Moments of Grace as Our Great Work   81
    in the Thought of Thomas Berry
    JOHN GRIM

13. Reflective Thinking About Place as Part of a   87
    Curriculum for Ecological Studies
    GARY N. McCLOSKEY

14. Endocrine Disrupting Chemicals Threaten   97
    Fetal Health
    FREDERICK S. von SAAL

Part III
Innovative Study-Abroad Programs
Centered on Thomas Berry's Cosmology

15. Imaging the Earth in San Francesco & Dante: 117
    Some Reflections with Tom Berry
    JAMES CONLEY

16. The Universe Story & the Earth Community: 137
    Reflections on Thomas Berry's Teaching in Assisi
    DREW DELLINGER

17. The Great Work Within: a Journey   149
    in Search of the Universe
    EUGENIA PIA FERRERO

18.	Sacred & Civic Engagement BÉATRICE COLASTIN SKOKAN	155
19.	An Assisi of the Mind STEVE SNIDER	161

Part IV
Sacredness & Interconnection with the Natural World

20.	Mystical Prophet for the Postmodern Global Ecological Era JOE HOLLAND	179
21.	Beyond the Bird Baths PETER DAMIAN MASSENGILL	191
22.	Earth at Risk Redux: Sustainability Grounded in Spirituality RODNEY L. PETERSEN	197
23.	Ecological Reflections in Theology ROBERTO TAGLIAFERRI	215

Part V
Economics & Sustainable Development

24.	GEN, GAIA Education and GAIA Economics as the New Story HILDUR JACKSON	223
25.	Can We Achieve Thomas Berry's Dream for our Earth? MARTIN S. KAPLAN	229
26.	Chicago Wilderness: New Allies for Urban Sustainability LAUREL M. ROSS	247

27. Is an Ecological Society still Believable? KARL-LUDWIG SCHIBEL	257
28. Sustainability & Emotional Education JACQUELINE WAGNER	273

Part VI
A New Global Ethic: The Earth Charter

29. The Earth Charter: an Ethical Framework of Spirituality and Sustainability RICHARD CLUGSTON	283
30. The Earth Charter as a New Global Ethic ELISABETH M. FERRERO & JOE HOLLAND	301
31. Tribal Link and the Sacred Map PAMELA KRAFT	315
32. "A Unique Community of Life" – The Earth Charter in Assisi. A German View in a Global Context FRANK MEYBERG	323

Concluding Poem

33. Carolina Prophet: Poem for Thomas Berry DREW DELLINGER	337

Appendices

Contributors	343
Letter from Thomas Berry	353
Photographs	359

ACKNOWLEDGEMENTS

I am indebted to a student from Saint Thomas University, Vanessa Navarro, for her important editorial assistance and expertise throughout the entire process of editing this manuscript.

Also, my deepest thanks to Dr. Jonathan Roach for all his invaluable help with THE CHICAGO MANUAL OF STYLE, 16th Edition, as well as to Dr. James ("*Cosimo*") Conley for reading many of the essays and for his precious insight.

A very special thanks to Dr. McGregor Smith for introducing me to Thomas Berry many, many years ago, and to Dr. Joseph Iannone for allowing my dreams at St. Thomas University to unfold.

I am especially grateful to my daughter, Eugenia, and to my friends whose support made everything seem worthwhile.

All my thanks to Dr. Joe Holland for making it possible for this book to come to life – together with all the colleagues, friends and former students in Assisi who contributed to this book on Thomas Berry.

And my gratitude for Tom's presence that continues to live magically in all our lives.

INTRODUCTIONS

1

NATURE

Rashmi Mayur

In Memoriam

O Mother!

Let me be your chilld

In all manifestations
And countless expressions.

O Majestic One!
Let me join in your
Endless voyages
To go beyond
The abyss of space.

O Glorious One!
Let me join
In your inexorable march
Just to fathom
The mystery of eternity.

O Eternal One!
Let me be devoured
In the womb of time
To be immortal.

O Dancer!
Let me join in your

Ceaseless dance
To experience madness

O Creator
Let me partake in
Your countless grand performances
Of the unfolding drama

O Dreamer!
Let me sleep with the night
And the stars
To be
In reverie.

O Enlightened One!
Let me know all
The secrets of existence
To liberate myself.

O Sun!
Let me
See a ray of light
To know truth.

O Singer!
Let me sing with you
To harmonize myself
With the music of life.

O Omnipotent!
Let me embrace you humbly
Just to express my
Reverence and love for you.

Assisi, July 1997

2

INTRODUCING THOMAS BERRY[1]

Brian Thomas Swimme

"I'm having coffee with Pythagoras."

The above words were my first attempt to identify Thomas Berry some three decades ago. The notion came to me right in the midst of our conversation in the Broadway Diner. Listening to him was to be transported into another domain of soul. It was not just that his knowledge was so vast. It was the evocative power of his presence. As you listened, you regularly found yourself in what is called an "altered state." Quite literally, Thomas' reflections on the nature of things catapulted one into the archetypal realms of classical myths and psychedelic dreams and the greatest philosophy and art. Everything became more real. You found yourself at the very center of the universe and you were given a vision of the inner harmony of things. Suddenly you knew exactly what you had to do with your life. As all of this was happening to me I thought of Pythagoras, that great sage of the ancient world whose spiritual impulse would develop into so much of western philosophy and science. I felt certain that the deep joy and wonder filling my soul were similar to what the students in Pythagoras' mystery school must have experienced twenty-six hundred years ago.

---

[1] Copyright © 2015 Brian Swimme

That I would identify Thomas Berry with a personality of the axial age -- other notables would include Heraclitus, Confucius, Lao Tzu, the Hebrew Prophets, and Siddhartha -- that I would dare to locate Thomas in that rarefied company is easily understood as the exaggerated enthusiasm that often accompanies an initial meeting with a great person. And indeed, as the years went by and I began speaking, teaching, and writing with Thomas, I got to know him more closely which inevitably altered my initial enthusiasm. But, as hard as this might be to believe, the alteration was in the other direction.

Over the decades of my association with him, I came to the conviction that Thomas Berry is not just similar to Pythagoras or to Confucius or to Lao Tzu. Amazing to say, he was someone who went beyond them in certain ways. He was, to my mind, a person in the very midst of giving birth to a new order of human beings, an order made possible by the great teachers of history, but an order that was, in crucial ways, not available in the forms of consciousness found in the various world religions. A new, planetary mode of human being was emerging, one that was rooted in classical spiritualities, but one that reached back into the shamanic worlds and carried forward into the modern scientific forms of understanding. The entire human journey was undergoing a seismic shift and Thomas was aware of this and of his role in this transformative process.

In future centuries, many volumes will be written on the nature of this change in the structure of human consciousness that Thomas Berry both pointed to and, in part, enacted. Future scholars will have knowledge we do not have. Where today we can only intuit darkly that the transformation amplified by Thomas will lead to a vibrant Earth Community, they will know the overall effects of Thomas's life as historical fact. But what they will not have is what many of the writers and readers of this volume have been given -- the actual, ineffable experience of having been in Thomas's presence. How they will burn with envy! To have actually had coffee with Thomas Berry! What amazing historic good fortune!

As an aid to these future scholars as they contemplate the significance of Thomas Berry, I would like to end by describing just one splinter of the form of consciousness Thomas awakened in us by his personal presence.

We all fell in love. With sunshine -- with the rising moon -- with the rainbow trout as they hover in the shadows of Chambers Creek. With everything. And certainly with each other. The awakenings took place in every imaginable event. While driving to New York City in his little Mazda. Or while sitting with some two dozen people in those uncomfortable plastic chairs of his Riverdale library while listening to a presentation. All of a sudden an energy would come sweeping into your body, filling every artery and bone until it could no longer be contained and just gushed out as radiance from our eyes. Everything, each person, would be exploding with beauty. You would find yourself simply overwhelmed with a desire to get married. With anyone nearby. Did I say with anyone? I meant with everyone. With the Great Red Oak sheltering the library. Even with the sky overhead. That's just the sort of idea that made perfect sense to the form of consciousness Thomas awakened. That you'd marry the sky -- that Sky would become your central devotion -- that you'd dedicate your entire life to praising its nourishing beauty until everyone fell in love with it just as deeply as you did.

3

THOMAS BERRY
AS TEACHER, SCHOLAR, AND MENTOR

MARY EVELYN TUCKER

Thomas' reflections on the need for a New Story arose from his remarkably rich life as a monk, scholar, teacher, lecturer and writer. His early contemplative life allowed him time for reading and thinking which he avidly sought, often reading into the depths of night. It was as if he was possessed to see and understand a larger vision for human-Earth flourishing in this most critical moment for the planet.

His scholarly life began upon completing his doctorate from Catholic University with a thesis on Giambattista Vico. Directly after that he went to study in China in 1948-1949. There he met Theodore de Bary who was to become a life-long friend and one of the most renowned Asian scholars in the West. Along with his wife, Fanny de Bary, they were among Thomas' earliest supporters. Many an evening at their home in Tappan NY, Thomas and Ted would discuss the spiritual dimensions of the Asian classics, especially Confucianism. Fanny shared Thomas' interest in Teilhard and always arranged delicate spring flowers at the annual Teilhard Association meetings. At Columbia University Ted established a groundbreaking Asian studies program highlighting the classical texts and history of India, China and Japan. With Thomas he founded an Oriental Thought and Religion Seminar at Columbia which continues into the present. It was a rich and sustaining friendship when few understood Thomas' keen interests in Asian religions and his fascination with the universe story that Teilhard had articulated.

Thomas began his teaching at Seton Hall University in New Jersey and then moved to St. John's University on Long Island. The Jesuit, Christopher Mooney, later invited him to come to Fordham to teach in the Theology department. There he founded and directed the History of Religions program for more than a dozen years before retiring from teaching in 1977. This was the only program of its kind at any Catholic University in North America. Regrettably, it did not endure beyond his tenure at Fordham. Yet many of his students continue to teach at universities across the United States and Canada.

Thomas was somewhat anomalous in Fordham's department of Theology. He was not a Jesuit and he was not a theologian. Instead, he was trained in western history and in the world's religions. Yet, he was a charismatic figure and an engaging speaker. Thus, the History of Religions section that he directed drew more students than any other program in the Theology department. Students came from around the country, some turning down admission to religious studies programs at Columbia or Yale to study with him.

This is where I first met Thomas in 1975 recently returning from Japan and keen to study the Asian religious traditions. I had been reading Thomas' Riverdale Papers for the two years I was in Japan, having been given them by Fanny de Bary before I left.

It was an exhilarating time at Riverdale and Fordham as we gathered to study with this brilliant thinker and incomparable mentor. We thrived on the challenges he presented to us: learn the textual language of at least one tradition, know the history of many, feel the bass notes of the spiritual wisdom of each tradition, and read widely in an interdisciplinary fashion so that the living context of a tradition might be opened up.

Thomas himself set a high bar for his students, having read widely in the world's religions and learning the languages needed to appreciate their ancient texts and commentaries. His library at the Riverdale Center for Religions Research reflected this passion for breadth and depth. The Center was a beautiful old Victorian house along the Hudson just outside New York City. We gathered there under the spreading limbs of a four hundred year old red oak and across from the 200 million year old rock cliffs of the Palisades. There for over twenty-five years friendships were formed, talks were held, and lasting memories were made.

Thomas had collected his library of some ten thousand books in this rambling house. In the large front room the Latin Church Fathers faced the Greek philosophers and the Chinese Classics, all in their original languages. The Sanskrit texts of the Hindu Classics were in the next room and he initiated many of us into the *Bhagavad Gita* in Sanskrit before we read the other Indian texts. Some of his students wrote dissertations that were translations of these texts with original interpretive commentaries.

Not only did his library hold the classical scriptures of the Asian and Abrahamic religions, but also ethnographies and studies of indigenous peoples. Upstairs overlooking the Hudson was the American Indian room, filled from floor to ceiling with books on the various tribes that populated the North American continent.

On the sun-porch we would join Thomas for lunch or dinner. Music such as Beethoven's Archduke Concerto was background for wide ranging conversations from the state of the world to the state of Sung China, Heian Japan, or Moghul India. His historical versatility and religious understanding were stunning.

Thomas' appreciation for the wisdom of the world's religions was legendary. Well before interreligious dialogue became a topic of inquiry and discussion, he was immersing himself in the texts and traditions of India, China, and Japan. He wrote a book on *Buddhism* and one on the *Religions of India*, both of which are still in print from Columbia University Press. He would remark, in light of the Vatican II document *Nostrum Aetate* that spoke of "rays of Truth" in the world's religions, that, indeed, they held not just rays but floods of illumination and truth.

Poetic, insightful, and playful, Thomas moved through diverse religious traditions with a profound empathetic feel for the pulse of their spiritual dynamics. We recall afternoons after class when a group of us would gather with him in the campus dining area or ratskellar. We would explore the Pali texts of Buddhism, the Sanskrit scriptures of Indian *dharma*, and the enigmatic turn of the hexagrams in the Chinese *Book of Changes* (*I Ching*).

More than once he guided us through a throwing of coins to build a hexagram from this classical text in response to a question. Rather than dwell on the divinatory dimension of the *I Ching*, however, he urged us on to deeper reflection on the poetic lines of the text. We still ponder the possibility in our driven, acquisitive world that, as one hexagram indicated, "the small get by" (*hsiao kuo*). Perhaps, he observed, we may even move toward a world where Fritz Schumacher's notion, "Small is Beautiful" may come to be realized.

While those graduate school days focused on historical and textual developments in the many religions, Thomas encouraged us also to explore the cosmology of religions. Under his guidance we related rituals, texts, teachings, and vast commentarial studies to the stories of creation and metaphysical speculation about the world as it was. We struggled to understand the history, anthropology, and sociology embedded in those stories. Thomas forged ahead articulating broad understandings of historical interactions and cultural relationships.

Gradually, we sensed some of his feel for cosmology as the ground for investigation of a depth level of human reflection on placement and orientation in the world. "With a story," he would say, "people can endure catastrophe. And with a story they can gather the energies to change their lot." For him the first place to look for story was in history. He began with Western history and later moved to Asian history. He was part of the early group of world historians seeking to define the contours of our human movement across the planet.

He mused that the West was in search of a comprehensive story and cited historians such as Oswald Spengler, Arnold Toynbee, Christopher Dawson, and Eric Vogelin to give nuance to his views. He drew on the philosopher of history, Giambattista Vico, stitching his arguments together with a Vicoesque sense of the sweeping ages of history -- both human and Earth. In Vico he found a mind that could roam amidst the large-scale dimensions of earlier eras and uncover a passageway into modernity. It was because of his remarkable grasp of world history that he could eventually make the transition into evolutionary history.

In his classes he would grope for a thought, searching for a word that could capture the transition between the great ages of evolutionary time. And, then, he would cough. That cough became emblematic for us of his searching for articulation -- looking for the words to move us forward into a new and deeper understanding of our historical moment. Gradually, Thomas connected his study of history and evolutionary cosmology to the environmental issues of our day. This came slowly, maturing like some fine wine that carries the texture and taste of soils, sun, grapes, air and aging.

Reaching into his own past he recalled his boyhood experience in North Carolina of a summer meadow filled with white lilies. This experience began to define his commitment to preserve and protect such beauty. Increasingly he spoke of a deep affectivity and authenticity imparted by Earth itself in its biodiversity. It was in the early 1980s that these ideas coalesced in his term "Ecozoic." This was his way of naming the terminal destruction of Cenozoic life in the industrial-technological bubble of consumer acquisitiveness. He observed that scientists were telling us that we were in the midst of an extinction period. Nothing this devastating had occurred since the dinosaurs went extinct 65 million years ago. But rather than leaving his audience in despair, his use of the term Ecozoic was to name that emerging period in which humans would recover their creative reorientation in the world.

Sensing his way, he drew increasingly on the thought of Pierre Teilhard de Chardin for insight into the story of our times, namely, the emerging, evolutionary universe. Teilhard provided a large-scale vision of humans as situated within the vast context of universe evolution. Teilhard had a profound sense of the unfolding of ever-greater complexity and consciousness in the arc of evolution from the molecular to the cellular to multi-cellular organisms to the explosion of life forms.

It was at this time in the early 1980s that he met Brian Swimme who came to the Riverdale Center for a year of study with Thomas. Coming from the Pacific Northwest and earning a doctorate in mathematical cosmology at the University of Oregon, Brian was the ideal partner for collaboration. Thomas' years of study of world history and religions flowed into conversation with Brian's comprehensive study of evolutionary history. From out of a decade long intense collaboration including research, lectures and conferences there emerged the jointly authored book, *The Universe Story*. This was the first time the history of evolution was told as a story in which humans have a critical role.

Rather than settling on Teilhard's insights, however, Thomas pushed beyond to explore the conjunction of cosmology and ecology.

While appreciating Teilhard he also critiqued his optimistic view of "Building the Earth" with new technologies and scientific discoveries. He balanced Teilhard's technological optimism with a strong dose of realism -- highlighting our current patterns of environmental degradation. He wanted us to see that in a geological instant we were extinguishing life -- species, ecosystems, rivers, wetlands. Our moment was as significant as the change implied in a geological era.

When flying back from an environmental conference in the Seychelle Islands, looking down over the Nile River at 30,000 feet, he realized that he was not a theologian simply studying Christian theology, but rather a "geologian." That is, he viewed himself as a human being who emerged out of eons of Earth's geological and biological evolution now reflecting on our world. This reflection was a way to reinvent the human at the species level.

It was due to the great inspiration of Thomas' comprehensive vision that Brian Swimme, John Grim, and I spent a decade creating the *Journey of the Universe* PBS film with a remarkable group of talented people. Complemented by a book and a series of Conversations, this *Journey of the Universe* trilogy is moving out in to North American culture and indeed in to the world with various translations. Without Thomas' immense erudition in history and religion and without his understanding the power of the story of evolution this project would not have emerged. He has called each of us to participate in the Great Work of our times, inspired by the new story and dynamized by human energies for the flourishing of life into the future.

4

REMEMBERING THOMAS BERRY

Elisabeth M. Ferrero

On June 18, 1991, twenty-one students traveled to Italy to spend six weeks participating in Saint Thomas University's new ecological study abroad program, *Study Abroad For Earth* (S.A.F.E.) in Assisi, the European environmental capital and the birthplace of Saint Francis. They came from colleges all over the United States and stayed at a local family-owned hotel in the heart of Assisi, *Posta Panoramic*, eating simple but delicious vegetarian meals, without air-conditioning but with breath-taking views of the Umbrian countryside. Many of the classes were held outside, amongst the millenary olive trees overlooking the valley that were so dear to Francis of Assisi.

Since the days of St. Francis and St. Clare, Assisi has been a *locus* of activities to promote an ecologically sensitive spirituality as well as the site of educational initiatives. However, S.A.F.E. was different from other environmental study abroad programs; it had the specific intent to embrace another bioregion's culture while studying environmental and social justice with top scholars in the humanities and the sciences from all over the globe. Moreover, its most unique feature was its Visiting Scholar, the Rev. Thomas Berry, since all the humanities and sciences courses were centered in his cosmology.

As an educator, I have always been keenly aware of the difficult task of bringing about a truly transformative education in the classroom. In the late 1980s, Dr. Joseph Iannone, Dean of Religious Studies at St. Thomas University, started a discernment process amongst faculty and students through a 'base community' concept. Thomas Berry's cosmology was at the center of our gatherings, with frequent visits by Dr. McGregor Smith, Director of the Environmental Center at Miami Dade College; Miriam MacGillis from Genesis Farms; and others. The resulting intellectual ferment changed many people's lives and work. *Healing the Earth* was conceived with important events open to the entire South Miami community. In October 1990, I knocked on Dean Iannone's office with a unique idea: a summer ecological study abroad program in Assisi, Italy, centered on Thomas Berry's cosmology. The following June, *Study Abroad for Earth* was underway in Assisi with Fr. Berry as the Visiting Scholar for the next seven years.

S.A.F.E. attracted numerous students from various colleges interested in Fr. Berry's work. The same students would return summer after summer. At St. Thomas University the students who had participated in the Assisi program engaged regularly with other students to discuss what they had learned and many included an ecological component to their major. The synergy that Thomas Berry created was contagious among all participants. Each summer Berry was flanked by eminent scholars in the humanities and sciences. One of the highlights in 1993 was the presence of Dr. Brian Swimme who came to Assisi with his entire family and often taught his classes in the fields surrounding San Damiano. One day he asked each of his students to get close to one of the millenary trees growing there and to feel its energy. It was an amazing sight to see thirty-five young adults quietly and deeply connected to all those olive trees! Other prominent scholars and professors who taught in the Program were Drs. Enzo Cannata; James Conley; Joe Holland; Rupert Sheldrake;

Fred vom Saal; and Jill Pierce; Miriam MacGillis, as well as many, many others.

In the Spring of 1992 Saint Thomas University, mostly because of the uniqueness of the S.A.F.E. program, received a prestigious environmental award from the Rodale Foundation, Washington D.C., for "The University in the Ecological Age." Saint Thomas University was selected from over 1600 institutions, in recognition of its innovative environmental projects to serve as environmental models.

In 1995, while S.A.F.E. was underway in Assisi, Saint Thomas University and the Center for Respect of Life and Environment of the Humane Society of the United States, co-sponsored six yearly summer *Spirituality and Sustainability* Conferences in Assisi with The Archdiocese of Assisi; The Assisi Nature Council; The City of Assisi; The Gaia Trust and The International Franciscan Center For Dialogue, Commission for Justice, Peace and the Safeguarding of Creation.

Eminent leaders from various fields once a year participated in a week-long series of intensive conferences. Moral questions, as they related to a sustainable future, such as international relations, medical and legal ethics, justice and equity, education and so forth were researched and discussed in a participatory format with the goal of implementing these transformative changes in one's life and work.

One of the important outcomes of having both the S.A.F.E. program and the Conferences running alongside was the incredible synergy produced; students and scholars alike participated in the many presentations and interfaced with one another often resulting in life-changing transformation. The primary purpose of these conferences was to identify and celebrate developments in religion, economics, science, educations, politics and the arts to promote eco-justice and sustainability.

Thomas Berry was the keynote speaker of the *Spirituality & Sustainability* Conferences while the presenters and participants were from the humanities and the sciences, NGOs, and religious groups who returned summer after summer. Some of the most eminent presenters were Rev. John Brinkman, Rev. Gary McCloskey, Drs. Tony Cortese, Richard Clugston, John Grim, Steven Rockefeller, Karl-Ludwig Schibel, Mary Evelyn Tucker, and Mirian Vilela.

The presence of Fr. Berry in Assisi was not just the focal point of intellectual dialogue within the study abroad programs and the conferences, for the entire city participated in the extraordinary events taking place during the summer months. The owners of the shops around the fountain in Assisi's main square would wait impatiently for *Padre* Berry's presence and open smile. The *Posta Panoramic*'s cook would always think of new treats to prepare him. At sunset, as the colors of the sky take on muted and splendid shades in Assisi's *piazza*, at one of the coffee-shop-outside tables, the one closest to the florist shop, observers would find Thomas Berry and a large circle of students, colleagues, friends from Assisi and abroad all around him. More than once someone had to go and fetch him letting him know that dinner was getting cold.

Fr. Berry loved children. In Assisi, a few participants came with their young children. He spoke to them with the gentleness and kindness of a child himself, and the children flocked to him; at meals they all wanted to sit right next to him, and during his presentations they quietly sat mesmerized by his presence.

This is a book whose main objective is to commemorate the 100th Anniversary of Fr. Thomas Berry's Birth through the words, emotions and memories of former participants of the Study Abroad for Earth (S.A.F.E.) study program as well as the *Spirituality & Sustainability* conferences where Fr. Berry was both visiting professor and keynote speaker. The rationale for doing this book almost twenty years after the study abroad programs and the conferences was to allow time to unfold in the participants' lives and to try to understand the impact that Fr. Berry's presence and his ideas had on them. The underlying assumption is that a special kind of energy was created during those summers in Assisi with Fr. Berry in the 1990s. The book's intent was for the participants to look back and to ask themselves what recollections and interactions in Assisi seemed to have been important in their transformation on a personal level and in one's profession. Many of the former students in the S.A.F.E. programs now hold leadership positions in their community while all participants' lives and careers were transformed partly due to the encounters with Fr. Berry, either in the formal discussions in the auditorium/classroom or/and informally in the *piazza* of Assisi over *espresso* or *gelato*.

I had the good fortune to be present with Tom Berry at the S.A.F.E programs as well as the *Spirituality and Sustainability* conferences in Assisi during all those summers. It is my fervent hope that this will be a portrait of Fr. Berry hardly found in the many books written by him or/and about him; a portrait depicted through the eyes and hearts of those students whom he mentored as well as the colleagues with whom he interfaced; a portrait of the incredible humanity and passion which he shared with every single human and non-human life alike.

5

AN ECOLOGICALLY
SENSITIVE SPIRITUALITY

Spirituality and Sustainability Conference
Assisi, 1996

THOMAS BERRY

(Reprinted here with permission and in memoriam)

Here we are in Umbria, on the western slope of the Apennines, bathed in the soft summer light of this region such as was experienced by Giotto and the Umbrian school of painters. What we see now is of course only a remnant of the scene experienced by St. Francis and his early companions. The quiet lanes have been replaced by paved roads, the donkey-drawn carts of these earlier times have been replaced by automobiles. We feel an intimacy with these earlier times. But we also breathe an atmosphere less refreshing. A crowded world has emerged on the scene. The beginning of the modem commercial world that St. Francis perceived with a certain foreboding in the opening years of the 13th century has developed into the industrial centers of the late 20th century. The consequent assault on the natural world is leading to a certain anxiety concerning the future course of human affairs.

It is appropriate then for us to come here for a few days of thoughtful brooding over the decisions we must make in these terminal years of the 20th century and the opening years of the 21st century; for the period of Saint Francis, the opening years of the 13th century, was the period when our present world began to take shape. This time of high spiritual accomplishment of the European world was precisely the time when the commercial spirit entered into the western soul. The cities of Europe were reborn in these years after their long period of decline following the dissolution of Roman order in the 6th century. The Hanseatic League of commercial cities in central Europe was formed in the 13th century. Venice had begun its commercial empire during the period of the crusades from 1095 until 1291.

All of this culminated in the 15th and 16th century overseas ventures of the seacoast peoples of Europe, ventures leading to the discovery of America. With this discovery, the European dominance of the entire planet was begun. It seems appropriate then to speak somewhat concerning the European occupation of the North American continent, for this was in some sense the most momentous deed carried out in these years of discovery.

The historical role of America is especially significant as something of a parable of the larger human process; for when that first tiny mast of a European ship appeared over the Atlantic horizon every living being on the American continent might have shuddered with foreboding at what awaited it. These peoples from across the sea might have come to join the great community of life on this distant continent. They might have responded to the spiritual grandeur of the forests, the rivers and the woodland creatures, to the mountains and valleys, with the reverence and wonder that were appropriate. They might have learned something of the spirituality appropriate to this land from the native peoples here.

The difficulty was that these people from across the sea thought they already knew everything that they needed to know. They brought with them a Book as their primary referent as regards reality and value. This Book, I would say, while recognizing its vast spiritual significance, has caused endless difficulty not only in America but eventually in the larger community of all the living and non-living components of the great community that constitute the planet Earth; for, validly or invalidly, it has served to block the spiritual understanding communicated to humans in the world of natural phenomena.[2]

The North American continent was ready to communicate a profound spirituality to the incoming peoples. In the magnificence of its natural splendor, in the grandeur of its forests, in the beauty of its rivers, in the abundance and variety of its wildlife, this continent still had something of its primordial vigor, something of the innocence that older civilizations had lost long ago. In all these ways, it was a more immediate manifestation of the divine than the incoming peoples had experienced for centuries.

Yet to have responded in any worthy manner to this all-pervasive presence of the spiritual world would have been considered as heretical, as unworthy of a people accustomed to experience the spiritual order of things in terms of the biblical world. This incapacity to enter into any significant rapport with the primordial world, we might consider as the deep source of our present problems of spirit-

---

[2] *EDITORIAL COMMENT. Thomas Berry refers here to the book of the Christian Bible, which many European and American Christians have read in terms of "sola scriptura" (Scripture alone). But that contradicts the ancient Christian teaching of Saint Augustine of Hippo, that God gave us two books of revelation, the first being the "Book of Nature" and the second being the "Book of the Bible." For an authentic Christian reading, the Book of Nature can be read only against the horizon of the Book of Nature, which is the chronologically primary Divine revelation. Again, reading the Book of the Bible without simultaneously reading its companion volume The Book of Nature, does not seem authentically Christian.*

uality and sustainability. Because the spiritual dimension of this continent could not be responded to in any adequate manner there was no proper reverence for the continent to mitigate the exploitation of the immense wealth that was available here.

This alienation was further strengthened by the humanistic formation of western civilization which fostered the exaltation of the human throughout its education program. Both the spiritual and the humanist dimensions of the western tradition had only minimal concern for the natural world. Education that should be orientated toward deepening the intimacy of the human inhabitants with the larger earth community and the comprehensive universe community was turned away toward the self-appreciation of the human and the exploitation of the nonhuman.

This attitude was further strengthened by the Newtonian cosmology set forth in 1687. After the material explanation of the universe given there, the natural world could no longer carry any significant spiritual significance. Everything was explained as a world of objects to be manipulated for the benefit of the human. Already in the first part of the 17th century, Descartes had effectively killed the life systems of the planet by his division of the universe into mind and matter. What was not mind was mechanism.

With this background, it is little wonder then that when they arrived in America the incoming peoples had no deep feeling for the natural world; they had none of the reverence or even aesthetic appreciation due to the continent. Above all they had no awareness that humans form a single integral community with the other components of the continent, with the planet Earth and ultimately with the universe.

The non-human world could be seen only as a collection of objects to be exploited not as subjects to be communed with. This exploitation we have carried out in these past four centuries with such a passion that the devastation has flowed over into the larger dimensions of the planet, until now we are at a planet-wide impasse as regards human consumption and Earth limits. These two are on a collision course. What is not limited is our understanding, aesthetic appreciation and spiritual celebration of the Earth. We do need endless progress; not however in material development. Only such trans-material advance in aesthetic appreciation and spiritual experience can be without limits. Advance in material possession and use is severely limited.

Our universal need at the present time is a reorientation of the human venture toward such intimate experience of the world around us. If we would go back to our primary experience of any natural phenomena we would recognize that immediately on seeing the stars splashed across the heavens at night, on looking out over the ocean at dawn, on seeing the brilliant autumn colors of the oaks and maples and poplars in autumn, on hearing a mockingbird sing in the evening, or breathing the fragrance of the honeysuckle while journeying through a southern lowland; our immediate response to any of these experiences or parallel experiences on other continents, is a moment of something akin to ecstasy. There is wonder and reverence and inner fulfillment in some overwhelming mystery. We experience a vast new dimension to our own existence.

A return to a mystique of the Earth is, I would say, a primary requirement if we are ever going to establish a viable rapport between humans and the Earth. Only in this context will we overcome the arrogance that sets us apart from all other components of the planet and establishes a mood of conquest rather than of admiration. To assume that conquest and use is our primary relation with the natural world is ultimate disaster.

We have an absolute need of the natural world for activation of our inner world. To lessen the grandeur of the outer world is to limit the fulfillment available to our inner world. For the stars in the night sky over our cities to be so blocked from view by the particle and light pollution is not simply a loss of a passing visual experience, it is a loss of soul. This is a special loss for children. For it is from the stars, the planets and the moon in the heavens as well as from the flowers and birds and forests and woodland creatures of earth that some of the more profound inner experiences take place in children. To devastate any aspect of the natural world is to distort the more sublime experiences that provide ultimate fulfillment to the human mode of being.

We need to move from a spirituality of alienation from the natural world to spirituality of intimacy with the natural world, from a spirituality of the divine as revealed in verbal revelation to a spirituality of the divine as revealed in the visible world about us. From spirituality concerned with justice merely to humans to a spirituality of justice to the devastated Earth community. From the spirituality of the prophet to the spirituality of the shaman. The sacred community must now be considered the integral community of the entire universe, more immediately the integral community of the planet Earth.

Our western Christian-humanist world has come to a period of the reversal of values. We live in a time when the saving of humans can only be achieved by saving the natural world upon which humans depend for both their psychic and physical survival. While we have already outlined the basic psychic need that we have for the natural world, we need also to mention our need for water and air and nourishment and shelter and a sense of security in the presence of the grand complex of living and non-living forces that make up the integral community of life.

The pervasive flaw in western civilization is the attitude that only the human is capable of moral and legal rights. The attitude that the non-human world has its primary purpose and its primary value in its use by the human. This attitude more than any other single cause has brought about the devastation of the natural world by its human component.

In reality, every being has three basic rights: the right to be, the right to habitat, and the right to fulfill its role in the great community of existence. Negatively every being has rights not to be abused by humans, not to be despoiled of its primary dignity whereby it gives some manner of expression to the great mystery of existence, the right not to be used for trivial purposes.

To bring about recognition of this new sense of our human role in relation to the natural world, we need a radical transformation throughout the entire human venture. The dynamics of the industrial-commercial-financial empires of these times is driving the Earth into a termination of the Cenozoic period in the geo-biological story of the planet. This period, the Cenozoic, the last 65 million years of life development, has been the culmination of the most brilliant phase of life expansion on the planet. Only at the end of this period, when the planet was at its most gorgeous expression, was the time appropriate for humans to appear. For only in a world of such magnificence could the human mode of being be fully developed, only then could the divine be properly manifested, only in such a world could the burden of human sensitivity and responsibility be sustained, the human condition be endured, and the constant healing needed by the human soul be communicated.

This magnificence was rejected by the settlers of the North American continent and later throughout the planet with all the industrial development that has taken place. During this time the spiritual and intellectual guides of our western tradition have shown themselves to be inadequate to their task, however adequate they have been in past. A new type of spiritual guide is needed. At one time, it was the Benedictine monks who by their patterns of cultivating the soil and by their intellectual work in copying and explaining the great intellectual works of the past established themselves as the guides for our western endeavor. Later in the medieval period when the cities of Europe were reestablished after the dark ages, it was the new spirituality of the cathedral builders, the universities, the mendicant friars who guided the course of human affairs. Later in the 18th century came the political and social Reformers who brought about a new sense of nation identity, and also a new sense of the people as competent to determine their own destiny.

Toward the end of the 19th century came the research scientists, the technologists, the engineers, but above all the corporations as the controlling persons and institutions guiding the course of human affairs. These last mentioned are the persons and the institutions determined to lead humans into a new golden age through technological exploitation of the planet and its resources. The corporations, supported by the dominant political forces, were determined to take control of the planet in its every aspect. This effort at control has led to our present impasse in human -earth relations. But especially it has led to the radical dysfunction of the planet in all its major life systems.

Throughout this modem period, the earlier spiritual types have themselves been incompetent in providing guidance. They failed to recognize that the basic issue is not simply divine-human or inter-human relations but our human relations with the larger community of the planet Earth and beyond that with that comprehensive community of the entire universe, the ultimate sacred community. This failure has led to the plundering of the planet by good persons, even deeply religious persons, for the supposed temporal and spiritual benefit of the human. This plundering of the planet to serve human purposes is what must change. The industrial movement with its ideal of subjection of the planet must give way to the ecological movement toward supporting the integral functioning of both the human and non-human components of the planet in a single integral community.

This we might say requires a new spirituality. No longer can we identify the guiding person of our society primarily with the prophet or priest or saint, with the guru, the yogi, the Buddhist monk, the Chinese Sage, the Greek philosopher, or the modem scientist. Each of these types and their teachings are immensely important in their own proper field of functioning, Yet they might all be considered deficient as guides to the human process in its rapport with the natural life systems of the planet in these times. We now have a new understanding of the universe, how it came into being and the sequence of transformations through which it has passed. This new story of the universe is now our sacred story. None of the traditional spiritual guides seem able to accept this new understanding as a revelatory experience. Only an ecologically sensitive personality can do this. The traditional spiritual ties in all their various cultural manifestations seem to have reverted back to neo-fundamentalist attitudes.

An ecological spirituality seems to be indicated. The integral ecologist is the type of spiritual guide that is needed. While we can expect this type to be realized in only a partial and inadequate manner in any individual, we can say that this is the spiritual type that is needed. We can also say that, just as the spiritual ideal of former ages was realized in an unlimited variety of individual realizations, and rarely in any striking manner sufficient to become a referent for imitation by others, so too with the ecologists as a guiding personality for these times, it is the type that establishes the basic referent; for the great spiritual mission of the present is a renewal of the entire western religious-spiritual tradition in relation to the integral functioning of the bio systems of the planet.

Until recently there has been a feeling in the spiritual formation of the western personality that spiritual persons were not concerned with any detailed understanding of the biological order of the Earth. The spiritual person was in some manner abstracted from concern with the physical order of reality in favor of the interior life of the soul. If attention was given to the physical order this was simply in the service of the inner world. The natural world had no inherent spiritual dimension; it was not an integral part of the larger spiritual reality. This neglect of attention to the natural world permitted those concerned with the more material things of life to take possession of the land and the wealth of the planet. It permitted the exploitation of the entire natural world for human gain and the ultimate ruin of the planet.

The integral ecologist, as the type needed, can now be considered as the normative guiding personality of our times. The saint of former times would be spiritually deficient in these times. The integral ecologist would understand the spiritual aspect of an emergent universe from the beginning. The sequence of transformation moments of the universe would be understood as cosmological moments of grace to be celebrated religiously with special rituals. But above all, these moments would appear as revelatory of the ultimate mystery of the universe itself.

The Ecologist is the spokesperson for the planet in both its spiritual and its physical meaning, just as the prophet was the spokesperson for deity, as the yogi is the spokesperson for the interior spirit, as the saint is the spokesperson for Christian faith. In the ecologist, our scientific understanding of the universe becomes wisdom. For we can finally appreciate that our new understanding of an emergent universe that comes into being through a sequence of irreversible transformation has a revelatory dimension. This new understanding of the universe establishes a new horizon under which all the traditions will henceforth need to function in their integral mode of self-understanding.

This issue of our human disturbance of the most basic life systems of the planet Earth is such that from here on, for an indefinite period, the main difference between human beings will not be the difference of conservative or liberal, based on social or cultural orientation, as has been a primary difference of humans in the western world throughout the 20th century; it will rather be the difference between the entrepreneur and the ecologist, the difference between those who exploit the planet in a deleterious manner and those who sustain the planet in its integral functioning. This difference will provide not only the public identity of individuals; it will also be a primary designation in all the professions; in law, in medicine, education, religion, politics or whatever. The prefix "eco" will occur in a multitude of words that will refer to the coherence on any thought or deed or institution with the integral life systems of the planet.

The seriousness of the situation we are discussing here can hardly be exaggerated for it is the issue of life and death, not for human individuals, or for the human community; it is rather the issue of survival of the most gorgeous expression that the ultimate mystery of the universe has given of itself, as far as we know. In designing a program that can adequately deal with the issue we need to be concerned with Principles, Strategy and Tactics.

Tactics involves ten thousand things such as recycling materials, limiting our use of energy, composting, conserving water supplies, insulating our buildings, and a multitude of adaptations of a similar nature.

Then there is the question of Strategies. This would involve teaching children about the natural world and how living systems function and how humans fit into these systems. This might also involve dealing with corporation enterprises to have them control their emissions from industrial production. It might also involve city planning boards that determine the use of land in a given territory.

One of the most significant strategies would be concerned with the universities. The universities need to understand that Ecology is not a course, it is not a program; it is rather the foundation of all courses, all programs, all professions -- because Ecology is a Functional Cosmology and the Universe or the Cosmos is the only self-referent mode of being in the phenomenal world. Every other being is universe-referent. Cosmology or the Universe Story is the implicit basis of every particular course or program.

Beyond these is the question of Principles governing the course of human actions. This is what we have been dealing with here in this presentation. We are involved in a deep cultural pathology. What is most needed – in addition to the new technologies for integrating our human needs with solar energy and with the organic functioning of the life systems of the planet – is a deep cultural therapy that will identify the sources of our pathology and provide a way of returning to the jubilant life expression that should characterize any human mode of being.

I am proposing that the most fundamental source of our pathology is establishing a discontinuity between the non-human and the human and giving all the inherent values and all the rights to the human. The only inherent value recognized in the non-human is its use by the human. By this discontinuity between the human and the non-human we break the great covenant of the universe, the covenant whereby every being exists and has its value in relation to the great universe community. Nothing bestows existence on itself. Nothing survives by itself. Nothing is fulfilled in itself. Nothing has existence or meaning or fulfillment except in union with the larger community of existence.

As Saint Thomas Aquinas saw so clearly, "The integrity of the universe is the ultimate and noblest perfection in things" (*Summa Contra Gentiles*, II, 46). In the phenomenal world, only the universe is self-referent. Every being in the universe is universe-referent. Only the universe is a text without a context. Every other being has the universe for context. To challenge this basic principle by trying to establish the human as self-referent and other beings as human-referent in their primary value subverts the most basic principle of the universe.

Once we accept that we exist as a component member of this larger community of existence then we can begin to act in a more appropriate human way. We might even enter once again into that great celebration, the universe itself.

REFERENCES

Aquinas, Thomas. 1955. *Summa Contra Gentiles*. Translated by Anton C. Pegis. Notre Dame, IN: University of Notre Dame Press.

PART I
OPENING REFLECTIONS

6

THOMAS BERRY &
SAINT THOMAS UNIVERSITY

REV. MSGR. FRANKLYN M. CASALE

Saint Thomas University is fortunate to have called the late Father Thomas Berry a friend. A Passionist priest and a passionate teacher whose dedication to the environment was unmatched, Tom Berry left his mark on our University in several ways.

On our campus in Miami Gardens, Florida, Tom Berry's presence was felt throughout the 1990s, during which time he was frequently featured as the keynote speaker at the University's numerous symposia and conferences focusing on spirituality and sustainability. In 1992, his symposium entitled "Healing the Earth is Good Business" was attended by the entire University community as well as many members of the South Florida community. In 1994, St. Thomas University recognized Tom Berry for his life's work by awarding him an honorary doctorate, *honoris causa*.

Fr. Tom also served as a visiting professor in St. Thomas University's summer abroad programs in Ecuador and Italy. He mentored students from around the world, and taught these students to appreciate the Earth and all her resources. Many of Tom's former students have inherited from him his same passion for the environment, and today they represent the next leaders in the field of human and environmental sustainability.

Tom Berry always believed that higher education had a distinct and profound role in society. Any discussion about the environment and human ecology needed to begin in the university, the primordial setting being its law school, as he once told me. Indeed, in his own book, *The Great Work: Our Way into the Future*, Berry wrote,

> *Of the institutions that should be guiding us into a viable future, the university has a special place because it teaches all those professions that control the human endeavor.* (Berry 1999)

Tom Berry would be pleased to know that St. Thomas University is doing its part to live up to this important responsibility. Our law school currently offers an LL.M. degree in environmental sustainability, providing graduates a strong foundation in environmental sustainability and natural resource laws, and preparing them to be advocates for the environment – so that they may continue "the great work" of Tom Berry.

REFERENCES

Berry, Thomas. 1999. *The Great Work: Our Way into the Future*. New York, NY: Bell Tower.

7

THOMAS BERRY IN ITALY
EMERGENCE OF A MYTHIC VISION

Miriam MacGillis O.P.

"We are now experiencing a moment of significance far beyond what any of us can imagine. What can be said is that the foundations of a new historical period, the Ecozoic Era, have been established in every realm of human affairs. The mythic vision has been set into place ... the dream drives the action. In the larger cultural context the dream becomes the myth that both guides and drives the action." (Berry 2009).

Whether it gathered us with political, business or religious leaders in the chambers of its historic city hall, or with students in the formal classrooms of the Franciscan monastery, or in the open-air cafes of its piazza, the Umbrian town of Assisi lavished us with a unique setting for the emergence of a *mythic vision*. The vision arose from the excited conversations among students and pilgrims, old and young. It settled into exchanges around evening dinner in the family *pensione* which hosted us. It rose from the steamy cobblestones and winding narrow streets where the concert music of visiting groups from all over Europe filled the evening air along with the chatter of families and children, the comings and goings of cyclists, pilgrims and tourists.

A *mythic vision* was indeed forming in this small but potent opening created through a study program in Assisi by St. Thomas University, an American liberal arts university in Miami, Florida. It was mythic because it was committed to bringing together the best of its two traditions: its intellectual search for truth and its religious commitment to meaning, in a world ripped apart by ecological devastation, human injustice and savage wars.

It was also a rare opening in time. The *Study Abroad for Earth* program created by Professor Elisabeth Ferrero with *confreres* from a diversity of disciplines at St. Thomas University had drawn together a growing network of scholars, scientists, ecologists and individuals from all walks of life. They had journeyed to Assisi to engage with one of the most significant thinkers of the twentieth century, cultural historian and author, Thomas Berry.

Miami had become a seedbed for the perspectives of Thomas Berry. The seeds were planted in the late 1980s, by Dr. McGregor Smith, innovative creator of a New Literacy Program at Miami-Dade College. His commitment to bringing greater exposure to Thomas Berry resulted in a network of educators desiring to bring Berry's thought, especially as expressed in his classic work, *The Dream of the Earth*, into curriculum materials for students and faculty alike. *The Earth Literacy Communion* was a pioneering expression of this vision. It sought to bring new cosmological foundations to the context of higher education.

Thus, a small, unpretentious effort born in south Florida wrought collaboration between Miami-Dade College and St. Thomas University. But it took further visionary efforts of even more creative faculty and administrators to press for academic accreditation. With that achieved, and with a growing cohort of colleagues, courses in Earth Literacy were born. When Thomas Berry and mathematical cosmologist, Brian Swimme, published *The Universe Story* in 1992, a seminal scholarly text became available. New graduate courses were designed. And because the narrative history of the Universe was told as a spiritual as well as a physical evolutionary story, a *mythic vision* became possible for a generation of students hungry for meaning and for reasons to hope.

When S.A.F.E., *Study Abroad For Earth,* proposed the Assisi program with Thomas Berry coming to teach, it drew an enthusiastic response, not only from seekers of the heritage of the 'poor man of Assisi.' But to this modest, soft-spoken scholar who perhaps more than any other twentieth century Christian thinker had ignited a mythic vision of hope that could give scientific and practical substance to the mystical communion Francis felt for the natural world, some would say the "mystique of Francis of Assisi entered its cosmological phase," strengthened by contemporary scientific insights into the evolutionary nature of the Universe and by rigorous ecological ethics and practices that would challenge the inadequacy of earlier models of biblical stewardship.

So many moments, conversations and meetings fill my memories of the program . . . and the insights shared by Thomas Berry. He was so accessible to everyone. But in formal and informal settings, his message was uncompromising in its challenge to face into the enormity of the problems the planet was experiencing due to human activity. He focused on the inability of the four major western institutions to correct these activities in their devotion to economic growth. All four, the governmental, the educational, the economic and the religious seemed powerless to stem the tide of plundering every aspect of the living planet.

Here we were, then, gathered in Assisi representing two of these institutions: the educational and the religious. It provided a rare, historic opening for each of them to transform themselves at the level of their cosmological foundations. So much progress had been made. St. Thomas University was at the cutting edge.

I remember a very poignant session where a young student, obviously disillusioned by the state of the world, was equally challenged by Thomas not to settle for any easy answers or cosmetic fixes. He turned his frustration toward Thomas, attempting to discredit him as he was describing the ecological realities which were threatening the future. He was visibly shaken and angry. Thomas paused and spoke quietly but with a deliberate boldness rare for him. "This is hard stuff." he said. The student and the rest of us all fell into silence. Maybe we were all feeling that our escape routes into denial were shutting down, were closed off. We had to make choices. Some of us for our institutions, religious or academic. All of us for our personal lives and values.

There was one door still open. It was the consideration that a new cosmological story was providing light into the future from a small, darkened passage. This idea would take courage, determination, vision and imagination to nurture. It would ask much of us and give much in return.

On many occasions in his life Thomas would ask, "Are you enabling people to *survive* in the terminal phase of the Cenozoic era, or are you enabling them to *thrive* in an emerging Ecozoic Era?" The responses to these questions are very different. And they elicit different dreams. And, he would say, "the dream drives the action" (Berry 1999, 172). We might add, it also drives the curriculum or the educational philosophy. In his concluding chapter "Moments of Grace" in *The Great Work* he reminds us,

> *But even as we make our transition into this new century we must note that moments of grace are transient moments. The transformation must take place within a brief period. Other-wise it is gone forever. In the immense story of the universe, that so many of these dangerous moments have been navigated successfully is some indication that the universe is for us rather than against us. We need only summon these forces to our support in*

> *order to succeed. It is difficult to believe that the purposes of the universe or of the planet Earth will ultimately be thwarted, although the human challenge to these purposes must never be underestimated.* (Berry 1999, 201)

As you read the stories and testimonies of the authors who share their perspectives on Thomas Berry, the significance he played in the history of St. Thomas University and the *Study Abroad For Earth* program, you may sense how they were "summoning the forces of the Universe" in those brief and transient moments of grace.

REFERENCES

Berry, Thomas. 1999. *The Great Work: Our Way into the Future*. New York, NY: Bell Tower.

8

THOMAS BERRY IN ITALY
RELATIONSHIP, STORY AND PLACE

GARY N. MCCLOSKEY O.S.A.

When Professor Elisabetta Ferrero asked me to write a preface for *Thomas Berry in Italy*, I was filled with a rush of pleasant memories of relationships, stories and places. As I have reflected on these memories, they reminded me that dialoguing with Thomas Berry was always about reflection, relationship, story and grounding in place. Thomas' impact at Saint Thomas University predated my involvement in programming related to his work. In particular, it was the Italy dialogues that took us to a deeper level of embracing the great work. Our Italy experiences enabled us to grow closer to Thomas and others who connected to him. Involvement in these Italy experiences were truly a blessing for me that continue to bless me.

Thomas Berry had a real penchant for connecting to people. In his interactions, he was always inviting others, through dialogue, to reflect on the deepest of issues. While his work as a geologian presents a theoretic construct for understanding the evolving nature of our universe, conversations with him always contained openings for others to join him reflecting on their own experiences. Unlike some professors who are so involved in the theoretic that they have trouble working with people new to a field, Thomas thrived on conversing with students whose eyes were being opened for the first time by the reflection he was inviting them into. Through him, Saint Thomas' Study Abroad for Earth (S.A.F.E.) broadened the horizons of first generation university students, making available to them an opportunity rarely available to such students.

Through the connections that Thomas had built up in sharing his learning, Saint Thomas University was able to become involved in dialogues that normally would have been unavailable to a minority-serving institution like Saint Thomas. Dialoguing with Thomas was a gift that challenged us intellectually. But, the greatest gift he gave us was the challenge to form a relationship with him and with others in the wide circle of conversation that he had developed. Via Thomas Berry's connections, Saint Thomas was able to be an active co-sponsor with the Center for Respect of Life and Environment of the Humane Society of the United States of our series of *Spirituality and Sustainability* Conferences. It was my privilege to be one of the leaders of these conferences. Even though it was later in his life, Thomas' presence and involvement were a youthful gentle breeze among us.

The *Sustainability and Spirituality* conferences were a platform for discussions on the crafting of the Earth Charter as well as discussions on advancing religious and spiritual dialogues on ecology and sustainability that were occurring in other higher education settings. Thomas Berry served as a focal point easily bringing these disparate endeavors together. Because of his involvement and his thought, these conferences were also able to gather people to find common ground who normally would not cross paths. Thus, people who struggle with religion were able, through Thomas and the conferences, to think about the possible spiritual dimensions of their work in a venue of safety. Others versed in spirituality and religious thought were able to dialogue on the issues beyond the confines of their spiritual and religious structures. Building relationships enabled participants from different starting points to venture into reflecting beyond the limits that their starting points may have created and to broaden their circles of dialogue.

An important way that Thomas Berry was able to be invitational was through some of the metaphors that he used. His ingenious terming of the description of the focus of his thought as *The Universe Story* is an example of his use of metaphor to make theory accessible. His use of the term, "universe," takes us beyond our small earth world and the small worlds we create in our minds and lives. Yet, even more importantly the use of the metaphor, "story," is a way his thought draws us in. We all have our own stories. Too often, however, we do not listen to each other's stories but talk over each other rather than with each other. When Thomas listened to people's stories and invited others to do the same, he opened all involved to listen to and for the Universe's story.

In the Judeo-Christian scriptures, there are two creation stories. One describes the creation of the universe and the other the creation of humans. For Thomas, we have spent too much time focusing on the second story and not enough time reading the scripture of the created universe. We might say that in his view a good deal of the ecological crises we face comes from overvaluing the centrality of humans and not having sufficient respect for the sacred place humans have in the sacred story of the universe. Humans are part of the story rather than the totality of the story. With our ecological crises exposing the impacts of human errors, Thomas saw the great work of his life as sharing the universe story in ways that we would change what we do in our own stories to align ourselves with the sacred creation of the universe. In his use of the metaphor, "great work," he conveyed to us in his writings and in the Assisi dialogues, a double entendre. Sharing the message was his great work, but in reality the focus of his work was the great work, that is the story of the universe itself. In sharing his work as story, he enabled all of us to identify with him and his story to have an accessible entry point into joining with him in being guided by the truly great work of the sacredness of the Universe Story.

One cannot underestimate the importance of place with Assisi as a backdrop for the dialogues of Saint Thomas University and those we were blessed to collaborate with. While Assisi is the home town of Saint Francis, the religious and secular patron of respect for creation and ecology, it is in its own right a mystical place. At times, experiencing Assisi was finding a place often teeming with hordes of people and souvenir shops and all those things connected to a tourist attraction. Yet, in the midst of the hubbub it was always possible to find a nook or cranny for meditative reflection. The spirit of the place somehow was able to break through and rise above the din and connect to the spiritual dimension of the work we were engaged in. While we were able to appreciate the valley below the city, it was somewhat sad to know that the lush forest of the time of Francis was nowhere in sight. This reminded us that the work of Francis needed to continue and that Thomas Berry's work had a real urgency. Yet still available to us, was our glimpse into the countryside in which Francis found his brothers and sisters in nature at the *Eremo delle Carceri* outside the city. Our "pilgrimage" to the *Eremo* was a real moment in spiritual grounding where we could get out of the head and embody connection to the creation around us. In the caves of this isolated place, Francis and his brothers were able to commune through nature with their God. What might seem to be a jail (*Carceri*) for some was for Francis and us a place, freeing us for commitment to the spiritual work.

Our dialogues were not only spiritual and ecological. Dialoguing in the *Piazza del Comune* of Assisi over a cappuccino or a beer was a crucial part of our activities. There we were able to connect with one another very personally in our relationships and stories. The Piazza was a wonderful place to be with Thomas. He could easily move from responding to a question from an earlier discussion to offering a kind word to one of the local people we came to know. Those gentle and basic conversations evidence how truly grounded Thomas was and how fundamental to him was his care for the earth and others.

The Mystical City of Assisi is very different from Miami, the Magic City, where Saint Thomas University finds itself. In our meals and excursions, we were exposed to the Umbrian bioregion where Assisi is located. The differences between Assisi and Miami were great yet helpful because in juxtaposing them in our minds we were called to look more deeply into the South Florida bioregion of Saint Thomas University. To see the ecological losses since Saint Francis' time and the opportunities still available to connect to his ecological spirituality in Assisi, gave us insights to look at the area around Saint Thomas University through different lenses. Thomas Berry's message reminded us that we need to act locally as that is part of the great work that is unfolding in the Universe story. As a minority-serving institution of limited resources, we were not one of the big players in higher education. Yet, being in Assisi with Thomas Berry enabled him to encourage us to know that we could be part of a great work in joining him in conveying to others the Universe Story.

As you read the wonderful contributions of others in this text, I hope that you feel the vibrancy of the relationships and stories inspired by a wonderful place and a wonderful man. Hopefully, you will be inspired in your part of *The Great Work*.

9

REFLECTING ON THOMAS' LEGACY, THE ASSISI EXPERIENCE, AND THE WAY FORWARD

RICHARD CLUGSTON

Reading *The Dream of the Earth* in 1988 helped propel me into working for the well-being of the whole Earth community. When I arrived at my new job in 1989, at the Center for Respect of Life and Environment (CRLE) in Washington DC, Thomas was on our board, and soon became our Senior Scholar in residence. We adopted his phrase, "Existence is a communion of subjects, not a collection of objects" as our organization's theme, and embraced, as central to our mission, the tasks of promoting the new story and transforming key institutions (higher education, religion and economic development policy) toward mutually enhancing human Earth relationships.

Over the next twenty years CRLE engaged in many projects to realize Thomas' dream, drafting an Earth Charter, publishing *Earth Ethics*, helping create the Forum on Religion and Ecology, promoting humane and sustainable food systems, running the Association of University Leaders for a Sustainable Future. In 1991, I began working with St Thomas University, exploring the changes in curricula, operations, and student life that would reflect a Catholic university's commitment to the human vocation and caring for creation.

Building on S.A.F.E.'s work with Thomas in Assisi, CRLE and STU decided to create an annual conference to bring together leaders in spirituality and sustainability to walk in the footsteps of Francis, Claire and Thomas and to chart the way forward in catalyzing the great transition.

It was a remarkable convergence of commitment and action. Yet, despite our, and many others' efforts, we have made little real progress toward ushering in the Ecozoic Era. In fact climate disruption, species extinction, inequitable economic development continue apace and many institutions, particularly universities and churches, have been unable to realize their commitments to sustainability.

Our great work now is to more effectively demand and embody the transformative changes needed in our lifestyles, communities and workplaces, and social policies: to live in a way all can live, providing opportunities to all for full human development within a flourishing Earth community.

We need to be bold in affirming the fundamental task in life is spiritual growth and sustainable living. We are here to awaken to our cosmic selves, which involves: coming into relationship with numinous power, the creative force; experiencing a sense of profound interconnection with all life (e.g., Schweitzer's reverence for life; seeing the Buddha nature of all beings; honoring all my relations): and finding our great work, our vocation in developing mutually enhancing human Earth relationships.

A major task emerging from the nexus of spirituality and sustainability is understanding why it is so difficult to awaken and to live right. Why is existence so filled with suffering and ignorance, so many lives cut painfully short? Why do bad things happen to good and innocent people? What happens when we die?

We must engage more effectively in the critical cultural debates of our time, for example, intelligent design vs. evolutionary theory. Neo-Darwinian theory can't explain the "sudden" bursting forth of animal life in the Cambrian (let alone the big bang, or the emergence of life). The Universe Story describes the amazing, miraculous transitions in history, where something dramatically new, differentiated and integrated, with more interiority, emerged, something hard to explain purely materially. From universe expansion through Earth formation, in cultural and personal human history, Thomas sensed such moments of grace were crucial in understanding the spiritual dynamics of evolutionary emergence. So the "moments of grace" hypothesis is an alternative to, and in some ways a variation on, the "intelligent design" hypothesis. And we should be plunging into this debate, a place of deep cultural ferment and struggle for a new narrative.

I think one of the great lessons learned in the fifteen years since our *Spirituality and Sustainability* conferences in Assisi and since the Earth Charter was completed, is the need to reorient education and development policy to cultivate our capacities to:

1. Engage deeply and effectively in contemplative and transformative practices that awaken and orient us toward the creative force or radiant source informing the universe and to our vocations, our greater selves;

2. Experience our interconnectedness and interdependence with the whole living world embracing diverse cultures of people and animals, agriculture and wilderness, the cycles of life and the seasons, as well as the unfolding cosmos;

3. Feel and act from compassionate concern for others, seeking to do no harm, reaching out to assist all beings;

4. Live in ways that all can live, consuming no more than one's fair share of Earth's bounty -- choosing products and services (e.g., food, energy, transportation, housing) that are ecologically sound, socially just and economically viable (e.g., local, fair trade, organic, carbon and pollution neutral, humane);

5. Ensure that our decision-making and conflict-resolution processes are open, enabling all to participate and clarify their preferences and grievances. Our process capacities -- to be humble, honest and respectful; to not blame and to forgive; and to compromise for the good of all -- are foundational for arriving at structures and solutions that further everyone's development;

6. Act to shift policies to support a just and sustainable future by voting, lobbying, and participating in political decision-making at all levels to promote policies to better care for future generations and the whole community of life, e.g., creating better measures of genuine progress than GDP, internalizing social and environmental costs in pricing goods and services, eliminating perverse subsidies and creating ethical assessment and trusteeship structures at all governmental levels.

In a sense, our Assisi conferences and the Earth Charter were ahead of their time. The various actors involved in the UN deliberations on sustainable development were not ready to recognize the need for a deep shift in fundamental assumptions about the nature and purpose of development, nor see the interconnectedness of the economic, social and environmental challenges we face, and to create new goals and indicators for development grounded in a new narrative and a new bottom line that integrates these three dimensions and consideration for future generations. Now the time is ripe.

We now have a promising opportunity to reorient the guiding framework for sustainable development and education for global citizenship, to support a viable future for all members of the life community.

PART II

THE UNIVERSE & THE UNIVERSITY

Transformative directions in higher education for the 21th Century, in order for humans to enhance their relationship with all beings on Earth and to become aware of their deep connection with the Universe. Research and learning assume a new ecological significance for our changing world.

10

THOMAS BERRY TO HIGHER EDUCATION: LEAD US ON A HEALTHY, JUST & SUSTAINABLE PATH

ANTHONY D. CORTESE

What would higher education look like, how would it organize and act if creating a healthy, just and sustainable world was its central purpose? How can we build on and rapidly expand the current exciting higher education efforts in the next decade? Dr. Cortese will explore how Thomas Berry's call to action, philosophy and teaching has and can influence higher education to urgently move beyond knowing to action.

Thomas Berry's Challenge

More than any other individual, Fr. Thomas Berry has helped us understand how deeply cultural and historical are the roots of the current unhealthy, inequitable and unsustainable path of humanity. In his 1999 book, *The Great Work: Our Way into the Future*, he called on the four major establishments that determine human life in its most significant functioning – government, the religious traditions, the university and commercial-industrial corporations – to change course for our own sake (Berry 1999, 73). His call to higher education was clarion and appropriate in nature.

Higher Education: A Critical Institution

Higher education has been granted tax-free status, the ability to receive public and private funds, and academic freedom in exchange for educating students and producing the knowledge that will result in a thriving civil society. It prepares most of the professionals who develop, lead, manage, teach, work in, and influence society's institutions, including the most basic foundation of K-12 education. Higher education has been a crucial leverage point in making a modern advanced civilization possible for an unprecedented number of people in almost every important way. In addition, college and university campuses are microcosms of the rest of society – they are like mini cities and communities that mirror society. Society looks to higher education to solve current problems, anticipate future challenges, develop innovative solutions and model the action and behavior that society must take to continue to evolve in a positive direction.

Humanity & Higher Education at an Unprecedented Crossroads

Higher education now has a challenge bigger than any other it has ever faced because humanity is at a crossroads without historical precedent. Because of the extraordinary and exponential growth of population and of the technological/economic system, humans have become pervasive and dominant forces in the health and well being of the earth and its inhabitants. The sum of humanity and the expansive dynamic of industrial capitalism constitute a *planetary* force comparable in disruptive power to the Ice Ages and the asteroid collisions that have previously redirected Earth's history. Despite the impressive array of environmental protection laws and programs in the industrialized countries since 1970, all living systems (oceans, fisheries, forests, grasslands, soils, coral reefs, wetlands) are in long-term decline and are declining at an accelerating rate, according to all major national and international scientific assessments.

There are also huge social, economic and public health challenges worldwide, e.g., nearly 3 billion people are without sanitation and make less than $2.50 per day; over 1 billion lack an adequate supply of safe drinking water and/or adequate nutrition. The gap between rich and poor within and among countries (including the U.S.) is increasing and is greater than it was in the "robber baron" days of the early 20th century. The challenge that will accelerate all the negative trends is human-induced global warming, primarily from the burning of fossil fuels that is destabilizing the earth's climate and other life supporting systems. As Dianne Dumanoski asserts in her recent book, *The End of the Long Summer*,

> *Our way of life depends on a stable climate. Through most of our species 200,000-year existence, our ancestors had to cope with a chaotic climate marked by extreme variability, a climate that could not support agriculture. The world as we know it, with agriculture, civilization, and dense human numbers, has only been possible because of a rare interlude of climatic grace – a "long summer" of unusual climatic stability over the past 11,700 years. The human enterprise has become a risky agent of global change. What lies ahead is a time of radical uncertainty.*
> (2009, 2)

This is happening with 25% of the world's population consuming 70-80% of the world's resources. The crucial question for all of humanity is: how will we ensure that current and future humans will be healthy, live in strong, secure, thriving communities and have economic opportunity in a world that will have 9 billion people and that plans to increase economic output 2-4 times by 2050?

As Fr. Berry has pointed out repeatedly, this is arguably the greatest civilizational, moral and intellectual challenge that humanity has ever faced. It is not about saving the planet. The planet has survived 5 major biological extinctions, the last being 65 million years ago in the age of the dinosaurs, and it will survive the 6th, which is being caused by humans. It is about saving civilization by remaking the human presence on earth in a way that allows all present humans to have their health, social and economic needs met while ensuring that future generations can also meet their needs. It is also built on the understanding that all human activity and survival is completely dependent on the earth for all of its resources and key ecosystem services including converting waste products into useful substances. We are imbedded in and part of the Earth's biosphere. We can only live about 3 minutes without breathing, 3 days without water and 3 weeks without food. We count on the Earth's biosphere for f ood, shelter, fuel, pharmaceuticals, water and many other goods and services including sophisticated ecological services that help convert our waste products into useful substances.

Changing Our Collective Mindset

The routine business of our civilization is threatening its own survival, and by putting Earth's living system in jeopardy, it also risks foreclosing the conditions for any civilized life.

How did we get here? In the industrialized world, we are guided by a myth of human separateness from and domination of nature for our purposes. This myth suggests that because it has worked in the last three centuries, continued physical economic growth will increase the quality of life for most of the world's population and solve all its problems. It contains an implicit assumption that the earth will be the gift that keeps on giving — providing the resources and converting our wastes into useful substances -- *ad infinitum*. This myth assumes that human technological innovation will allow us to ignore planetary limits. In western industrialized culture, we tend to view increasing material consumption as the principal measure of success, despite its negative effects on health, society and the environment.

Moreover, we are dominated by linear short-term thinking that makes it difficult to recognize the magnitude of our cumulative actions, and the danger of their impacts. Our collective impacts are now global, intergenerational, sometimes irreversible and prone to rapid, unexpected shifts.

One example of the many undesirable consequences of this current paradigm, is that the ecological, health and social footprint of our activities is largely *invisible* to most of us and almost completely absent in the price of products. As a result, the average person in an industrialized country does not know that we consume the equivalent of our body weight in solid materials daily, over 94 percent of which goes to waste before we ever see the product or the service. Consequently, the market fails in efficiently and effectively allocating resources. It allows us to practice a kind of group self-deception about the impact of our daily living. An important part of education must be to make the *invisible* impacts (positive or negative) of our daily living, *visible*.

We need a *transformative shift* in the way we think and act. As Einstein said, "we cannot solve today's problems at the same level of thinking that created them." We currently view the array we have of health, economic, energy, political, security, social justice, environmental and other societal issues as separate, competing and hierarchical when they are really *systemic* and *interdependent*. *We have a de facto systems design failure.* The 21st century challenges must be addressed in a systemic, integrated and holistic fashion with an emphasis on creating new and more desirable ways of helping society succeed, e.g., local, sustainable food production that provides healthy food, local jobs, protects soils and water supplies.

The current state of the world is also a *prima facie* indicator that the current higher education system is reinforcing the unhealthy, inequitable, and unsustainable path that society is pursuing. As David Orr has said, "it is not a problem *in* education it is a problem *of* education "(1994, 1). This is not intentional. The structure of higher education and its evolution in the last one and a half centuries is based on and is reinforcing the deep cultural (and therefore hidden) assumptions referred to above.

Thomas Berry tells us the need for a transformative shift in the purpose, focus and modus operandi of higher education is both urgent and profound.

> *While our universities have gone through many since they first came into being in the early medieval period, they have never experienced anything like the transition that is being asked of them just now. The difficulty cannot be resolved simply by establishing a course or a program in ecology, for ecology is not a course or a program. Rather it is the foundation of all courses, all programs, and all professions because ecology is a functional cosmology. Ecology is not a part of medicine; medicine is an extension of ecology. Ecology is not a part of law; law is an extension of ecology. So too, in their own way, the same can be said of economics and even the humanities.* (Berry 1999, 84)

A New Human Story

We need a new human story in which we recognize and celebrate our presence as members of all life on earth. To do so we must make several conceptual shifts. First, we must move from *problem solving* to *creating*. Problems are negative conditions that we desire to eliminate, e.g., environmental degradation or pollution. Eliminating the negative neither motivates large-scale action unless it is a serious immediate threat nor does it engage broad scale societal adoption.

Moreover, we often frame the problem in such narrow terms that solutions create other problems in time and space. A focus on *creating the kind of world that we want* shifts our thinking to a desired outcome, one that can motivate individuals and institutions to rapid action, e.g., the advent of cell phones and the ability to spread communication worldwide quickly.

Secondly, we must focus on how to create an *economy designed for the well-being of people, communities and nature,* not one that hopes the by-products of market success and growth for growth's sake will benefit all people and not harm natural systems.

We need new design principles for a sustainable society. Imagine future scientists, engineers and business people designing technology and economic activities that sustain the natural environment and enhance human health and well-being, operating completely on solar/renewable energy. Imagine an industrial and consumption system in which the concept of "waste" is eliminated because every waste product is a raw material or nutrient for another species or activity, or returned into the cycles of nature. (The human species is the only one that operates in a linear 'take, make, waste' fashion.) Imagine that we are managing human activities in a way that uses natural resources only at the rate that they can self-regenerate – the ideas embodied in sustainable forestry, fishing and agriculture. By doing so, we could live off nature's "interest," not its capital, for generations to come. This is the concept of *biomimicry* – learning from and imitating nature, tapping into a model that has figured out what works and survives after 3.4 billion years of experimentation (biomimicry.net 2012).

Let us imagine that all current and future generations are able to pursue meaningful work and have the opportunity to realize their full human potential both personally and socially. Imagine that communities are strong and vibrant because they celebrate cultural diversity, are designed to encourage collaboration and participation in governance and emphasize the quality of life over the consumption of stuff. The latter is critical because human wants can be insatiable while the earth's ability to meet our wants is finite and shrinking. In an August 5, 2007 New York Times story, "In Silicon Valley, Millionaires Who Don't Feel Rich," executives with a net worth of more than $5 million discussed how their families were unhappy with their lifestyle because they compare themselves with neighbors whose net worth is 5-10 times greater. As one executive put it, "here, the top 1 percent chases the top one-tenth of 1 percent, and the top one-tenth of 1 percent chases the top one-one-hundredth of 1 percent. You try not to get caught up in it," he added, "but it's hard not to" (Rivilin 2007, para. 57-58). The road to sustainability is one of culture and values as much as it is about scientific and technological development. It must be guided by the arts, humanities, social and behavioral sciences, religion and other spiritual inspiration as well as the physical and natural sciences and engineering.

These are the design principles of a healthy, just and sustainable society -- principles that include a human consciousness in which we apply the Golden Rule to our dealings with all current and unborn humans as well with the rest of life on earth. To work, these principles must become the basis for society's economic and governance framework and, therefore, a fundamental part of all education.

Higher Education's Future Role

It is clear that today's and tomorrow's businesses, government and professionals -- architects, engineers, attorneys, business leaders, scientists, urban planners, policy analysts, cultural and spiritual leaders, teachers, journalists, advocates, activists, and politicians – will need new knowledge and skills that only Higher Education can provide on a broad scale.

What if higher education were to take a leadership role in helping to make this a reality? A college or university would operate as a fully integrated community that models social, economic and biological sustainability itself and in its interdependence with the local, regional and global community. In many cases, we think of teaching, research, operations and relations with local communities as separate activities; they are not. Because students learn from everything around them, these activities form a complex web of experience and learning. All parts of the college or university system are critical to achieving a *transformative* change that can only occur by connecting head, heart and hand. The educational experience of graduates must reflect an intimate connection among *curriculum* and (1) research; (2) understanding and reducing any negative ecological and social footprint of the institution; and (3) working to improve local and regional communities so that they are healthier, more socially vibrant and stable, economically secure and environmentally sustainable.

What if the educational experience of all students is aligned with the principles of sustainability outlined above? To achieve this...

The content of learning would reflect interdisciplinary systems thinking, dynamics and analysis for all majors and disciplines with the same *lateral rigor* across, as the *vertical rigor* within, the disciplines.

The context of learning would change to make human / environment interdependence, values and ethics a seamless and central part of teaching of *all the disciplines*, rather than isolated in programs for specialists, or in special courses or modules.

The process of education would emphasize active, experiential, inquiry based learning and real-world problem solving *on the campus* and *in the larger community*.

Higher education would *practice and model sustainability*. A campus would *practice what it preaches* and model economically, socially and environmentally sustainable practices in its *operations, planning, facility design, purchasing and investments*, and tie these efforts to the formal curriculum.

Finally, the *learning and benefit to society* of higher education forming partnerships with local and regional communities to help make them socially vibrant, economically secure and environmentally sustainable will be a crucial part of successful higher education – especially because the 4,100 higher education institutions in the United States are, themselves, large economic engines with annual operational budgets totaling $350 billion annually and endowments of $450 billion – this is about 3% of US GDP and greater than the GDP of all but twenty-five countries in the world.

Frank Rhodes, former president of Cornell University suggests that the concept of sustainability offers, "a new foundation for the liberal arts and sciences" (2010, 1). It provides a new focus, sense of urgency, and curricular coherence at a time of drift, fragmentation, and insularity in higher education, what he calls "a new kind of global map." Sustainability provides a vital source of hope and opportunity for facilitating institutional renewal and revitalizing higher education's sense of mission.

The Current Reality in Higher Education

The great news is that there has been unprecedented, exponential growth in distinct academic programs related to the *environmental dimension* of sustainability in higher education, especially in the last decade. Exciting environmental (and now sustainability) studies and graduate programs in every major scientific, engineering and social science discipline, business, law, public health, behavioral sciences, ethics and religion are abundant and growing.

Progress on campuses modeling sustainability has grown at an even faster rate. Higher education has embraced programs for energy and water conservation, renewable energy, waste minimization and recycling, green buildings and purchasing, alternative transportation, local and organic food growing and 'sustainable' purchasing -- saving both the environment and money.

The student environmental movement in the U.S. is the most well-organized, largest and most sophisticated student movement since the civil rights and anti-war movement of the 1960s. And higher education environmental efforts have become publicly visible to a degree that was unimaginable a decade ago. These developments represent one of most encouraging trends in higher education innovation since World War II.

Unfortunately, higher education is doing a poor job on the health, social and economic dimensions of sustainability. The overwhelming majority of graduates know little about the importance of sustainability or how to lead their personal and professional lives aligned with sustainability principles. Moreover, most of the excellent and exciting sustainability-oriented innovation in higher education have been led by (1) individual groups (students, a subset of the faculty, a subset of the business and operations staff -- often working together), (2) have primarily focused on the environmental dimension of sustainability and (3) have largely focused on educating environmental and sustainability professionals within the framework of existing academic disciplines. Few have been integrated with social efforts such as civic engagement, social justice, economic development, poverty alleviation, and human rights. With a few exceptions sustainability, as an aspiration for society, is not a central institutional goal, or *lens* for determining the success of higher education institutions.

A Beacon of Systemic Change:
The American College & University Presidents'
Climate Commitment

One of the brightest beacons of light for the systemic change in the U.S. is the American College & University Presidents' Climate Commitment (*PresidentsChangeCommitment.org* 2007),/ launched in January of 2007 by twelve college and university presidents, working with Second Nature, the Association for the Advancement of Sustainability in Higher Education (AASHE) and EcoAmerica. It is a high-visibility, joint and individual, publicly accountable commitment to achieve carbon neutrality in all its operations and develop the capability of all students to help the rest of society do the same.

As of the January 2014, 679 colleges and universities in all 50 states and the District of Columbia representing 6.3 million students (45% of the college student population) are members of this network. Every type of school is represented – public, private, community colleges, tribal and other minority-serving colleges, religious-affiliated schools, baccalaureate, graduate degree granting and large research universities. There have been impressive results – a 25% overall reduction in carbon emissions and financial savings of over $2 billion during a time of rapid growth in campus expansion and enrollment.

This is unprecedented leadership by higher education. Higher Education is the first and only major U.S. sector with a significant number of its members to commit to climate neutrality. These schools are doing what is scientifically necessary, not what is easily doable within their current mode of operation. They are sending a strong signal to society that climate change and other large scale unsustainable societal practices are real, that urgent action is needed and that higher education is taking action to model sustainable behavior and to provide the knowledge and educated graduates necessary for society to do the same.

For the members of the network the ACUPCC has created a successful learning community among the participating institutions. Participating institutions are sharing plans and experiences, working together to address challenges and helping to create new knowledge and financial resources to benefit all of the institutions in higher education. Finally, the ACUPCC has begun to fundamentally shift attention on sustainability from a series of excellent, distinct programs to a *strategic imperative* of presidents, academic officers, business officers and trustees. Sustainability is becoming a *key lens for measuring success*. It represents an unprecedented *institutional and cultural shift* to focus on all aspects of social, economic and ecological sustainability.

Achieving Thomas Berry's Vision

Can Higher Education respond and lead this cultural transition? Many argue that it is too difficult, impractical or impossible to shift toward a deep culture of sustainability of all life. What we must do is make the seemingly impractical or impossible *inevitable* as we have done so many times in society – witness the elimination of many infectious diseases, modern medicine, space travel and improving human rights among many human achievements. Colleges and universities are anchor institutions for social, community and economic development as full partners in anticipating and informing society of the challenges we face as well as finding and modeling solutions. Higher education is the primary secular sector in society designed with a *long-term focus*. The unprecedented challenge we now face provides the greatest opportunity that higher education has ever had to demonstrate its crucial and ever-growing importance to society, especially in a time when higher education is under pressure because of accessibility and affordability issues. If we don't who will? It is not likely to be the government with its 2, 4 and 6 year election cycles, nor business with its focus on quarterly earnings. As Thomas Berry has told us, "from here on, the primary judgment of all human institutions, professions, programs and activities will be determined by the extent to which they inhibit, ignore, or foster a mutually-enhancing human/Earth relationship" (Webb 2006).

REFERENCES

Berry, Thomas. 1999. *The Great Work: Our Way into The Future*. New York, N.Y.: Three Rivers Press.

Biomimicry. 2012. Last modified http://biomimicry.net/.

Dumanoski, Dianne. 2009. *The End of the Long Summer: Why We Must Remake Our Civilization to Survive on a Volatile Earth*, New York: Crown Publishers.

Orr, David W. 2004. *Earth in Mind: On Education, Environment, and the Human Prospect*. Washington, D.C.: Island Press.

Presidents' Climate Commitment. http://presidentsclimatecommitment.org/.

Rhodes, Frank H.t. "Sustainability: the Ultimate Liberal Art - The Chronicle Review - The Chronicle of Higher Education." *Home - The Chronicle of Higher Education*. Web. 15 July 2010. <http://chronicle.com/article/Sustainability-the-Ultimate/29514>.

Rivlin, Gary. August 05, 2007. "Age of Riches: In Silicon Valley, Millionaires Who Don't Feel Rich." *The New York Times*.

Webb, Caroline. "Interview with Dr. Berry."(Personal Interview. February 2006.)

11

PRESCRIPTIONS FROM THE CLASSROOM[1]

Elisabeth M. Ferrero

This essay elaborates the re-connections of the human to the natural world in higher education curricula.

Thomas Berry's presence in Assisi of twenty years ago still echoes in me today as I ponder about education and how our students' needs are not met.

What I believe is at the root of our multifaceted problems in our youth is the total body\soul disconnection stemming from the disconnection of the human from the natural world; thus, unless this two-fold connection is re-established at all levels and in all areas of education, all curricular and structural changes will not amount to any real transformation in our students. Humans cannot function independently from the rest of creation. By seeking human well-being at the expense of the wider community of life, we diminish our own well-being as well as the well-being of all creation. A utilitarian approach to the environment and the non-human world can only increase the *dis*order of the universe, along with the spiritual and the physical degradation of humankind (Berry 1999).

---

[1] A version of this essay was published under the title "The Educator of the Twenty-first Century" in *Earth Ethics*. 1997-98. Vol. 9.1&2: 18-19.

The *dis*order and the *dis*connection from the natural world represent an historical break from Catholic theological tradition as well as from natural law (Berry 1999). Over the last three hundred years, this faulty perception of the relationship of the human to the natural world has done immeasurable harm and truly is at the root of the plagues of our times (Berry 2009). What is needed in education – as in all other institutions – is a fundamental shift, as a society, to adopt a new paradigm along with a change of values and views (Berry 1999).

To reconnect the human to the natural world is obviously the solution; however, we must re-connect emotionally, not simply come forth with an intellectual critique or plan of action. We must shift from the predominant and exclusive employment of *'logos'* to include *'pneuma.'* A polarized perception of the world, the way we know it today, can no longer co-exist. We must move beyond the world of dualities. Darkness needs to embrace light; reasoning and imagination must become one; female defines itself in the dialogue with male; below and above must become part of the same continuum in the spiral of life. The East has always known that a polarized world is a fragmented one and thus a weak one; therefore, it has reconciled all opposites – something which is lacking in our Western civilization.

My students of ethics at Saint Thomas University, as part of the service component of their course requirement, grow a few vegetables and flowers at the corner of the University's spacious grounds. On their first day, their impeccable white sneakers meld in the brown terrain. They farm in the worst of conditions – an old-fashioned irrigation system and only a handful of tools – yet they are "nourished" by this humble task in a simple, non-verbal, non-linear, non-logical relationship to the natural world. I never try to make farmers out of them. I talk to my students a lot about empowerment – but little do we know, as educators, that it is the natural world which can open, rekindle and nourish their hearts.

Today, this re-connection to the natural world, not in fragmentary terms, but as a whole being, is the number one pedagogical remedy essential for real transformation in our students. As Tom Berry repeatedly said, the natural world is the context for the human, and the devastation of the natural world will bring about the desolation of the human, and both will perish or grow as one (Berry 2009).

By connecting with the natural world, one develops an openness which becomes compassion for all forms of life. There is so much that is mysterious in life that can only be experienced with a deep sense of awe, by walking with gentleness and dignity towards all forms of creation. By doing so, we reconnect our heart and soul to our body -- a long lost connection. We live at a time when the cult of the body prevails, and yet there is no real connection with the body because such a bond is only possible where the heart and the body meet in stillness, beyond logic. The role of the human on this earth is a privileged one, but somehow we have trivialized our sense of being sacred. How can we continue to talk about spirituality and refer only to our spirit?

Medieval mystics saw the inter-relationship of body and soul in a universe permeated by the divine. However, the Cartesian split of matter and spirit by removing the soul from nature and from the human body – except for the pineal gland in the human brain – not only alienated the human from the natural world, but also impoverished our inner life, which is dependent upon the exchange of spiritual energy and wisdom from the natural world; and in this exchange of energy and wisdom the divine is evoked, and through this deep bond we are healed and transformed (Berry 2009).

This is why we cannot speak of disease of the body without understanding that the soul is also suffering, that it too is diseased and that it is no longer working in harmony but is out of sync with the body. Action, or work, has to become the work of the body *and* the soul connected and working as one. As the body and the soul work together, the person comes to trust one's heart without anxiety. With a deep sense of tranquility, one has a clear perception and is open to go beyond oneself, entering into a real encounter with the world. When body and spirit are synchronized, one feels grounded in a particular place, like a tree whose roots expand under the ground and draw nourishment from all surroundings. This causes a feeling of belonging. Everything is where it needs to be and it cannot be controlled, eradicated, or used but exists in a common destiny on this Earth.

We need to talk about prescriptions, not lofty intellectual critiques of the *malaise* of our times, on how to educate today's youth. The natural world needs to become the primary context of all forms of education (Berry 1999). Within this context, all curricula need to reflect the expression of the student through movement, sounds, words, shapes, and colors as the way by which s/he can experience what s/he is learning. The fine arts, creative writing and music in our educational systems and programs are often separated from other disciplines; they are labeled "artistic subjects" *vis-a-vis* "cognitive" disciplines. All departments and disciplines need to recognize how inter-connected the cognitive and the artistic subjects are in the learning process.

What we need is to embody in our educational system the very fundamental laws and principles of nature. Today, students are almost always excluded from the subjects that they learn, and thus they do not see themselves and their own story as part of the wider story of what they are learning and of the universe (Berry 2009). Science courses must incorporate the arts as a way to teach scientific concepts. In 1993, when Brian Swimme came to Assisi to teach physics, his students learned the Big Bang theory not only by studying it from the textbook but also by embodying the various elements present at the beginning of time through song, poetry and dance.

We, as educators, must become co-creators with our students in order for a real transformation to occur in their lives and in the universe.

REFERENCES

Berry, Thomas. 2009. *The Christian Future and the Fate of Earth.* Eds. Mary Evelyn Tucker and John Grim. Maryknoll, New York: Orbis Books.

---. 1999. *The Great Work: Our Way into the Future.* New York: Three Rivers Press.

Spretnak, Charlene. 2011. *Relational Reality.* Topsham, ME: Green Horizon Books.

12

KNOWING MOMENTS OF GRACE
AS OUR GREAT WORK
IN THE THOUGHT OF THOMAS BERRY

JOHN GRIM

This essay explores a phrase that Thomas Berry originated to describe moments in evolutionary emergence which involves great tumult and great creativity. Thomas described, for example, the development of our solar system from an earlier proto-star as a moment of grace. This was an explosive sequence in which the collapse and rapid explosive expansion of a supernova led to the formation of elemental materials composing the planets, moons, comets, and asteroids that we now observe. From universe expansion through Earth formation, in cultural and personal human history, Thomas sensed such moments of grace were crucial in understanding the spiritual dynamics of evolutionary emergence.

For Thomas Berry, "moments of grace" refers to ineffable "sacred moments of transformation" that are numinous, namely, awesome and compelling. They are irreversible and set a pattern for what comes after. Such transformative events occur at all levels of reality from the monumental collisions of galaxies to the inner workings of cellular life. Thus, just as there are cosmological moments of grace so also there are such historical moments when events in human communities focus them and change them forever. Similarly, we all know our own personal moments of grace when something happens and we awaken in ways that after which we are never the same. Berry explains it this way,

> *In this emergent process we recognize transformation moments as those instants when the numinous presence in the phenomenal world manifests itself with special clarity. These moments include the time of the supernova collapse of a second – or third-generation star that produced the ninety-some elements needed for the solar system, for planet Earth, for life and consciousness. These transformation events can be considered cosmological moments of grace. Just as there are historical moments of grace and sacramental moments of grace, so, too, there are such cosmological moments. These are times that deserve ritual commemoration, just as moments in the annual solar cycle do; solstice and spring equinox are given ritual expression in nativity and resurrection liturgies. In most religious traditions, diurnal moments of transformation, dawn and dusk, the mysterious transition from day to night and from night to day, are profoundly religious moments to be observed with appropriate prayer and ritual.* (Berry 2009, 55)

For Berry, this idea, moments of grace, in its cosmological occurrence provided a lens into understanding the creative tensions underlying the dynamics of the unfolding universe. The term "moments" suggests an historical focus on, and understanding of, crucial events in universe evolution that determine patterns of evolutionary unfolding. These historical moments are also cosmological in that they are happening on the scale of universe processes. From the standpoint of us, the human observers, they are also numinous moments simultaneously dangerous and filled with promise. Finally, and perhaps most importantly for we endlessly optimistic Americans, moments of grace are not bound to happen. Concomitant events can interfere and distract or prevent such a moment of grace from having its transformative and enduring change.

This phrase — moments of grace — reveals several influences on Berry's ideas that might be seen as simply intellectual, but which also provide insight into what he understands about the depth and breadth of transformation. Three of these influences are the cosmopolitan thought of the Greek Stoics, thinking about "grace" among Christian theologians, and the perspectives on evolution and genetic coding among scientists.

The ancient Stoics thought that a living cosmos could orient individuals causing some of them to form a deep cosmopolitan citizenship that connected them to all reality. Thus, the grace of civilization enabled a cultivation of city life that was in direct relationship with the whole of the cosmos. Secondly, for many Christian theologians, grace is a term associated with divine, providential assistance that can be interpreted differently. One perspective on grace says that it is an unearned award, or gratuitous gift, that is, it is something freely given not earned. Another interpretative understanding is that grace once given determines future formation. Finally, another understanding sees grace as fully earned by personal actions, grace flows to a person by merit. Obviously, Berry realizes that these different interpretations come into play if we consider a cosmological moment or an historical moment or a personal moment of grace.

Another influential current in understanding moments of grace comes from those many thinkers who have grappled with Darwinian evolution. Thomas received from this evolutionary lineage a sense of dynamic change in the cosmos and an awareness of pattern that seeks to move beyond itself. Thus, a moment of grace is both in accord with the endless change observed in the universe, on Earth, and in our own person. Yet, moments of grace refer to those exceptional moments when forces coalesce in such a way that they determine future change.

In this context, moments of grace describe those incredibly delicate interweavings of chance and necessity in evolution that need not have occurred the way they did, but having done so provide a pattern for all that comes after. Such moments are the flaring forth of the universe, the coalescence of particulate matter, the springing into reality of galaxies, the creative explosions of supernovae, the formation of solar systems with encircling planets, such as our Earth, the emergence of life throughout our Ecosphere, and many more. Such evolutionary moments of grace are coming into human awareness in the twenty-first century. One challenge that we face in considering such moments is to recognize how what has happened in the evolution of the outer world has shaped, and continues to affect, our inner world.

Understanding and responding to moments of grace is for Berry a Great Work, namely, aligning with the larger sacred purposes of the universe and the planet Earth. He was especially interested in the relationships between cultural traditions, what Berry called cultural coding, and the biological structure of life that he termed genetic coding. Berry became increasingly interested in the relationships of these codings. He pondered their alignments in human moments of grace. This occurred, as he saw it, when cultural expressions align with the spontaneities expressed in biological genetic coding. That is, genetic coding prompts humans to exist, to eat, to produce, and to propagate. Cultural codings express symbolic formations that align individuals and societies with these inner genetic drives. Awareness of these correspondences of culture and biology can bring humans into a more comprehensive participation with the cosmos within. A singular feature of moments of grace for Thomas Berry, then, is that they manifest to the human the deepest cosmological dimension of oneself. Everything in the universe is shaped by such moments of grace.

But just as these moments of grace allure and call the human, so also they present moments of danger that transcend our rational powers. This numinous dimension of moments of grace highlights the challenge, opportunity, and potential misreading of such moments. That is, one may try to understand them by relying exclusively on reason alone. For example, science as a way of knowing brings reason in powerful ways to knowing the world. But it may fall short of the guidance we need to know a moment of grace as well as the great work we must undertake to realize such a moment in our lives. Becoming aware of the cosmic spontaneities within us requires a sensitivity that Thomas associates with the ancient healing and divining practices of the shaman. Now, he observes, we need to cultivate the shamanic dimensions of our psyche. Just as shamans among indigenous peoples evoked symbolic consciousness from their spiritual experiences of the cosmos, so also we must assemble a living "ecology of the mind," as Gregory Bateson described in his book with that title (Bateson 1972). The special sensitivities that arise from mutually enhancing relationships with the natural world may prepare us for establishing limits and creating detachment needed for the healing of the Earth. Much is given to us, according to Berry, and much is expected of us. We know the deep wonder that we are, but we also sense how detached we have become from the source of that wonder. Now, our challenge is not only to understand and align with the moments of grace that we are, but also to undertake the "Great Work" of our times implementing that realization in the flourishing of the Earth community.

REFERENCES

Berry, Thomas. 2009. *The Christian Future and the Fate of the Earth.* Edited by Mary Evelyn Tucker and John Grim. Maryknoll, NY: Orbis Books.

Bateson, Gregory. 1972. *Steps to an Ecology of Mind; Collected Essays in Anthropology, Psychiatry, Evolution, and Epistemology.* Northvale, New Jersey: Jason Aronson Inc.

13

REFLECTIVE THINKING ABOUT PLACE AS PART OF A CURRICULUM FOR ECOLOGICAL STUDIES

Gary N. McCloskey, O.S.A.

A curriculum based on ecological studies must connect not only to the ecology of the world, but most especially to the concrete reality of the people of the bioregion where a curriculum is being experienced and learned.

When I first worked on the role of place as part of a curriculum for ecological studies (McCloskey 1997-98) during the gatherings with Thomas Berry in Italy, I had less of a realization of how unreflective so many people are about knowledge. With the continued popularity of the thought of global warming deniers and now climate change deniers, it is more clear to me how knowledge is seen by some as factoids which can be marshaled or ignored willy-nilly to fit their predispositions. In a recent study Chew (2014), posits that underlying similar types of thinking are four misconceptions that people generally have about learning. For him, students think that learning is fast, knowledge is composed of isolated facts, being good at a subject is a matter of inborn talent rather than hard work, and that they are good at multi-tasking. To overcome these misconceptions there is a need to teach and design learning opportunities that aid students to develop sustained interaction in learning, ability to find connections among the elements under study, a "growth mindset" for working "towards mastery" (Chew 2014, 217), and a focus to assist in overcoming "inattentional blindness" (2014, 217). To equip learners studying in an ecological studies curriculum to be able to respond to the continuing climate change denial, the curriculum must teach them to address, in particular, two of the student misconceptions -- finding connections and overcoming intentional blindness.

One means that curriculum for ecological studies can use to face these misconceptions is by enabling learners not only to study ecology on the macro/world-wide level, but also to foster reflection on the application of macro-level thinking to the concrete reality of the bioregion where the curriculum is being experienced and learned. In a spiritual sense, to prepare learners to overcome misconceptions, ecological studies curricula must assist in reconnecting us to the very ground out of which we grow. In the Judeo-Christian understanding, it is reconnecting us to our own creation. One translation the Book of Genesis has captured the relation in this way,

> *At the time of YHWH, God's making of earth and heaven,*
> *no bush was yet on the earth,*
> *no plant of the field had yet sprung up,*
> *for YHWH, God, had not made it rain upon the earth,*
> *and there was no human/adam to till the soil/adama*
> *but a surge would well up from the ground*
> *and water all the face of the soil;*
> *and YHWH, God, formed the human, of dust from the soil,*
> *he blew into his nostrils the breath of life*
> *and the human became a living being.*
> *YHWH, God, planted a garden in Eden/Land of Pleasure,*
> *and there he placed the human whom he had formed.*

> *YHWH, God, caused to spring up from the soil*
> *every type of tree, desirable to look at and good to eat,*
> *and the Tree of Life in the midst of the garden*
> *and the Tree of the Knowing of Good and Evil.*

(The Five Books of Moses, Genesis 2:4-9)

If we reflect on this and apply it, ecological studies must connect us with the reality of the very soil *(adama)* of which we *(adam)* are a part. Through such studies, the human person *(adam)* must recover the sense of connectedness with the earth *(adama)* in the particular place out of which he or she draws life. A Judaeo-Christian biblical spirituality of Genesis can be a point of recovery of this connectedness. With the soil/roots *(adama)* of our own selves *(adam)* as a part of an ecological studies curriculum, how can we talk about saving the earth and renewing the planet, if we do not understand our concrete daily connection to that which we proclaim to care for? In such a curriculum, we would understand that we are not really talking about saving the earth *(adama)* outside of us, we are talking about saving ourselves *(adam)*, children of mother earth.

If the identification of this connection is so simple and apparently straight forward in the Judeo-Christian religious understanding and spirituality, why is it so difficult for people to see it in our current world? They probably have difficulty, because this understanding of the creation story is not the prevalent understanding within our culture. Bowers (2000) may have the reason in what he calls "root metaphors." As he describes it, "the root metaphors of a cultural group are based upon its ancient mythopoeic narratives (or cosmology)" (2000, 26). Specifically, he notes that, "the Book of Genesis extolls (sic) the mythopoeic narrative that led to viewing men as dominant over both women and the environment" (2000, 27). This root metaphor understanding of Genesis is of "a distinctly modern origin" (2000, 27). This modern domination metaphor is a reading into scripture not found in the Hebrew *adama/adam* relationship.

When an ecological studies curriculum raises issues of our connectedness to the earth, it brings up issues that go to the core of the root metaphors of our culture and the spirituality that pervade the culture. In the face of such entrenched root metaphor thinking, learners in an ecological studies curriculum will need to develop deep thinking to be able to make the case for a grounded thinking about human to environment relations. The deep thinking that needs to be involved in an ecological studies curriculum is reflective thinking. According to Dymore and Harrison (2008), reflection in learning is "the capacity of an individual to think thoughtfully and deeply, to remind oneself of past events and to consider alternative courses of action" (2008, 302). Full consideration of alternative courses of action will be enhanced by application of global environmental issues to the local place. This application in the local bioregion is grounding in both the practical and spiritual senses.

Such a practical use of place in an ecological studies curriculum involves a second sense of place that any effective curriculum of ecological studies must address. While educators emphasize theoretical constructs to guide teaching, we forget that talking too theoretically, too abstractly, too philosophically can take us away from who we are with and where we are. Such distance unfortunately encourages students to maintain their "intentional blindness," because they cannot connect to the distant theory and easily drift into thinking about ideas more close at hand. In universities, where abstract ideas are held in high regard, we may forget that they should never be too far from the soil of the learner's reality.

Even when they do not appear to do so, the theories that universities teach shape the spirit of the university itself as much as they shape the students in the university. While spirituality is seen by many as a religious concept to be discussed only in classrooms where the study of theology or religion takes place, every course of study shapes the student's sense of meaning and fundamental direction, thus embodying a spirituality of its own. This understanding of spirituality is what the secular theorists term an ethos: common attitudes, values, and beliefs that bond disparate individuals into a community. An ethos also is the mores, or folkways, of central importance to a group. They are accepted without question and embody the fundamental moral view of a community (Bellah et al. 1985) following de Tocqueville, have called these mores, or folkways, "habits of the heart."

Beyond the modern root metaphor of domination over (interpreted from Genesis), an ecological studies curriculum must help in the reappraisal of the varieties of our modern modes of thought, particularly dualism that are alive in both university and culture. Our study of the environment must critique modern thought and reconnect us to ground on which we walk. As Brent Waters (1986) has observed about the general move to post-modern thinking, "It invites a deepening suspicion of the rigid dichotomies modernity has created between objective reality and subjective experience, fact and imagination, secular and sacred, public and private" (1986, 113). Every curriculum contains hidden assumptions. Rather than thinking of sacred vs. secular or even objective reality vs. subjective experience, a curriculum of ecological studies needs to go beyond the study of the science at hand to foster reflection on the ethos of the whole learning environment in which it is located as carrying spiritual and ethical messages.

Global warming and climate change deniers are not the only deniers that an ecological studies curriculum faces. In modern universities we often deny the reality that there is an ethos of deeply held fundamental convictions underpinning the education and working against ecologically sound points of view. We make a crucial mistake in believing and acting on the belief, that we are without what Kenneth Sirotnik (1991) calls rhetoric *of inquiry* no matter what our ontological, epistemological, and methodological persuasions. By "rhetoric of inquiry," Sirotnik means, "the gestalt created through considerations of how rational human beings generate knowledge, communicate it, and act with it. This gestalt includes our methods of sense-making, our metaphors and other figures of speech, and our ethical, moral, and political interests" (Sirotnik 1991, 253). While there are many similarities among universities, each as a particular place has certain rhetoric of inquiry that is fundamental to its direction. Any development of an ecological studies curriculum in a particular university must take into account the relation of that curriculum to the rhetoric of that place. Since almost all, if not all, universities remain imbued with the world view of modern dichotomies, the development of curricula of ecological studies must recognize the challenge that an eco-centric curriculum presents to the fundamental direction of other learning directions within the university.

St. Thomas University in Miami Gardens and its dialoguing with Thomas Berry and his ideas provides a case in point. While we found through these dialogues that we were a place, fundamentally open to ecological thinking, we still had our problems. In trying to shift directions, we suffered from the proponents of new ideas at times trying to borrow too much from other places. This was not a surprise, since modern universities in their construction of curriculum have fostered the belief that you can transplant a course of study from one place to another with great ease. In modern thinking, the particularity of place means nothing and does not need to be reflected upon. Place in modern thinking is something about which we can have intentional blindness. In its educational bioregion, not all that worked at other places, worked at St. Thomas. Even though many seeds from other places were planted in our soil but did not take root, the watering and tending of those seeds enabled the plants and flowers of our own place to begin to grow and flourish. For example, much of our original curriculum thrust was oriented toward a traditional framework of major and minor in ecological studies for undergraduate students. This did not bear much fruit. More fruitful was the development of courses in the various departments to educate students in business, education, etc., in environmentally sound thinking in their own disciplines. From this a foundation emerged, an approach reflecting the points of view of various disciplines related to ecological studies, rather than a separate discipline of ecological studies. This reflects the reality of our specific place. While it is our university mission to share in the ecological healing of the earth, our students were and are self-directed toward professional disciplines of study. More recent developments of St. Thomas University's structures have developed further in response to this student orientation. We had to work through the disappointment of things not working as planned, but in seeing the lovely unintended fruit, we were not discouraged for a great length of time and learned to serve our students in better ways.

Even though faculty members at St. Thomas have enjoyed a place with much interchange across disciplines, they still focus on the basic rhetoric of inquiry of their own discipline. Throughout higher education, disciplines work as if place does not exist, and this blocks hearing all the voices in a place and the opportunity for fully reflective thinking. The block comes in great part from the modern disciplinary assumption of the teacher as expert. In the modern discipline system, the teacher is the focus of the learning environment. The rhetoric of inquiry limits the dialogue to one among experts. Where can the knowledge, which our created universe provides to us, be assured of an un-manipulated or unfiltered hearing? Robert Welker (1992) reminds us that, "education implies freedom, personal responsibility over what one learns, and ownership of the knowledge one acquires. Education implicates the ability of the learner, not the ability of the teacher who has been able to manipulate events so as to promote the desired response in the subject" (Welker 1992, 136). The modern discipline system makes the student dependent on the teacher rather than empowering the student to explore and understand the universe in as many ways and places as possible. Welker takes us to the heart of things when he further notes that, "the teacher whose knowledge has not been used to make the student less dependent has failed" (1992, 136).

Part of the failure in developing ecological studies curricula may be because of this culture of focusing on the teacher rather than the learning environment. We focus on teaching rather than learning. We focus on disembodied, decontextualized factoid knowledge rather than on the story of the universe among all its forms, as Thomas Berry encouraged us. We focus only on people's knowledge, and only some people at that. What John Cobb (1992) identifies as a problem for the church in speaking about environmental issues may apply to teaching as well, "its distorted commitment to anthropocentrism has blocked it"(1992, 118). It is easy for us to fall into this. Even environmentally concerned educators use language that reinforces the problem. The expression "crystallized pedagogy" is gaining some currency as a way of saying that the teaching, the curriculum, the buildings, and the place all need to reflect sound ecological directions in order to experience a consistent message in the study of ecological concerns. While I agree with the concept, the term still puts the teacher in charge. If the place with its entire people is to be taken seriously, then we must move to another language which focuses on what Maxine Greene (1995), following upon the ideas of Hannah Arendt, calls a "web of relations." Maybe better terms would be "crystallized learning" or "embodied learning," or "sustainable learning."

For Greene the "web of relations" has, "to begin in local places, in schoolrooms and schoolyards and neighborhood centers; it has to begin where people know each others' names. But it can reach beyond, toward an enlarging public space where more and more common interests are articulated. It can radiate to inform the "conversation" and to empower individuals to open themselves to what they are making in common. Once they are open, once they are informed, once they are engaged in speech and action from their many vantage points, they may be able to identify a better state of things -- and go on to transform (Greene 1995, 59). In an ecological studies curriculum the web must include all in the place: the students, the workers, the most insignificant of persons whose work impacts the lives of the learners, and, most especially, the often most insignificant member of the web, the physical place itself.

Further, while finding at St. Thomas that traditional modes of teaching in relation to ecological concerns was burning out those who strove to continue with the teacher as focus, we also discovered that an ecological studies curriculum needs to have teachers who take a different stance. In pedagogical terms they must move, as devotees of cooperative learning say, from "sage on the stage" to "guide on the side." They must move from a place where they "stand and talk" to one where they freely "sit and listen" to other persons and the earth itself. An essential part of this is for teachers to assist the ethos of the place to become supportive of the learning they are trying to foster. They must be able to believe that the very landscape in which they work can help to bring knowledge to students and other participants in learning. They have to sense the ethos or spirituality of the landscape of the place. As Lane (1988) observes, "even ordinary landscapes -- those least expected to offer entry into mystery -- can sometimes prove the most profound."

In our dialoguing with Thomas Berry in Italy and Miami, we at St. Thomas University were led to work on changing teaching and begin involving the ethos, the spirituality of our place, as a source of knowledge to facilitate learning. In the ordinary landscapes of Italy and Miami we entered into mystery, found connections, examined our root metaphors and overcame intentional blindness through reflective dialogues with Thomas. As a result, students and faculty at St. Thomas University -- a very ordinary, a least expected, place --

explored through reflective thinking profound changes in the ways we learned, taught and constructed curriculum around the ecology of our local environment and our universe.

REFERENCES

Bellah, R. M., Madsen, R., Sullivan, W.M., Swidler, A. and Tipton, S.A. 1985. *Habits of the Heart: Individualism and Commitment in American life*. Berkeley: University of California Press.

Bowers, C.A. 2000. *Let them Eat Data: How Computers Affect Education, Cultural Diversity and the Prospects of Ecological Sustainability*. Athens, GA: University of Georgia Press.

Chew, S. 2014. "Helping students to get the most out of studying". In V.A. Benassi, C.E. Overson, & C.M. Hakala (Eds.). *Applying Science of Learning in Education: Infusing Psychological Science into the Curriculum*. Retrieved from the Society for the Teaching of Psychology web site: http://teachpsych.org/ebooks/asle2014/index.php

Cobb, J. 1992. *Sustainability: Economics, Ecology and Justice*. Maryknoll, NY: Orbis Books.

Dymoke, S. and Harrison, J. 2008. *Reflective Teaching and Learning; a Guide to Professional Issues for Beginning Secondary Teachers*. Los Angeles: Sage Publications.

The Five Books of Moses: Genesis, Exodus, Leviticus, Numbers, Deuteronomy: A New Translation with Introductions, Commentary, and Notes. 1995. Translated by Fox, E. New York: Schocken Books.

Greene, M. 1995. *Releasing the Imagination: Essays on Education, the Arts, and Social Change.* San Francisco: Jossey-Bass.

McCloskey, G.N. 1997-98. "Knowledge of place as part of a curriculum of ecological studies." *Earth Ethics,* 9 (1 & 2) 33-35.

Lane, B. C. 1988. *Landscapes of the Sacred: Geography and Narrative in American Spirituality.* New York. New York: Paulist Press.

Sirotnik, K. 1991. Critical inquiry: a paradigm for praxis. Edited by Short, E C. *Forms of Curriculum Inquiry.* Albany, NY: SUNY Press.

Waters, B. 1986. Ministry and the University in a Postmodern World. *Religion and Intellectual Life* 4(1) 113-122.

Welker, R. 1992. *The Teacher as Expert: a Theoretical and Historical Examination.* Albany, NY: SUNY Press.

14

ENDOCRINE DISRUPTING CHEMICALS THREATEN FETAL HEALTH

FREDERICK S. VOM SAAL

One of the most relevant contributions to the Spirituality and Sustainability conferences with Thomas Berry was the presence of renowned scientists, like Dr. Frederick vom Saal, adding an important dimension to the dialogue of sustainability.

A large number of chemicals in household products and commerce, referred to as endocrine disrupting chemicals (EDCs), can interfere with the hormonal signals required for normal fetal development. The functioning of the endocrine system in animals and humans is very similar, and adverse effects of EDCs on fetuses have been observed in wildlife (fish, frogs, reptiles, birds and mammals) and humans. Regulatory agencies have been slow to respond to published findings about the hazards of fetal exposure to EDCs and have resisted changing outdated approaches being used to assess the safety of chemicals.

Decades ago the Great Lakes in North America had many predatory birds that fed on fish in the lakes. Wildlife biologists noticed a dramatic decline in nests with live young, and between 1980 and 1983 there were very few birds that successfully reproduced. Biologists had known of the disastrous thinning effect of high levels of the pesticide, DDT, with the result that eggs would break prior to hatching; also, chicks were being found dead with gross deformities. With lower levels of pesticides and industrial chemicals in the lakes, the egg-shell thinning and gross deformities were not seen, and most people assumed that the problem of pollution had been solved by the regulations enacted during the 1970s. But, something was still happening to reduce reproduction. One strange observation that, at first, there was no explanation for was that nests contained more that the typical 2 to 3 eggs, and instead, double clutches, nests with 5 to 6 eggs, were being found. In some areas in which this was observed, populations of gulls were mostly females. There were very few males, and females were pairing with each other instead of with a male. Many of the eggs in these double clutches were not fertilized.

Where had all of the males gone? Why were these female gulls exhibiting abnormal reproductive behaviors and pairing with other females? An avian biologist provided a possible answer when he measured the levels of DDT in gull eggs found in nests, and then conducted an experiment and administered the same amount of DDT to gull embryos that he had measured in eggs found in the nests. The experimentally treated eggs were produced by gulls that had not been exposed to man-made chemicals. The DDT caused sex reversal in males, making the male embryos appear externally as if they were females. However, all of the DDT exposed embryos were actually intersex (they had some male and female reproductive organs), and they were sterile. DDT ingested by a female gull was being transported into her eggs and causing effects in male embryos that were similar to effects of treating embryos with the natural sex hormone, estradiol, the most potent endogenous estrogen; one of the chemicals present in commercial DDT is a chemical estrogen. Estrogen is critical as a regulator of sexual development in birds as well as all other vertebrate animals, including humans. The levels of DDT and other pollutants were no longer high enough to cause death or gross externally visible malformations, such as beaks that were crossed, but instead, more subtle damage that was not as easily detected was occurring in embryos that led to functional and behavioral abnormalities that became apparent much later in adulthood (Fry and Toone 1981, Fry 1995).

Biologists studying fish in the Great Lakes were also alarmed that so many different types of fish were showing abnormalities, including reduced fertility or sterility. There was not a top predator fish being found in the lower Great Lakes that did not show evidence of an abnormal thyroid. Entire populations of salmon and trout were not reproducing and their reproductive organs were also abnormal. Thyroid hormone is essential for normal development, particularly of the brain, in all vertebrate animals (Colborn and Clement 1992).

At the same time that these observations were being made, I was conducting research showing that the sensitivity of fetuses to sex hormones such as estradiol was much greater than had been realized. A change in the level of estradiol in the serum of a mouse fetuses of less that 1/10 of a trillionth of a gram per milliliter of serum (which we refer to in toxicology as 1/10 of a part per trillion or 0.1 picogram/ml serum) was sufficient to completely change the course of development of the brain and reproductive organs, resulting in changes in behavior and organ function throughout the remainder of life (vom Saal 1989, vom Saal et al. 1997). Importantly, the potency of estradiol in mice is similar to its potency in human tissues (Welshons et al. 2003).

By way of background to a discussion about chemicals in the environment that disrupt normal development because they can interfere with the functioning of natural hormones, which are referred to as endocrine disrupting chemicals or EDCs (Colborn, vom Saal, and Soto 1993), it is important to understand something about the endocrine system and how the hormone messengers that make up the endocrine system regulate the development of organs during prenatal life. The endocrine system consists of many different glands that produce hormones and tissues in the body that have receptors for specific hormones that allow cells in the tissue to respond to the hormones. Most important is that the developing fetus cannot be thought of as a little adult, who is capable of responding to changes in hormones by making physiological adjustments, which is the principle of homeostasis. This principle cannot be applied to fetuses as it can to adults, since the homeostatic systems are in the process of developing in fetuses.

Fetuses are incredibly sensitive to hormonal disturbance. As discussed above this can be shown by using as an example estradiol that can have a dramatic influence on sexual development due to a very small change in concentration in the blood in mice and all other vertebrates, including humans. Estradiol turns on and off genes in developing cells in a fetus based on minute changes in the amount in the fetal blood. Once a set of genes in turned on or off or modulated in terms of how active the genes will be, these genes have been irreversible or "programmed". The molecular mechanisms by which the function of genes in controlled is called "epigenetics", which refers to events outside of "classical" genetics that focused on gene mutations or factors that led to changes in the genetic code. For example, the relative amounts of estradiol and another sex hormone, testosterone, determines whether a fetus develops female reproductive organs or male reproductive organs, which is not a very subtle consequence of what would be considered by anyone to be minute changes in hormone levels. The same thing happens in the brain, leading to normal sex differences in socio-sexual behaviors, such as aggression, activity levels, and sexual orientation. If you have raised both a boy and a girl you understand the consequence of these small (parts per trillion to parts per billion) differences in the levels of hormones in male and female fetuses; these differences are not just due to how parents raise boys and girls (Hines 2011).

Our dependence on hormones to regulate development has made fetuses incredibly vulnerable to exposure to very small concentrations of EDCs during development (Welshons et al. 2003; Vandenberg et al. 2012). The recognition that man-made chemicals being released into the environment could alter development at very low concentrations led Dr. Theo Colborn to propose that it was possible that much lower levels of environmental pollutants than had previously been thought to cause effects might, in fact, account for the damage to wildlife that was being observed in the Great Lakes and elsewhere in the world (Colborn, vom Saal, and Soto 1993; Colborn, Dumanosk, and Myers 1996).

Why was this not previously found if the chemical revolution that led to the widespread use of man-made chemicals began in the 1950s? The reason is the very long generation time in people and many of the most affected species. If effects of endocrine disruptors are "programmed" during fetal life but do not become apparent until adulthood when attempts to reproduce continuously fail, it is logical that this problem took a long time to be recognized even though widespread exposure may have occurred decades ago. This was clearly demonstrated by the tragedy associated with doctors prescribing the estrogenic drug diethylstilbestrol (DES) to millions of women over about a 20 year period from about 1950 to 1970, when DES was finally banned for use in pregnant women due to the finding that the daughters exposed to DES as fetuses were being diagnosed with a rare cancer. More recently, DES daughters, now middle-aged, have been shown to be at increased risk for developing breast cancer 40 years after being exposed *in utero* (Soto et al. 2013).

Over 20 years after the first workshop on endocrine disrupting chemicals in 1991 (Colborn, vom Saal, and Soto 1993), there is now clear evidence that a wide variety of chemicals in use today can alter the endocrine system in developing animals and humans at exposure levels far below those established as "safe" based on the use of outdated testing methods by federal regulatory agencies in the USA and elsewhere. This has led Endocrine Society, the international society of medical and research endocrinologists, to issue a position paper calling for a change in the approaches used by regulatory agencies to assess the risks associated with exposure to EDCs (Zoeller et al. 2012).

EDCs are showing up in unlikely places. They are present in a wide variety of household products and are being released into the air we breathe, the water we drink and the foods we eat. None of these chemicals was thought to be a "hormone disruptor" when it was first synthesized for use as a pesticide or in some product, such as plastics or hand cream. It is only very recently that some of these chemicals have been discovered to be "environmental estrogens" that can mimic the hormone estradiol, environmental anti-androgens that can interfere with testosterone, or environmental thyroid hormone disruptors that can disrupt thyroid hormone function. In addition, many other aspects of hormone signaling, including disruption of fat cell (adipocyte) differentiation, insulin production, uptake of glucose into tissues, effects on the heart and kidney, as well as widespread effects on the brain, have been identified due to exposure to very small amounts of EDCs once presumed to be safe (TEDX 2014). However, most regulatory agencies will not acknowledge that the "old" approaches used to test for chemical hazards, which did not include examination of endocrine responses, is no longer valid. There is a large amount of evidence that effects of EDCs can occur at doses thousands of times lower that the doses predicted to be safe by the old crude testing methods currently used by industry to test for the safety of chemicals used in products. However, it is also important to note that only a very few of the approximately 100,000 registered chemicals have ever been directly tested for their health effects (EDF 1997).

For example, bisphenol A (BPA) is a chemical that has been found to mimic the effects of estradiol, block the effects of testosterone and thyroid hormone, and stimulate an increase in fat cell development in human and animal cells; the estrogen-mimicking and fat cell stimulating effects occur at very low exposures, far below doses that the public is assured are safe (Angle et al. 2013, Vandenberg et al. 2013). Based on prior animal tests with BPA, which is the chemical used to make polycarbonate plastic, the plastic coating in metal cans, dental sealants and fillings, thermal receipt paper, and as an additive in many other products, daily oral intake of BPA of 5-mg/kg body weight/day was estimated to be safe. In contrast, there are now about 90 epidemiological studies in humans and hundreds of experimental studies in animals, which are supported by hundreds of other studies using human and animals cells, showing that BPA can have effects at dramatically lower doses, thousands of times below the presumed safe dose (vom Saal et al. 2007, Rochester 2013, Vandenberg et al. 2013). The BPA studies conducted by independent scientists covered in these published reviews of the literature contrast dramatically with the relatively small number of studies conducted and funded by the chemical industry, that always concludes that BPA is safe; the difference in the conclusions regarding safety based on source of funding was dramatic when reviewed in 2005 (vom Saal and Hughes 2005), and is even greater today.

The US-FDA and European Food Safety Authority (EFSA) have conducted risk assessments over the last few years and both agencies have ignored all of this large published literature by independent scientists and based their assessment that BPA is safe on only two studies funded by the American Chemistry Council, the lobbying organization for chemical industries (FDA 2008b, EFSA 2006). The FDA's science board criticized and rejected the risk assessment conducted by the FDA (FDA 2008a) and the European Commission has challenged EFSAs risk assessment, but in the mean-time, no action by regulatory agencies is being taken to reduce exposure to this chemical.

The implications of evidence that using 21st century molecular techniques, effects of EDCs are found that are not predicted based on crude and outdated toxicological testing methods still in use by regulatory agencies, are profound (Zoeller et al. 2012). The challenge will be for the regulatory establishment to accept that there is overwhelming scientific evidence that their assurances of safety of EDCs are false. It is always a stressful and painful process to admit that a "paradigm shift" has occurred requiring a change in approach, and it is not surprising that the US-FDA and EFSA are currently unwilling to acknowledge this to the public (Kuhn 1962).

Not all endocrine disrupting chemicals are estrogen mimics. Other chemicals, such as polychlorinated biphenyls (PCBs), that were previously used in many products due to resistance to heat, and dioxin, an industrial waste produced as a consequence of manufacturing chlorinated chemicals, can interfere with normal thyroid function during embryonic life. Not only have effects of PCBs been shown to occur in laboratory animals and wildlife, but studies in humans have shown that fetal exposure to PCBs predicts the rate of postnatal neuromuscular development (which is delayed), a child's behavior and even IQ, which is lowered in fetuses exposed to the highest levels of PCBs. In one of a number of studies relating exposure to PCBs in the womb to subsequent abnormalities, mothers were recruited based on having eaten a few fish per month from the Great Lakes. But, sport fishing remains a multi-billion dollar a year business in this region and governments and industries that profit from this activity by taxes, fishing licenses and selling products do not want to take action regarding the health risks posed by eating contaminated fish (Jacobson and Jacobson 1996).

Particularly frightening about PCBs and other highly persistent chemicals, such as DDT, which can remain active in your body for decades, is that they "bioaccumulate or biomagnify" as they are transported up the food chain and finally reach animals, such as humans, at the top of the food chain, who are thus the most heavily contaminated by these chemicals (Colborn, vom Saal, and Soto 1993). In addition, we now know that PCBs and other persistent chemicals are being transported around the globe via the atmosphere. Thus, whenever a chemical is released into the environment, its impact is not local but global. This is truly a world-wide problem that no laws that focus only on local communities will solve. One sad commentary on the approach to global pollution in the USA is that whereas it became illegal to use DDT in the USA in the 1970s, it was not banned from production or sale by US companies abroad.

The finding that exposure of human fetuses to a man-made chemical predicts brain function later in life, and the confirmation of identical findings in animal experiments and studies of wildlife exposed to the same chemicals, now leaves no doubt that man-made chemicals in the environment can disrupt the endocrine system during development, with profound consequences for the functioning of the brain. The list of chemicals that can alter the normal functioning of the endocrine system in animals is growing, and this list is certain to get larger as testing for endocrine disruption finally becomes a part of the screening of chemicals for health effects (TEDX 2014).

The position of the chemical industry is one of denial that a problem has been shown with regard to effects of EDCs on human health. There is, on the other hand, acceptance that wildlife and laboratory animals are showing effects. The assumption underlying this argument is that humans are somehow disconnected from the rest of the animal kingdom, and that chemicals can have dramatic damaging effects that can be demonstrated in every class of vertebrate: fish, frogs, reptiles, birds, laboratory rodents and primates as well as mammalian wildlife (such as mink), but, somehow we can believe that this does not mean that we should also expect to see effects in humans.

With regard to the likelihood of significant species differences in the capacity for environmental chemicals to cause endocrine disruption, there is consensus among biologists that at the molecular, mechanistic level, the response system to hormones (hormone receptors in cells) as well as the hormones that make up the endocrine system, are so fundamental to development and normal life that they have changed remarkably little over 300-million years of vertebrate evolution. Thus, the sex hormone estradiol in fish and humans is identical, and the functioning of hormone receptors in fish and human cells is fundamentally the same. However, specific genes controlled by estrogen will differ in each species. Binding of natural estradiol or other man-made estrogenic chemicals to the estrogen receptor in fish has thus been shown to predict that a response (albeit a different response) will also occur in humans; this has been known for decades, it is not a new finding. Thus, if a chemical is an endocrine disruptor in fish or any other vertebrate, it can reasonably be expected to disrupt the endocrine system in humans. If we reject the relatedness of humans to the rest of the living world, we open up the possibility that global pollution will be viewed as only a problem for plants and animals, but not for humans.

Industry representatives state that until "solid scientific proof" of effects in humans is obtained, they should not be expected to alter production or use of chemicals, such as BPA, based only on information from animals. They also reject the large number of published human studies because they were not "experimental" studies that involved random assignment of people to be treated or not treated with a chemical (referred to as a randomized controlled study). The vast majority of epidemiological studies involve relating measured levels of a chemical (or a group of chemicals) in a population and relating the amount measured to some set of health outcomes. When the observed relationship is consistent with data from causal experimental studies in animals, and mechanistic studies in cell culture, one would expect that finding effects in populations of people to raise an alarm. It is important to remember that no study has provided "solid scientific proof' that cigarette smoking is dangerous to your health, since this would require a human experiment, which has not been conducted. My view is that if it gets to the point that there is evidence for harm being done by a chemical that can be detected in the human population, the regulatory system has failed to adequately protect the public. With regard to the standard of proof being set by industry whose products are being found to act as endocrine disruptors, we cannot expect experiments to be conducted with pregnant women to determine whether their fetuses are harmed in a manner similar to effects already observed in animals.

The regulatory system is supposed to base assessments of risk using a "weight of evidence" approach, such as is now accepted for cigarette smoking and adverse health effects. However, for chemicals such as BPA, regulatory agencies only include in their analysis industry-funded studies that meet government record-keeping requirements put in place due to finding extensive fraud in reporting by industry about the adverse effects of chemicals that they manufacture (Myers, Zoeller, and vom Saal 2009; Myers et al. 2009). These reporting requirements are based on the assumption that the study will not be repeated by anyone else. In contrast, in academic science findings are considered preliminary until they are independently verified. The very expensive / extensive record keeping requirements imposed on industry are thus irrelevant in academic science where independent replication is the major criterion for accepting results as valid.

Industry in the United States has tremendous control over environmental laws enacted by congress, as well as the federal agencies that regulate chemicals. The Toxic Substance Control Act (TSCA) that governs the regulation of environmental chemicals in the USA was determined by the courts to not provide the EPA with the authority to regulate asbestos. Everyone agrees that TSCA is a failure as currently written, but the chemical corporations have successfully blocked TSCA reform for decades. It has thus proven almost impossible to eliminate any chemical from the marketplace through federal regulatory action once it becomes economically valuable to an industry. Instead, civil lawsuits have been the only vehicle open to the US population to remove or restrict chemicals in commerce. A few examples are asbestos, Silicon and tobacco. Only through an intensive campaign of public education regarding the problem of global pollution and the long-term harm to the health of our children, those yet unborn, and all animal life, with resulting public and legal pressure on industry and regulatory, will any change from the status quo of regulatory inaction occur.

REFERENCES

Angle, B. M., R. P. Do, D. Ponzi, R. W. Stahlhut, B. E. Drury, S. C. Nagel, W. V. Welshons, C. L. Besch-Williford, P. Palanza, S. Parmigiani, F. S. Vom Saal, and J. A. Taylor. 2013. "Metabolic disruption in male mice due to fetal exposure to low but not high doses of bisphenol A (BPA): Evidence for effects on body weight, food intake, adipocytes, leptin, adiponectin, insulin and glucose regulation." *Reprod Toxicol*. 42:256-268.

Colborn, T. , D. Dumanosk, and J.P. Myers. 1996. *Our Stolen Future: Are We Threatening Our Fertility, Intelligence, and Survival? A Scientific Detective Story*. New York: Dutton.

Colborn, T., and C. Clement. 1992. *Chemically induced alterations in sexual and functional development: the wildlife/human connection*. Princeton, NJ: Princeton Scientific.

Colborn, Theo, Frederick S. vom Saal, and Ana M. Soto. 1993. "Developmental effects of endocrine-disrupting chemicals in wildlife and humans." *Environmental Health Perspectives*. 101 (5):378-384.

EDF. 1997. *Toxic Ignorance*. Baltimore, MD: Environmental Defense Fund; https://www.google.com/#q=Toxic++Ignorance+EDF.

EFSA. 2006. "Opinion of the Scientific Panel on Food Additives, Flavourings, Processing Aids and Materials in Contact with Food on a request from the Commission related to 2,2-BIS(4-HYDROXYPHENYL)PROPANE (Bisphenol A)." *The EFSA (European Food Safety Authority) Journal*. 428:1-76.

FDA. 2008a. FDA Science Board Subcommittee Report on Bisphenol A. http://google2.fda.gov/search?q=bisphenol+A&client=FDAgov&site=FDAgov&lr=&proxystylesheet=FDAgov&output=xml_no_dtd&getfields=*&requiredfields=-archive%3AYes, accessed October 1, 2013.

FDA. 2008b. Food and Drug Administration draft assessment of bisphenol A for use in Food contact applications, August 14, 2008.

http://google2.fda.gov/search?q=bisphenol+A&client=FDAgov& site=FDAgov&lr=&proxystylesheet=FDAgov&output=xml_no_ dtd&getfields=*&requiredfields=-archive%3AYes, accessed October 1, 2013.

Fry, D. M., and C. K. Toone. 1981. "DDT-induced feminization of gull embryos." *Science*. 213 (4510):922-4.

Fry, D. Michael. 1995. "Reproductive effects in birds exposed to pesticides and industrial chemicals." *Environmental Health Perspectives*. 103 (Suppl. 7):165-171.

Hines, M. 2011. "Prenatal endocrine influences on sexual orientation and on sexually differentiated childhood behavior." *Frontiers in Neuroendocrinology*. 32 (2):170-182.

Jacobson, J.L., and S.W. Jacobson. 1996. "Intellectual impairment in children exposed to polychlorinated biphenyls in utero." *New England Journal of Medicine*. 335:783-789.

Kuhn, T. S. 1962. "Historical structure of scientific discovery." *Science*. 136:760-764.

Myers, J. P., F. S. vom Saal, B. T. Akingbemi, K. Arizono, S. Belcher, T. Colborn, I. Chahoud, D. A. Crain, F. Farabollini, L. J. Guillette, Jr., T. Hassold, S. M. Ho, P. A. Hunt, T. Iguchi, S. Jobling, J. Kanno, H. Laufer, M. Marcus, J. A. McLachlan, A. Nadal, J. Oehlmann, N. Olea, P. Palanza, S. Parmigiani, B. S. Rubin, G. Schoenfelder, C. Sonnenschein, A. M. Soto, C. E. Talsness, J. A. Taylor, L. N. Vandenberg, J. G. Vandenbergh, S. Vogel, C. S. Watson, W. V. Welshons, and R. T. Zoeller. 2009. "Why public health agencies cannot depend on good laboratory practices as a criterion for selecting data: the case of bisphenol A." *Environ Health Perspect*. 117 (3):309-315.

Myers, J.P., T.J. Zoeller, and F.S. vom Saal. 2009. "A clash of old and new scientific concepts in toxicity, with important implications for public health." *Environ. Health Perspect.* 117:1652–1655.

Rochester, J. R. 2013. "Bisphenol A and human health: A review of the literature." *Reprod Toxicol.* 42:132-155.

Soto, A. M., C. Brisken, C. Schaeberle, and C. Sonnenschein. 2013. "Does Cancer Start in the Womb? Altered Mammary Gland Development and Predisposition to Breast Cancer due to in Utero Exposure to Endocrine Disruptors." *J Mammary Gland Biol Neoplasia.* 18 (2):199-208.

TEDX. 2014. TEDX (The Endocrine Disruption Exchange) List of Potential Endocrine Disruptors. http://endocrinedisruption.org/endocrine-disruption/tedx-list-of-potential-endocrine-disruptors/overview, accessed Jaunary 16, 2014.

Vandenberg, L. N., T. Colborn, T. B. Hayes, J. J. Heindel, D. R. Jacobs, Jr., D. H. Lee, T. Shioda, A. M. Soto, F. S. vom Saal, W. V. Welshons, R. T. Zoeller, and J. P. Myers. 2012. "Hormones and endocrine-disrupting chemicals: low-dose effects and nonmonotonic dose responses." *Endocr Rev.* 33 (3):378-455.

Vandenberg, L.N., S. Ehrlich, S.M. Belcher, N. Ben-Jonathan, D.C. Dolinoy, E.S. Hugo, P.A. Hunt, R.R. Newbold, B.S. Rubin, K.S. Saili, A.M. Soto, H-S. Wang, and F.S. vom Saal. 2013. "Low dose effects of bisphenol a: An integrated review of in vitro, laboratory animal and epidemiology studies." *Endocrine Disruption.* 1:E1-E20.

vom Saal, F. S. 1989. "Sexual differentiation in litter-bearing mammals: influence of sex of adjacent fetuses in utero." *Journal of Animal Science.* 67 (7):1824-1840.

vom Saal, F. S., B. T. Akingbemi, S. M. Belcher, L. S. Birnbaum, D. A. Crain, M. Eriksen, F. Farabollini, L. J. Guillette, Jr., R. Hauser, J. J. Heindel, S. M. Ho, P. A. Hunt, T. Iguchi, S. Jobling, J. Kanno, R. A. Keri, K. E. Knudsen, H. Laufer, G. A. LeBlanc, M. Marcus, J. A. McLachlan, J. P. Myers, A. Nadal, R. R. Newbold, N. Olea, G. S. Prins, C. A. Richter, B. S. Rubin, C. Sonnenschein, A. M. Soto, C. E. Talsness, J. G. Vandenbergh, L. N. Vandenberg, D. R. Walser-Kuntz, C. S. Watson, W. V. Welshons, Y. Wetherill, and R. T. Zoeller. 2007. "Chapel Hill bisphenol A expert panel consensus statement: integration of mechanisms, effects in animals and potential to impact human health at current levels of exposure." *Reprod Toxicol.* 24 (2):131-138.

vom Saal, F. S., and C. Hughes. 2005. "An extensive new literature concerning low-dose effects of bisphenol A shows the need for a new risk assessment." *Environ. Health Perspect.* 113:926-933.

vom Saal, Frederick S., Barry G. Timms, Monica M. Montano, Paola Palanza, Kristina A. Thayer, Susan C. Nagel, Minati D. Dhar, V. K. Ganjam, Stefano Parmigiani, and Wade V. Welshons. 1997. "Prostate enlargement in mice due to fetal exposure to low doses of estradiol or diethylstilbestrol and opposite effects at high doses." *Proceedings of the National Academy of Sciences.* 94 (5):2056-2061.

Welshons, W. V., K. A. Thayer, B. M. Judy, J. A. Taylor, E. M. Curran, and F. S. vom Saal. 2003. "Large effects from small exposures. I. Mechanisms for endocrine-disrupting chemicals with estrogenic activity." *Environ Health Perspect.* 111 (8):994-1006.

Zoeller, R. T., T. R. Brown, L. L. Doan, A. C. Gore, N. E. Skakkebaek, A. M. Soto, T. J. Woodruff, and F. S. Vom Saal. 2012. "Endocrine-disrupting chemicals and public health protection: a statement of principles from the endocrine society." *Endocrinology.* 153 (9):4097-110.

PART III

INNOVATIVE STUDY-ABROAD PROGRAMS CENTERED ON THOMAS BERRY'S COSMOLOGY

Mindful of our environmental and social degradation, Study Abroad for Earth (S.A.F.E.) was born first to discover the underlying causes of our current problems and then to change our way of thinking, our life-styles and our anthropocentric paradigm, to an eco-centered one based on Thomas Berry's Cosmology.

15

IMAGING THE EARTH
IN SAN FRANCESCO & DANTE:
SOME REFLECTIONS WITH THOMAS BERRY

James Conley

This essay briefly relates St. Francis of Assisi's "Cantico delle Creature" and Dante's Commedia to Thomas Berry's reflections on the living quality of the earth and universe, on the need for a conversion towards sustainability and on the importance of re-telling the story of creation in light of the impending environmental crisis.

In the summer of 1995 when Thomas Berry taught as part of the St. Thomas University Study Abroad for Earth (S.A.F.E.) program in Assisi, he shared with all of the program's participants his vision of the "Great Work" that faced civilization at the close of the twentieth century. His call to comprehend and act upon the story of the universe as explained by the extraordinary accomplishments of contemporary science and as manifested by the startling and often indifferent pollution of the natural environment had its particular influence on me while preparing lectures for a literature course presented that summer as a S.A.F.E. offering. Whether at the entrance of the chapel of San Miniato after a steep journey downhill from Assisi or beneath the arch of the Porta Romana before an arduous climb up Mount Subasio to the Eremo delle Carceri or simply gathered around the dining tables at the Hotel Posta Panoramic, Tom Berry's insights seemed to have parallels in San Francesco's famous song of creation, in Dante's *Divine Comedy* with its imaging of nature, and in the call to appropriately "tell the story" so often articulated by Dante.

San Francesco apparently composed the *"Cantico delle creature"* in what are now gardens just below San Miniato: there is a bronze statue of Francesco in these gardens sitting beneath an olive tree, pen in hand and folio on his lap, gazing out at the Spoleto Valley and reflecting on the beauty all creation has to offer. San Francesco starts the poem as a prayer,

> *Altissimu, omnipotente, bon Signore*
> *Tue so le laude la gloria e l'honore*
> *Et omne benedictione.*
> *Ad te solo, Altissimo, si confano*
> *et nullo homo ene dignu te mentovare.*
>
> *Laudato sie, mi Signore, cun tutte le tue creature...*
>
> (San Francesco, 8)

(Highest, all powerful, good Lord\yours are the praise and the glory and the honor\and every blessing.\They belong to you alone, Great Lord, \and no one is worthy to speak your name.\ Praised be You, my Lord, \With all your creatures...)

There is a gentle humility on the part of Francesco as narrator of these words, for the divine is as high (*"Altissimu"*) and deep and extensive as the heavens, as the billions of galaxies and more; and Francesco recognizes his own shortcomings, his human limitations and his failures in contrast to divine perfection, his inability and unworthiness (*"nullo... dignu"*) to even attempt describing the "most high." And yet this Lord as fundamentally and ultimately "good" ("*bon Signore*") shares power and blessing with humanity and every other creature, allowing Francesco and every person and all of creation to manifest the "Highest" ("*Altissimu*") of all existence.

Years before coming to Assisi, Thomas Berry had described the broad trends of civilization in global culture in terms of "three mediations." The first mediation he explained as

> *that between the divine and the human, a mediation begun in ancient Israel, continued in the redemption by Christ, and communicated to Mohammed in later centuries. This process has dominated most of the last three thousand years of human history in the West* (Berry 2009, 8).

San Francesco clearly addresses this first mediation in his poem, whereas a second and third mediation gained prominence later, emerging in the fourteenth century and dominating modern times.

> *We have found it necessary during the past two centuries to give special consideration to the Second Mediation, the inter-human mediation, the reconciliation of different human groups … [And] our preoccupation with this second mediation continues even while a Third Mediation has become so strong that it overshadows in its significance even its predecessor. I speak of the mediation between the human community and the Earth, the planet that surrounds and supports us and upon which we depend for our nourishment and our breath.* (Berry 2009, 8-9)

Re-reading San Francesco's "*Cantico delle creature*" in light of the third mediation calls attention to the poem's interest in inter-human and human-earth reconciliations as well as those between the human and the divine.

Francesco as the narrator of the "*Cantico*" images each particular creature of the universe as a member of the human family: "*frate sole … sora luna e le stele … frate vento … sor' aqua … frate focu*" (brother sun…sister moon and the stars … brother wind … sister water …

brother fire"). Each of these has its particular quality: the sun, for example, is beautiful (*"bellu"*) and radiant (*"radiante"*) and establishes the day (*"jorna"*) and brings light (*"allumini"*), with all the intellectual and spiritual as well as physical implications of that image. And "brother sun," like each of the creatures, gains its meaning from the divine, "… *De te, Altissimo, porta significatione,*" (from you, most high, has significance, 8).

All three mediations operate simultaneously here: the divine creates each member of the universal community, and each person is empowered to respond by praising the Creator and sharing in the blessings of creation (hence the first mediation, the human-divine); each creature, human or natural, also carries the moniker "brother" or "sister" functioning symbolically as a member of a human family and capable of so doing literally (thus the second mediation, the inter-human or more accurately here the human and the natural treated as human); the third mediation, that between the human community and the earth (and by extension all elements of the natural universe) occurs as a corollary to imaging nature as a member of the human family, where the symbolism of the image becomes acceptance and respect in reality.

The "*Cantico*" in its middle stanzas names seven natural elements (the sun, the moon, the wind, water, fire, the earth, and death), and the references to the earth and to death deserve commentary on their distinctiveness. Francesco the narrator of the poem describes the earth as follows,

> *Laudato si, mi signore, per sora nostra matre terra,*
> *la quale ne sustenta et governa*
> *et produce diversi fructi con coloriti fiori et herba.*
> (San Francesco, 8)

(Praise be you, my Lord, for sister our mother earth,\ she who nourishes us and directs us\ and brings forth diverse fruits\ with colored flowers and grass.)

The poem recognizes the earth as parallel to but different from the other natural elements: the earth as "sister" (*"sora"*) shares as an equal with the others and with humanity, but simultaneously earth bears the image of "our mother" (*"nostra matre"*); the first person plural (*"nostra"*) includes the narrator and all the poem's readers and all the natural creatures. Like the sun, the earth takes her significance from the divine and symbolically participates in the human family; but she has the dual function of sustaining and ordering while manifesting diversity ("*...sustenta et governa \ et produce diversi fructi,*" San Francesco, 8).

Moreover, the earth endures beyond the death of other natural creatures, the fruits and the flowers and the grass; the earth and the other natural elements must be treated differently when Francesco reflects on death, which he associates primarily with humanity, "*Laudato si', mi Signore, per sora nostra morte corporale, \ da la quale nullo homo vivente po scappare,* ("Praise be you, my Lord, for our sister corporal death \ the which no human living can escape," 10). Only humans can sin and die in a state of the deathly evil, mortal sin ("*...quelli che morano ne le peccata mortali*") and thus experience a second death (*"la morte secunda"*), which Francesco describes as the ultimate evil. Earth can suffer evil at the hands of humanity, what the Greek Orthodox Patriarch Bartholomew in a joint statement with John Paul II called "ecological sins" (Tucker and Grim 2009, xvii), but earth can never sin and will never experience the second death.

The story in San Francesco's "*Cantico*" ends with a call to readers to do what the poem has been doing, "*Laudate et benedicite mi Signore et rengraziate / Et serviteli cun grande humilitate*" ("Praise and bless my Lord and thank and serve him with great humility," 10).

In 1999 Thomas Berry published *The Great Work* where he described, "those overarching movements that give shape and meaning to life by relating the human venture to the larger destinies of the universe" (Berry 1999, 1). He recognized the "Great Work" of the classical Greek world as its "understanding of the human mind" and that of Israel as narrating, "the experience of the divine in human affairs" (Berry 1999, 1), and then he discussed how, "in the medieval period there was the task of giving a first shape to the Western world in its Christian forms" (Berry 1999, 1).

It is in the context of discussing the late medieval world that Berry praises both San Francesco and Dante.

> *The immediate achievement of the thirteenth century was the first integration of what became Western civilization. This was the period of Francis, the poor man of Assisi, who established in Western civilization both the spiritual ideal of detachment from Earthly possessions and an intimacy with the natural world … In literature the incomparable Dante Alighieri produced his Commedia in the early fourteenth century.* (Berry 1999, 8-9)

San Francesco used images from the natural world to praise the divine, mediating between the divine and the human but also between the human community and the earth. Dante, adapting a principle of symbolic retribution where choices in each person's earthly life determine each individual's spiritual and eternal identity, shapes natural images for each stage of the great journey beyond life, realms envisioned as deep within the earth (Inferno) or on its surface surrounded by the planet's own watery hemisphere (*Purgatorio*) or above the earth in one of the nine heavenly spheres below the Empyrean, the measureless dwelling place of the divine (*Paradiso*).

The journey narrated in Dante's *Commedia* functions on many levels: for it is the story of Dante's love of his lady, Beatrice, who died in Florence when the two were still young adults; and it is the story of Dante's love of learning and letters and worldly reputation as embodied in the figure of Virgil, who guides the character Dante through *Inferno* and *Purgatorio*; and it is the story of Dante's diverse encounters with family and friends, educators and allies and political enemies, and of course natural phenomena including plants and animals and contrasting terrains and ever-changing waterways and even weathers -- often threatening but potentially soothing. Dante narrates a story of the universe!

In an essay entitled "Women Religious: Voices of Earth," written during the years that he taught with the Study Abroad for Earth program in Assisi, Thomas Berry discussed the importance of such universe-stories for every culture and for every individual longing to understand the sacredness of nature and human life,

> *Religion itself is awakened in the human soul by our experience of the awesome qualities of the immense universe about us, its overwhelming grandeur, its terrifying as well as its entrancing qualities. As the grandeur of the natural world declines, the primordial manifestation of the divine is progressively diminished. All of this must find its expression in the story of the universe.*
> (Berry 2009, 80-81)

There is little wonder that Berry considered the *Commedia* "incomparable."

From the earliest scenes of *"Inferno"* to the depiction of Purgatory's shore and Earthly Paradise to the celestial spheres and the last and ultimate moment of revelation in *"Paradiso,"* Dante fills his lines with images from nature that show his fascination with the physical environment, both in its "terrifying" and "entrancing qualities." Dante's journey, of course, begins in mid-life and in a "dark woods," a forest that leaves him stunned with fear and anxiety, hopelessly lost,

> *Nel mezzo del cammin di nostra vita*
> *mi ritrovai in una selva oscura*
> *che la diritta via era smarrita.*
> *Ah quanto a dir qual era é cosa dura*
> *esta selva selvaggia aspra e forte*
> *che nel pensier rinova la paura...*
> (*Inf.* I, 1-6)

(In the midst of the journey of our life\I found myself in a dark woods\where the straight path was lost.\ Oh how saying what was there is so hard\that wooded forest, bitter and thick such that in thinking of it the fear returns.)

At the end of this dark, forested valley Dante encounters a hillside *("un colle")*; and gazing up to its top he sees the rays of the sun (*"raggi del pianeta\che mena dritto altrui per ogni calle,"* rays of the planet that leads one straight through every way, *Inf.* I, 17-18); and he chooses to climb towards the light, only to be forced back by three beasts, the lion and the leopard and the she-wolf (symbols – Dante would call them allegories -- of violence, and deception and weakness).

In his descent Dante encounters a figure who identifies himself as having been once a man (*"omo gia' fui,"* *Inf.* I, 67) but now is a shadow (*"ombra,"* *Inf.* I, 66), the soul of the Roman poet Virgil, whose writings Dante had studied at length. Virgil was sent by Dante's celestial patronesses to guide him back to the straight path. When he learns that this means journeying deep within the earth and far above the earth, Dante hesitates, meriting a gentle rebuke from Virgil, who now identifies Dante's patronesses: Beatrice (*"donna...beata e bella,"* a lady...blessed and beautiful, *Inf.* II, 53), the Queen of Heaven herself (*"Donna gentil nel ciel che si compiange,"* Our gentle lady in heaven who feels your sorrow, *Inf.* II, 94), and Saint Lucy. Dante responds immediately, of course, a reaction that solicits a fascinating image from the natural world, one that contrasts with the dark woods and threatening beasts. Dante the narrator describes his character's new-found eagerness and courage as follows, *"Quali i fioretti, dal notturno gelo\chinati e chiusi, poi che 'l sol li 'mbianca\si drizzan tutti aperti in loro stelo,"* (like the flowers from the nocturnal cold bent and closed, then when the sun whitens them stand straight all open on their stalks, *Inf.* II, 127-29). Dante's nature imagery, as indicated by such early scenes in *Inferno*, celebrates the power and beauty of the natural environment and underlines the spiritual and psychological realities that these images represent. Over and over again such images invite the reader to appreciate nature, indeed to take action in preserving the natural environment from its pollution and destruction, and to do so from both aesthetic and moral inspirations.

Each scene as Dante descends through the underworld offers examples of this depiction of the natural environment in its diversity and significance. At the very gateway of *Inferno*, for example, Dante and Virgil experience a moment when the stones of the earth themselves seem to speak with the written word; carved above Hades' gates are stern and threatening yet compassionate words, among the most frequently quoted verses from the *Commedia*,

> *Per me si va nella città dolente,*
> *per me si va nell' eterno dolore,*
> *per me si va nella perduta gente.*
> *Giustizia mosse il mio alto fattore:*
> *fecemi la divina potestate,*
> *la somma sapienza e 'l primo amore.*
> *Dinanzi a me non fuor cose create*
> *se non etterne, ed io etterno duro.*
> *Lasciate ogni speranza, voi ch' entrate.*
> (*Inf.* III, 1-9)

(Through me one goes into the sorrowing city, \ through me one goes into eternal sorrow, \ through me one goes among the lost people. \ Justice my High Creator moved, \ shaped me the Divine Power, \ the Ultimate Wisdom and the First Love.\ Before me no created things were\ but only eternal, and I endure or eternity.\ Leave behind every hope, you who enter.)

One senses compassion as these lines begin, suggested by the emphasis on "sorrow" through repetition (*"dolente...dolore"*) and the realization that those in the underworld are the "lost" (*"perduta gente"*) similar to the character Dante himself in the dark woods but dissimilar too as lost forever. Justice and wisdom and even love shaped this realm, an environment severe in its hopelessness and yet at this point in Dante's journey immensely pitiable.

Such are the ones whose tormented cries Dante now hears, those whom Virgil describes as the "anime triste" (sad souls, Inf. III, 35) of the indifferent, those who "lived without shame and without praise" (*"che visser sanza infamia e sanza lode,"* Inf. III, 36). Included among these figures are those whom both "mercy and justice disdain" (*"misericordia e giustizia li sdegna,"* Inf. III, 50) like the angels who neither rebelled against nor remained loyal to the Creator. Virgil abruptly dismisses them with the sharp command *"guarda e passa,"* ("look and move on" Inf. III, 51). What Dante sees is excruciating and embodies Thomas Berry's concept that nature can be both terrifying and entrancing,

> *Questi sciaurati, che mai non fur vivi,*
> *erano ignudi stimolati molto*
> *da mosconi e da vespe ch' eran ivi.*
> *Elle rigavan lor di sangue il volto,*
> *che mischiato di lagrime, a' lor piedi*
> *da fastidiosi vermi era ricolto...*
> (*Inf.* III, 64-69)

(These tortured ones who never were alive\ were naked and much attacked \ by the huge flies and wasps there.\ These lined their faces with blood\ which mixed with tears was grasped by fastidious worms at their feet.)

The souls of the indifferent cannot even brush away the flies and wasps that attack them, for an identity of avoiding choices defined their lives on earth and does so now and forever in eternity. Such might be those who cannot make up their minds about the crucial issues affecting the environment.

Out of the increasing darkness of *Inferno* emerges a group of souls awaiting Charon, the boatsman for the first of the Hellish, polluting rivers Dante will encounter, the Acheron with its *"livida palude,"* (smoldering swamp, *Inf.* III,98) and *"onda bruna,"* (darkened waves, *Inf.* III, 118). Subterranean waters border and permeate the realm of the damned where Inferno's winds (*"La bufera infernal"* *Inf.* V, 31), an earth-polluting hailstorm of filthy rain and snow (*"piova\...Grandine grossa, aqua tinta e neve\... pute la terra,"* Inf. VI, 7-12), and bone-crushing boulders rolled by their nameless sinners (*"voltando pesi per forza di poppa,"* Inf. VII, 27) provide punishment. Dante must cross the turbulent waters of the River Styx, the punishment for soul-damning anger, before passing through the Gates of Dis and entering the deeper Hell of the violent and the frauds and the consummate viciousness of betrayal. This last is the ninth circle of *Inferno,* the coldest and darkest space in the underworld, the eternal dwelling place of the source and prototype of all evil, Satan, buried in the frozen waters of Lake Cocytus. So the natural world in multitudinous diversity can serve as punishment for those who abuse God, fellow humanity, and nature herself.

All this changes as Dante ends his journey of descent, revolves on the very body of Satan, and climbs back to the surface of the earth (*"ritornar nel chiaro mondo,"* return to the clear world, *Inf.* XXXIV, 134) where he and Virgil can once again see the stars (*"riveder le stelle,"* *Inf.* XXXIV, 139). They emerge on the shores of the island mountain of *Purgatorio* with its seven ledges rendering temporal punishment for evils that can be purged in time. In the opening lines of *Purgatorio* Dante announces the significance of this change by referencing the contrast between the nature images of Inferno with what lies ahead, *"Per corer miglior' acque alza le vele\ omai la navicella del mio ingegno,"* (To run better waters now the little ship of my mind raises its sails, *Purg.* I, 1-2). Nature will still serve Justice and Divine Power in punishing evil but now with "better waters" will cleanse and renew and no longer terrify in portraying and contributing to the second and eternal death.

Seeking a way to begin their ascent of *Purgatorio*'s mountain, Dante and Virgil encounter the soul of the Roman statesman Cato, who explains that Dante must cleanse himself before proceeding and gird himself with the stalk of a rush growing along *Purgatorio*'s shores. Virgil leads Dante to a coastal meadow, spreads his hands upon the grass, and uses the fresh morning dew to remove the stains of Inferno from Dante's face,

> L' alba vinceva l'ora mattutina...
> Quando noi fummo là 've la rugiada
> pungna col sole...
> ambo le mani in su l'erbetta
> soavamente 'l mio maestro pose...
> ivi mi fece tutto discoverto
> quel color che l' inferno mi nascose.
> (*Purg.* I, 115, 121-129)

(The dawn was conquering the morning hour...\When we were where the dew fought with the sun...\both his hands in the new grass\my master gently spread...then he uncovered all that pigment which Inferno had hidden)

The images of the dawn, the dew, the new grass, the true and healthy color of Dante's flesh, and the gentleness of Virgil's gesture establish the tone of forgiveness and renewal that define this second realm of Dante's journey. When Virgil picks the *"umile pianta,"* ("humble plant" *Purg.* I, 135) to gird Dante, another immediately comes to life (*"rinacque," Purg.* I, 135), an allegory for nature and human life in an ideal pattern of environmental regeneration rather than destruction.

Nature dictates movement upward in *Purgatorio*, for climbing mountain paths and stairwells requires the light of the sun. During his first night in *Purgatorio,* Dante dreams of an eagle lifting him to the skies, and upon awakening he finds himself at the gates of *Purgatorio* proper, halfway up the mountainside. Dante and Virgil must pass through seven ledges on the mountain, settings for the punishment of pride, envy, anger, sloth, avarice, gluttony and lust. It is the last of these ledges, where lust is purged by jets of fire shooting from the mountain walls, that Dante suffers his greatest fears and pain; but with Virgil's encouragement (noting that Beatrice waits beyond the fire), Dante endures his punishment and climbs to the last step of *Purgatorio*'s rock-chiseled stairways and to the edge of Earthly Paradise. Dante and Virgil follow a path through the trees until their way is blocked by a stream and, on its far side, a woman by herself, singing and picking flowers (*"una donna soletta...* \ *cantando e scegliendo fior da fiore,"* Purg. XXVIII, 40-42). This is Matilda, a guardian of the realm; she explains to Dante that the stream is called Lethe and has a companion stream called Eunoe, rivers of forgetfulness and remembrance, *"Da questa...toglie altrui memoria del peccato;* \ *dall' altra d' ogni ben fatto la rende,"* (From this...it takes away one's memory of sin; by the other is recalled every good act, *Purg.* XXVIII, 127-129). And Matilda then points to the eastern horizon where the triumphal procession of Dante's longed-for Beatrice has begun to appear.

Seven grand candelabra precede twenty-four elders and four winged creatures and a triumphal chariot (*"carro...triunfale,"* Purg. XXIX, 107), pulled by a griffin and surrounded by seven angels dancing and singing and honoring the chariot's lone occupant, Beatrice,

> *...dentro una nuvola di fiori*
> *che dalle mani angeliche saliva*
> *e ricadeva in giù dentro e di fori*
> *sovra candido vel cinta d' uliva*
> *donna m'apparve...*
> (*Purg.* XXX, 28-32)

(within a cloud of flowers\ that from angelic hands rose and fell back down within and outside, \ below a white veil bound by the olive a lady appeared to me...)

The idealized nature imagery (cloud of flowers, band of olive) that initially characterized *Purgatorio* returns in this climactic scene and leaves Dante in ecstasy, briefly. Beatrice immediately chastises him for his failures in virtue; and, after Dante's distraught confession, Matilda plunges him into the River Lethe to drink of its waters and purge the memory of his flaws, after which he joins Beatrice's entourage. The second canticle of the *Commedia* ends with Dante's passage through Earthly Paradise's second river, Eunoe, from which he emerges "remade": "*Io ritornai\...rifatto\...puro e disposto a salire alle stele,*" (I returned...remade...pure and prepared to climb to the stars (*Purg.* XXXIII, 142-45).

Nature imagery plays significant and contrasting roles in the canticles of *Inferno* and *Purgatorio*, demonstrating nature's "terrifying" and "entrancing" qualities and adding to the grandeur of Dante's poetry. *Paradiso* deals more directly with the supernatural, yet here too Dante adapts an imagery that draws upon elements from the natural world including celestial lights of sun and moon and plants and stars culminating in the images of the Beatific Vision, far beyond the visible universe.

Paradiso opens with a reference to the divine as the Prime Mover, the supernatural present in every component of the universe, "*La gloria di colui che tutto move\per l'universo penetra e resplende...*" ("The glory of the one who moves all\penetrates and shines back throughout the universe" *Par.* I, 1-2). "*Paradiso*" depicts a sacred, earth-centered universe; and in order to describe his experience, Dante adapts an imagery that combines the visible and the transparent, the natural and the nearly immaterial, as he does with the portrait of the heavenly spirits in what Beatrice calls "*la prima stella*" (the first star, *Par.* II. 30). This is the sphere of the moon, described as "enveloped in a cloud" and "solid and polished like a diamond struck by the sun" (*"nube ne coprisse...solida e pulita, \ quasi adamante che lo sol ferisse,"* Par. II, 31-33). Here Dante meets Piccarda Donati, an admired cousin of Dante's wife Gemma and a saintly exemplar of vows broken; she and the other souls in the first sphere appear as reflections in a pane of glass or as "the traces of our faces return\ through clear and calm waters" (*"per acque nitide e tranquille \ ...tornan di nostri visi le pastille,"* Par. III, 11-13). This differs from the idealized nature imagery in *Purgatorio,* for here nature is transparent and translucent; it provides the simile, but the figure has a transcendent quality appropriate to the celestial where the natural and the supernatural operate in close union.

Together Dante and Beatrice ascend through seven planetary spheres (the Moon, Mercury, Venus, the Sun, Mars, Jupiter and Saturn) to the sphere of the fixed stars, the dwelling place of the apostles where Dante's power of vision is strengthened by looking back at all he has experienced from within the earth and upon the earth to the higher spheres of the heavens,

> *Col viso ritornai per tutte quante*
> *le sette spere, e vidi questo globo*
> *tal ch' io sorrisse del suo vil sembiante...*
> (*Par.* XXII, 133-35)

(With the power of sight I turned back to all the seven spheres, and I saw this world such that I smiled at its miniscule semblance ...)

The earth so celebrated as fearsome and a source of just punishment in *Inferno* and so idealized in its natural elements in *Purgatorio,* now inspires Dante's smile; for it seems so *"vil,"* vile in the sense of small in comparison to the rest of the planetary system as a whole. Miniscule it is, relatively, but also consummately significant in each human life because of its power and beauty and because for humanity eternity depends upon earthly decisions and finally because the divine became human on *"questo globo."*

While in the eighth sphere where this glance at the world occurs, Dante and Beatrice witness the triumph of the Incarnate God as living light ("*viva luce*" *Par.* XXIII, 31) and his mother as sacred rose surrounded by thousands of worshipping souls; Beatice says,

> *non ti rivolgi al bel giardino*
> *che sotto i raggi di Cristo s' infiora.*
> *Quivi é la rosa in che il verbo divino*
> *carne si fece...*
> (*Par.* XXIII, 71-74)

(Do you not turn to the beautiful garden\ that flourishes beneath the rays of Christ?\ Here is the rose in whom the divine word takes on flesh...)

Empowered by this vision Dante rises to the "*ciel velocissimo*" ("the swiftest moving heaven" *Par.* XXVII, 99), the ninth sphere, the Primum Mobile and eternal dwelling place of the angelic hosts. And beyond this lies the Empyrean, the tenth heaven of divine existence.

At the far edge of the Primum Mobile and the very border of the Empyrean Beatrice bids Dante to look up and experience the Beatific Vision in its infinitude, simultaneously microcosmic and embracing the whole created universe as a point of light that circumscribes all: "*un punto vidi che raggiava lume\ ...Da quel punto\depende il cielo e tutta la natura,*" (I saw a point that was radiating light from which point depends heaven and all nature, *Par.* XXVIII, 16, 41-42). From this point emerges the Primum Mobile which in turn generates the other spheres and appears as a Stream of Light ("*lume in forma di rivera,*" *Par.* XXX, 61) and, seen from above, an eternal rose ("*rosa sempiterna,*" *Par.* XXX, 124) by which Beatrice draws Dante towards the Empyrean ("*mi trasse Beatrice,*" *Par.* XXX, 128). And these visions of such grandeur are only prelude to the final imaging of the Beatific Vision itself, which ends Dante's *Commedia*.

Beatrice now returns to her eternal place in the sphere of Venus; and Dante has a third guide for this last part of his journey, the mystic

St. Bernard of Clairvaux. Bernard appeals to the Virgin Mother of God (*"Virgine madre" Par.* XXXIII, 1) to empower Dante to see the very face of God. And penetrating deeper and deeper into the ray of divine light Dante envisions " bound in love...a book" (*"legato con amore...un volumne," Par.* XXXIII, 86), three rainbow-like and self-reflecting rings of light (*"tre giri...\l' un da l'altro come iri da iri," Par.* XXXIII, 116-119), and humanity's own effigy (*"pinta della nostra effige," Par.* XXXIII, 131). Dante's story of the universe culminates with this vision as a story of love integrating the human and the divine and expressed in terms of images from nature idealized and transcendent and invoking a sense of grandeur for the great work that is nature's, humanity's, and God's.

The *Commedia* ends with this last canto of *Paradiso*, the one hundredth canto of the poem. Often throughout the *Commedia* Dante has been urged to tell his story, most prominently in the sphere of Mars, the heaven of the holy warriors, where Dante meets his ancestor Cacciaguida and gains insight into his own future as an exile from his beloved city of Florence. Dante will indeed suffer exile, says Cacciaguida, and learn "how salty seems\other people's bread" (*"come sa di sale\lo pane altrui..." Par.* XVII, 58-59). But he must tell his story for the benefit of all and regardless of the negative reactions of some,

> *Ma...tutta tua vision fa manifesta...*
> *Ché se la voce tua sarà molesta*
> *Nel primo gusto, vital nutrimento*
> *Lascierà poi, quando sarà digesta.*
> (*Par.* XVII, 128-32)

(But...make public your whole vision\...For if your voice will be troubling\at its first taste, life-giving nourishment\ it will then leave when it is digested).

This too is a great theme in the writings of Thomas Berry.

Time and again in Assisi at both formal presentations and the more intimate casual discussions during the summer of 1995 Tom Berry would urge his audiences to tell the new story of the earth and nature and the universe, as he often did in his writings.

> *Our great work, our historical role in its deeper significance, has to do with a new understanding of the planet EARTH: the radiant blue-white planet hanging in the sky, twirling upon its axis in the light of the sun each day, swinging in its solar orbit each year ... Such vistas create an overwhelming impression whether we look down from the heavens or across the landscape and up at the sky with its sun and clouds in the day and its moon and stars in the night.* (Berry 1999, 21)

Clearly such words echo the lyric prayer of San Francesco and the epic narrative of Dante. Berry taught his friends and colleagues and readers to tell the new story of the universe, to acknowledge the threatening consequences of ecological sins and present the harsh realities of today's environmental challenges, to re-shape the attitudes of a generation, and to strive personally to share in the "overwhelming grandeur" of nature in the context of an eternal universe.

His vision of the "Great Work" that faces civilization continues to live in a multitude of special ways through each of his readers and most certainly through each of those privileged to have learned from him as part of the Study Abroad for Earth (S.A.F.E.) in Assisi.

REFERENCES

Alighieri, Dante. 1994. *La Commedia Secondo l'Antica Vulgate*. Ed. Giorgio Petrocchi. Firenze, Italia: Casa Editrice Le Lettere.

Berry, Thomas. 2009. *The Christian Future and the Fate of the Earth*. Edited by Mary Evelyn Tucker and John Grim. Maryknoll, NY: Orbis Books.

---. 1999. *The Great Work: Our Way into the Future*. New York, NY: Bell Tower.

San Francesco d' Assisi. 1969. "Cantico delle creature." *Introduction to Italian Poetry: A Dual Language Book*. Edited by Luciano Rebay. New York, NY: Dover.

Tucker, Mary Evelyn and John Grim. 2009. "Introduction." *The Christian Future and the Fate of the Earth*. Edited by Mary Evelyn Tucker and John Grim. Maryknoll, NY: Orbis Books.

16

THE UNIVERSE STORY & THE EARTH COMMUNITY
REFLECTIONS ON THOMAS BERRY'S
TEACHING IN ASSISI[1]

Drew Dellinger

This essay explores Thomas Berry's cosmological teachings through the lens of Berry's lectures in Assisi, Italy. Drawing on Berry's ideas of the Universe Story and the Earth Community, Dellinger examines the significance of Berry's cosmological thought for our present times, as well as the future.

Our classroom was inside a monastery with a 700-year-old cathedral, the *Basilica di San Francesco d'Assisi*, built in the years after the death of St. Francis. Giotto's frescoes, depicting scenes from the saint's life, graced the walls. Thomas Berry settled into one of those school-type chairs with a desk attached and started to speak. With excitement, I pressed the "record" button on my handheld cassette player.

Berry's work and writings had already influenced me enormously as I had graduated from high school in North Carolina in the late 1980s and started college in Prescott, Arizona, in the early 1990s.

---

[1] Copyright © 2015 Drew Dellinger

I had been inspired deeply by Berry's collection of essays, *The Dream of the Earth* (1988), and the whole realm of New Cosmology and ecological spirituality expressed by thinkers such as Brian Swimme, Matthew Fox, Miriam MacGillis, Charlene Spretnak, Joanna Macy and others. Berry's teaching on cosmology -- the importance of understanding the universe as an unfolding story, and the place of the human within the cosmos and the Earth -- seemed to me to be revolutionary and yet common sense. His critique of environmental destruction, and the dysfunctional worldviews of the industrial, capitalist world, went to the deep roots of the ecological crisis. Berry's poetic evocation of the Earth and universe as unfolding sacred processes added cosmological and religious dimensions to environmental thought.

In the fall of 1990, my friend, Steve Snider, and I travelled to Seattle and met Thomas Berry at a conference. The following spring we organized a course at Prescott College exploring ecology, cosmology, and worldview, based on Berry's vision. During the class, someone brought in a flyer for something called Study Abroad for Earth, an opportunity to study with Thomas Berry that summer in Assisi, Italy.

For several weeks in the summer of 1991, Steve and I and a group of students had studied Berry's writings in depth, in a course called "New Cosmology" with Elisabeth Ferrero. We lived in Assisi, eating pasta and *gelato*, drinking *birra*, visiting the sacred sites of Francis' life, where his spirit still lingers, and anticipating Thomas Berry's arrival for nine days of lectures.

Berry was a light traveler, arriving with just a small vinyl shoulder bag, wearing grey slacks and a blue short-sleeve shirt with white buttons. In thin, dark socks and black shoes he traversed the steep cobblestone streets of Assisi, stepping carefully at 76 years old.

As Thomas began speaking on that first day, his immense learning and poetic vision of the universe quickly filled and transmuted the space. His opening statement on cosmology, the planet, and the ecological crisis is, to this day, one of the most sublime and inspiring teachings I have ever heard. Midway through, I looked at my tape recorder to make sure the wheels of the cassette were still spinning. After thirty or forty minutes we paused for a break, but already I knew my life had changed. I was more convinced than ever that Thomas' teaching held a healing for our culture. The students looked at one another, awed by Berry's wisdom.

I recorded many of his lectures, which I have to this day. Thomas' talks over the next nine days were stunning in scope, with topics and timelines ranging over centuries and millennia, and sweeping streams of thought that poured from Berry's mind. As a cultural historian, he recounted humanity's journey from the Paleolithic to the Neolithic, surveyed the three invasions of Eurasian history, summarized the fall of Rome, early and medieval Christian history, the rise of science and the mechanistic philosophy of Descartes and Bacon, the Industrial era, and the ascendancy of the corporation, as well as the development of the ecological movement.

He referenced an endless array of authors and thinkers from Dante, Vico and Aquinas, to Rachel Carson, Marija Gimbutas, E. F. Schumacher, Donella Meadows, Teilhard de Chardin, David Suzuki, Vladimir Vernadsky, Vandana Shiva, Wendell Berry and Carl Jung, among many others. He discussed Buddhism, Hinduism, Christianity, Taoism, Indigenous religions, Confucianism and more.

Weaving together centuries of history, Berry examined the various philosophical and religious threads leading to the present environmental predicament. The dysfunctional cosmology of Western culture was, in Berry's perspective, the deep cause of the ecological crisis.

When the recording picked up on the first day of class, Berry was speaking about "ways of understanding the universe," saying,

> *This, I think, is the single most important thing at the present time ... What I want to do is get to the sense of the numinous -- the divine from within the universe process, rather than a sense of creation from a transcendent, personal, monotheistic deity* (Berry 1991).

"Right now I want to begin with the universe," he said.

> *I want something that is available to everybody.... I don't use the word 'God' extensively. It's a valid word; I'm not sure it conveys what a person wants to convey by that term, or the reality of the thing* (Berry 1991).

This was my kind of priest. Thomas was never comfortable with the title "Father Berry," though he was in fact a Catholic monk and priest. He preferred to describe himself as a "geologian" rather than a "theologian," indicating that he was less interested in a transcendent God than with the divine as revealed in the universe and the Earth. At one point during his lectures on ecology and the universe, a student asked Thomas, "where does God come into all of this?" (Berry 1991).

"Well, I suggest forget about God," he replied, prompting laughter. "That is a tough thing to do, I guess, for most people," he continued, "but there's too much, I think, of 'God.' Sometimes people ask why I don't talk more about Jesus. I say, well, don't worry about Jesus... If he is who he's supposed to be, he'll show up somewhere" (Berry 1991).

For Tom, the ecological crisis was a far more pressing concern than traditional redemption narratives. Berry had a profound ability to convey the irreversible destruction of the Earth and its species taking place in our time. When he outlined the myriad assaults on the biosphere, it was more than one's heart could hold. Discussing overfishing, Berry said, "the most extreme devastation now, as I see it, is in the Pacific with these nets, 25-miles long and something like 30-

foot deep. These are out there night after night after night, or day after day after day, and everything is caught up in the net. This gulping up of life. We would find that the oceans could feed humanity indefinitely, with a vast amount of food, if only we would say something about it. Nobody seems to be saying anything about it" (Berry 1991).

Humanity is "closing down... the bio-systems of the planet," Berry stated, and causing "the termination of the whole 65 million years of the Cenozoic" period. "I don't know what else to say," he offered at one point. "It's the end of the civilization. It's not only the end of the human, it's the most extraordinary thing that has happened in the 4.5 billion years of Earth history" (Berry 1991).

Berry was one of the early voices emphasizing the significance of the mass extinction crisis. Along with his focus on more philosophical aspects of ecology such as worldview and cosmology, Berry stressed practical solutions for building an ecological culture, as well as direct action to protect the planet. "I think we need some revolutionary kind of actions, like Greenpeace and Earth First!," he said. "Some of these real obstructionists who will just stand in front of a bulldozer and say, 'No, don't do this.' It takes a lot of courage for people to do that, but we are going to need a lot of radical confrontation" (Berry 1991).

Berry always emphasized the primacy of the cosmos and the Earth, and the significance of understanding the universe as an unfolding story. He felt that the new cosmology -- the emergence of the universe, and the formation of the galaxies and planets -- had not been conveyed with appropriate grandeur by modern science. "One of the things that is most difficult," he said, "is to begin thinking of the universe as we know it empirically, but thinking of the emotional-aesthetic, or the psychic-spirit side of the stars" (Berry 1991).

This sacred dimension of the universe had been lost in Western culture. In contrast, Berry proposed a worldview that reconnected with ancient Cosmo visions such as the Great Mother of goddess civilizations, "The Great Mother, the feminine, is really very, very crucial," he stated (Berry 1991). He also stressed the importance of indigenous traditions, at one point describing the cosmological symbolism of the Sun Dance. To respond to the ecological crisis, Berry said, Western culture would have to overcome its cosmological alienation. "That's why I think that religiously, the sense of a religious personality now is not based on the prophet, but the shamanic personality. And when it comes to religious, spiritual experience at the present time, I think that there's a need to go to the shamanic experience" (Berry 1991).

In Berry's view, the cosmological connectedness expressed in indigenous thought could be brought to our understanding of the expanding galaxies of modern scientific astronomy. Even with the stunning new story of cosmic evolution and interrelatedness provided by science, the human-centeredness of the West, deeply rooted in our religious and scientific traditions, had kept us from seeing ourselves within the story of the cosmos. But Berry felt a new mystique was emerging in recent decades, the seeds of a more ecological culture.

The power of story, the significance of narrative, worldview and cosmology were central themes of Berry's lectures in Assisi that summer. Stories are the way in which humans understand anything, he said, telling the class, I recommend, "that you take narrative as the basic mode of understanding" (Berry 1991).

The basic problem with our cosmology in the West, as Berry saw it, is that we have a story of separation. Long-standing philosophical and religious dualisms separated spirit from matter, and earth from heaven. Anthropocentrism and arrogance separated humans from the rest of nature. Mechanistic science stripped the world of its soul. In contrast to the modern worldview of separation, Berry proposed two ideas, the Universe Story and the Earth Community, which he felt could help foster a new cosmology of connection.

The Universe Story

For Thomas, the environmental awakening, the photographs of Earth from space, and modern cosmology's new view of the universe all offered opportunities to expand our worldview beyond the human, reconnect with nature, and begin to read to story of the universe around us.

With the evolutionary vision of Darwin, Western culture was beginning to overcome its sense of separation. Berry called Darwin's "explanation of the evolutionary process" the "most important single" event of the nineteenth century "in our relationship with the natural world" (Berry 1991). In the twentieth century, the evolutionary vision was extended to the cosmos, with a scientific consensus gradually coalescing around the so-called "big bang" model of an expanding universe.

Berry placed great importance on the emergence of this evolutionary cosmology, one that linked our lineage to the galaxies, as cousins to the stars, and oceans, and all of life. "It's only a couple hundred years that there's been any idea at all of a universe that came into being over a vast period of time," said Berry. "In fact, my generation is the first generation to have a very clear idea of an evolutionary universe" (Berry 1991).

In Thomas' view, this new sense of a developing cosmos was a radical break from previous cosmologies, which he termed "spatial" in their mode of consciousness. As late as Einstein, "the universe was seen as a fixed entity," Berry noted. "So it's only in this century" that we have "moved into this as the first generation that moved into a sense of the universe as cosmogenesis rather than an established cosmos" (Berry 1991).

In earlier views, stated Berry, the world was seen as moving in ever-renewing cycles within a fixed cosmos. In "our times, however, the traditional modality of a spatial consciousness, and ever-renewing seasonal cycles, is not the way we are thinking. We know, as part of our consciousness now that we are at a certain phase of the universe that is in a sequence of irreversible transformations" (Berry 1991).

This sequence of transformations makes the universe a story. Moving from a "spatial" to a "time-developmental" mode of consciousness means seeing the narrative arc of the unfolding cosmos: exploding into existence fourteen billion years ago; billowing out in galaxies; creating stars and planets, life and music. "It's enormously important for us to know the story of the universe," said Tom, "and it's the only way in which we're going to know who we are" (Berry 1991).

The major contours of the universe story, Thomas taught, can be conveyed in four simple stages: the galactic phase, the Earth phase, the life phase, and the human phase. "My recommendation," he told the class, "is that you always go back to the story. These four chapters in the story: the universe story [or galactic story], the Earth story, the life story, the human story, and the continuity of these four stories. And then, of course, you have the personal story" (Berry 1991).

In Thomas Berry's conception, the universe story provides the basis for a sacred cosmology for Western culture, a worldview of connectedness between humans and Earth. This new story addresses the void created by our current dysfunctional worldviews. "What I think needs to take the place of [our earlier religious orientations] is a sense of the Earth, a sense of the story and our place in the story," Berry said. "So what I am suggesting is a renewal of the civic society, not on a religious basis exactly, because I don't think that's possible anymore, but on a mutual understanding of our common destiny, and of the common thread, and of the mystique. A new sense of the spiritual, even a new sense of the divine, is contained within the story of the universe... I think the universe story has become enormously important, and the Earth story, and that this is our revelation of the divine. And this does have a spiritual dimension. It does have religious import" (Berry 1991).

The Earth Community

Seeing the universe as story leads to a new appreciation of the Earth as community. The creativity of the cosmos unfolds most immediately, for us, as Earth, a precious reality that required the entire history of the universe to bring forth an almost unimaginable display of biological flourishing. As Wendell Berry once said, "If you don't know where you are, you don't know *who* you are" (quoted in Stegner 1989). By waking up to the unfolding story of the cosmos, humans can identify themselves as members of the integral Earth Community. By telling us *where* we are, and *when* we are, the universe story and the Earth story help us realize *who* we are.

"How old are we? We are as old as the universe," said Berry, "because it took 15 billion years to make us who we are ... There is one universe, there is one sacred community, there is one context of existence" (Berry 1991).

Re-visioning our cosmology involves overcoming Western culture's separation from the Earth. "Human society is an abstraction," Berry stated. "We are nothing without the water, and the soil, and the growing things, and so forth. So there's a need to stress the sense of integral community and to work toward the integrity of the community of life" (Berry 1991).

For Thomas, the Earth is primary; the human secondary, not only because our survival depends on the functioning of the Earth Community, but because the Earth gave rise to the human. The story tells us that our elements come from stellar nuclei, our cells from lightning-addled oceans, our breath from the delicate grace of Gaia's atmosphere. The Earth has manifested millions of creatures in richly complex ecosystems, and now our human activities are decimating the web of life. Such destruction of the very source of our existence was, for Tom, the ultimate expression of our cosmological crisis.

In his teachings in Assisi, Italy, in July of 1991, Thomas Berry hoped to nourish the seeds of a new connected cosmology, one that could lead us into an ecological future. "We have our human self, our Earth self, our universe self," Thomas said. "These are modalities of one reality. These are dimensions of the one reality" (Berry 1991).

On the last day of the course Berry restated his overall thesis and collective call-to-action: "The commission of our times is to reinvent the human at the species level, and do it by means of story and shared dream experience," he said. "Because this is not only a communication, it's an evocation. It's an evocation of a vision. It's an evocation of energies" (Berry 1991).

In the twenty-three years since our course together in Assisi, I have struggled to unpack all that Berry taught us that summer, both in words and through his presence. I have sought to carry Thomas's thought to new audiences in my work as a teacher, poet, and speaker. On a personal level, Berry's cosmology continues to inform and inspire me deeply. "The universe is best described, I think, as celebration," he told us in Assisi. "I say it this way: the universe, throughout its vast expanse in space, and throughout a sequence of transformation in time, is a single, multiform, celebratory event. In other words, what do the birds do? Well, they celebrate; they sing. The flowers blossom, the rivers flow, the clouds form, and the rain comes" (Berry 1991).

Thomas defined the entire universe as celebration, so naturally the human being is celebration, too. "The human activates a dimension of the universe," he taught us. "My definition of the human is, the human is that being in whom the universe reflects on and celebrates itself, and its numinous origin, in a special mode of conscious self-awareness" (Berry 1991).

Through his teachings in Assisi, as with his writings, and his speeches and lectures around the world, Thomas brought his students and the universe into communion with each other. As Berry said during our unforgettable encounter, "What we bring to the celebration -- or the great liturgy, or the great spectacle of the universe -- is the capacity of the universe to know itself" (Berry 1991).

REFERENCES

Berry, Thomas. 1988. *The Dream of the Earth*. San Francisco: Sierra Club Books.

---. 1991. "The Assisi Lectures." Audiotapes of lectures by Thomas Berry transcribed and edited by Drew Dellinger. Course sponsored by St. Thomas University (Miami Gardens, FL) in Assisi, Italy, July 1991.

Stegner, Wallace. 1989. *A Sense of Place*. Louisville, CO: Audio Press.

17

THE GREAT WORK WITHIN

A JOURNEY IN SEARCH OF THE UNIVERSE

Eugenia Pia Ferrero

"We need to move from our human-centered to an earth-centered norm of reality and value. Only in this way can we fulfill our human role within the functioning of the planet we live on"
(Berry 1999, 56).

To have had the opportunity to be in the presence of Fr. Thomas Berry from the time I was sixteen years old is purely magical. To say that I was fortunate does not capture the depth of my gratitude to have been able to listen, dialogue and be in Thomas Berry's presence. Since my mother was directing the S.A.F.E. study abroad programs and the *Sustainability and Spirituality* conferences in Assisi, I could have easily stayed home with my grandparents; however, I truly believe that my passion for environmental justice and sustainability was greatly fostered by attending the study abroad programs and conferences in Assisi for those nine years.

At the time the study abroad programs began, I was a sophomore in high school and the youngest person attending. The entire experience at times seemed surreal. Even though I did not have a depth of knowledge or experience on the issues being discussed, everyone was open and welcomed a teenager being part of these dialogues. Engaging with Fr. Berry, Drs. Brian Swimme; Rupert Sheldrake; Mary Evelyn Tucker and the other participants had a critical impact on my personal growth and development at a subconscious level; thus, re-surfacing in recent years.

Looking back, I now realize and appreciate what Thomas Berry awakened in me – a desire for something that at that time I could not explain in words. There were many memorable evenings when we would sit outside in the piazza after dinner having a gelato with Fr. Berry and the rest of the participants. Being in Tom Berry's presence and listening in awe to his passion, seeds were planted in my heart and soul. And now, all those experiences have given me the courage to be a voice for the voiceless.

Prior to the S.A.F.E. programs, I did not give much thought to environmental justice and sustainability. However, being in Assisi with Fr. Berry and the other faculty members helped me to realize that we are, "a communion of subjects, not a collection of objects" (Berry 1999), and my perception of the world started to change. I began to view myself no longer separate but rather an intrinsic part of the universe, with a purpose. During those summers, besides the lectures, we were encouraged to engage with the surrounding community. One experience I vividly recall was when several of us volunteered several times a week at a local animal shelter which was about to close its doors because of lack of personnel and in the process we helped save the shelter.

Another of my memorable experiences occurred in 1993. That summer, Dr. Swimme took his students to San Damiano, a monastery built in the 12th century overlooking the valley of Assisi. Brian Swimme had us all perform as a play the story of the universe in the olive groves. Then, we were asked to feel the energy of the olive trees surrounding us. I wrapped my arms around the large trunk of an olive tree; I felt a calmness which I had never experienced before, and an intense feeling of joy. This connection to nature continues to play a central role in my journey to be a voice for the voiceless.

My journey has been like a boat ride through the Amazon's rain forest. My life experiences took me to law school, focusing on environmental justice. And now, I am completing a Ph.D. in environmental communication, focusing on the sacredness and the inter-connectedness of all beings. The impact of Thomas Berry remains an integral part of how I define myself and how I view the world.

Fr. Berry continuously reminded us how critical it was that we all work together, men and women. He especially reminded us that, "the wisdom of women is to join the knowing of the body to that of the mind, to join soul to spirit" (Berry 1999, 180), and yet today the presence and the powers of women are not prominent in the decision-making processes in our communities. Moreover, Berry emphasized that the appropriation and domination of the reality and value of the Earth by men has been dysfunctional and detrimental to all species (Berry 1999, 180). This resonates within my being, especially now that I am a grown woman and a mother. Women today have a duty to themselves as well as to future generations to undo the patriarchal dominance men have imposed. This is a moral obligation that all women today feel at a very deep and primal level. Since the first study abroad program, my identity as a woman has changed significantly. The traps of our patriarchal system have been entrenched in our communities for too long as Thomas Berry has said, not allowing a woman's identity, perspective and dreams to flourish. Even law schools still perpetuate the patriarchal system, often suppressing the courage and strength of women to assert themselves. As I continue my journey, I am discovering my own voice and personal dignity as a woman, as Thomas Berry reminded us in Assisi many years ago.

The awesome mystery of the universe exists in each and every one of us. I vividly remember this dominant thought in all of Thomas Berry and Brian Swimme's talks in Assisi. It is amazing to realize how life-generating the universe truly is, and how the stars are our ancestors, as it is so eloquently portrayed in the *Journey of the Universe* (Swimme and Tucker 2014). That same energy is in our cells and in our DNA -- we are genetic cousins to all living beings (Swimme and Tucker 2014). What reverence for life we experience when we become aware that our water-based eyes are the same eyes of the fish! Life did not just happen by accident, but all the elements had to line up perfectly to allow for this incredible and beautiful universe to emerge (Swimme and Tucker 2014).

On Earth, humans have exploited nature and other species, at times for humanitarian reasons such as eliminating diseases. Our destructive patterns have plundered our forests and polluted our oceans reducing the habitats for various species. The damage does not stop there; and humans are now being affected too. How very sad that the fish which once swam in the oceans are now contaminated with endocrine disruptors (vom Saal and Hughes 2005). The Earth is changing before our very eyes and it is frightening. Nature is not a resource to exploit. The air we breathe, the changes in our climate, the oceans we depend on, even our DNA are being forever changed, all because of these human-made changes (Swimme and Tucker 2011). It is difficult to understand the depth and magnitude of these changes. Yet at the same time, humans cannot ignore what is occurring to our Earth, home not only to us but to all beings. We need to speak up and give the rivers and oceans and animals and plants a voice too.

As we strive to envision a new dream, let us take the time to absorb all the magic which surrounds us, just like the caterpillar which dies into life and transforms itself into a beautiful monarch butterfly.

This is our responsibility as children of the universe. Let us feel compassion for the mutated frog with four eyes, just like a mother nurturing her baby with love and sensitivity. The sacred and awesome mystery of the universe is in each of us and realizing that we are one with the universe allows me to be a voice for the voiceless; and together with others, we can dream a new dream for our home, the universe.

REFERENCES

Berry, Tom. 1999. *The Great Work: Our way into the future.* New York: Three Rivers Press.

Brian Thomas Swimme and Mary Evelyn Tucker. 2014. *The Journey of the Universe.* New Haven, Connecticut: Yale University Press.

----. 2011. *The Journey of The universe.* Directed by Patsy Northcutt, and David Kennard. n.d. San Francisco, CA: Northcutt Productions. DVD.

Vom Saal, F.S., and C. Hughes. 2005. "An Extensive new literature concerning low-dose effects of bisphenol A shows the need for a new risk assessment." *Environ. Health Perspect.* 113: 926-933.

18

SACRED & CIVIC ENGAGEMENT

BÉATRICE COLASTIN SKOKAN

The Study Abroad for Earth (S.A.F.E.) program in Assisi, Italy, was at the forefront of academic institutions placing emphasis on community and civic engagement as an essential component of a university education. Thomas Berry's vision of a sacred world serves as foundation towards being in and loving the world.

Only the Earth held a creative balance between the turbulence and the discipline that are necessary for creativity. (Berry 1993, 18)

Over the past twenty years I have cherished the S.A.F.E. summers in Assisi, Italy, as an epiphany, one of those rare turning points and a gift. In the 1990s, Elisabeth Ferrero, my ethics professor, organized a series of study abroad programs in Italy to introduce students to new modes of understanding the human relationship with the Earth. The program was six weeks long, primarily stationed in Assisi, and the readings and discussion centered on the works of eco-theologian Thomas Berry.

Teilhard de Chardin, the French Jesuit priest who is so familiar to the discourse of the U.S. environmental movement, was undeniably present in Father Berry's work and reflections on the sacred dimension of the natural world. As a teenager I had "accidentally" discovered the biographical work *La Vie et L'âme de Teilhard de Chardin* by Nicolas Corte many summers before in Haiti while rummaging through my father's library. While I remained puzzled and continuously drawn to the book, much of its analysis remained beyond my reach until I studied the works of Thomas Berry as an undergraduate student. As I read the narrative of his *Dream of the Earth*, the assigned text for our religion class, an inborn aesthetic experience of the natural world was rekindled. Thomas Berry's understanding of the "Universe [as] the primary sacred reality" (Berry 1993, 14) was a conscious encounter and validation of my intuitive attraction to the "liturgical" (Berry 1993, 9) dimension of the natural world. In the "Meadow Across the Creek" Thomas Berry writes, "dawn and Sunset are the mystical moments of the diurnal cycle, the moments when the numinous dimension of the universe reveals itself with special intimacy" (Berry 1993, 10). Over the years, I've revisited De Chardin's books by remembering Tom's lectures in the Assisi Papal palace where our courses where taught, outdoor cafés where we enjoyed a cappuccino or a glass of wine, and the beautiful little courtyard of the family-run hotel where we were staying.

In retrospect, Assisi was the ideal context for this "academic retreat" from our usual campuses into the new domain of sacredness in nature. Francis of Assisi, the city's patron, is the quintessential figure of Christian companionship with other figures of divine creation. Most interesting are the many stories of Francis' encounters with the wild when he made peace with the wolf who terrified the town of Gubbio or humbly asked the birds to be quiet. This juxtaposition of a culture's own legends was put in correspondence with the academic discussions on the western evolution of ideas that had shaped industrial civilization and its apparent mechanistic treatment of the planet. At an experiential level, it was also impossible to travel the many paths of Italian cities' *piazzas* and cultural symbols and not become imbued with the various "mythical" or "historical" narratives that determine modes of being in the world. What are the stories we tell ourselves about who we are, and at a time of environmental crisis, what are the stories we tell ourselves about the Earth and our relationships to it?

A couple of years after the S.A.F.E program, I started a graduate degree in International Studies and felt surprisingly comfortable with the epistemological exploration of modes of knowledge acquisition. I was also ready to understand schools of critical thought since Thomas Berry's lectures of cultural history had already introduced these new methods of study. I enjoyed graduate school and benefited from the expertise of many great academics while keeping the Assisi experience in dialogue with the new knowledge. The challenge posed by the quasi-idyllic experience of the S.A.F.E in Assisi experience is to bring a changed self and new awareness into the world as it presently stands. It is a call for a reverential and creative resolution to the environmental crisis.

Here again in his address on the "Sacred and the Wild," Thomas Berry reflects that, "artists have something in them that is wild, something guided and controlled ultimately by imagination, Divine imagination in the words of William Blake. So the philosopher and the artist are both poised between the wild and the disciplined. In this mysterious balance the universe in all its grandeur and all its loveliness becomes possible. Exactly here the presence of the sacred reveals itself" (Berry 1993, 19). S.A.F.E in Italy did not provide idealistic undergraduate students with the means of "saving the world." Thomas Berry's informed and gentle presentation, in a most interesting manner, set us on a path of exploration and meditation to find our own way of being in a sacred world.

> *The artist needs to greet this new era as Dante greeted Beatrice after his long journey through the Inferno and the Purgatorio, with bowed head and a soul to experience its entire being caught up in the love that moves the sun and the other stars* (Berry 1993, 23).

The eco-theologian's vision of a sacred world serves as a foundation towards being in and loving the world in all its diversity. The attention, acceptance and mutuality that are essential to the deepening of any loving relationship find a concrete articulation within the concept of bio-regionalism or a radical rootedness to the spaces we inhabit and their unique ecological manifestations. S.A.F.E in Italy's gift was to send one back home in the most profound way to be guardians of the hearth, listen to the tales and honor Hestia.

As the manuscripts and outreach librarian at the University of Miami Libraries, I am the curator of many stories narrated through diaries, letters, old photographs, slave registers and scrapbooks to name a few of the ways people choose to share experiences. Our repository has a special collecting focus on Florida and its narratives of space and discovery. As I reflect on the university's role in community engagement and focus my documenting activities on the region, I have encountered environmental awareness in its multiplicity of manifestations.

My first archival project focused on a digital exhibit for the Papers of Marjory Stoneman Douglas, the *Lady of the Everglades*. The Florida environmental movement experienced a marked conceptual shift when inhabitants started to understand the Everglades as a "River of Grass," nourishing a whole ecosystem instead of a swampy obstacle to "development." In my most recent documenting activities I reached out to Miami activists such as Max Rameau and his "Take Back the Land" movement and to Denise Perry's "Power U for Social Justice" to purposely add the voices of the African diaspora to the ongoing discourse on housing and economic disparities in South

Florida. Conversations with these grassroots organizations have renewed a preoccupation with the social justice and racial component tied to the environmental movement. I remember the sometimes heated discussions that took place in Italy in the 1990s around the topic of environmental justice and the silence surrounding diversity of people in the environmental movement.

As I reflect on these debates, it is not surprising that at the 2011 Special Collections event "Archiving the Fringe," Max Rameau acknowledged that his work dealt with subsidized housing, disenfranchised black residents, or homelessness, but he emphasized that the primary issue is about "land" and our society's conceptual framework of land ownership. Are there human rights for the homeless between real estate booms and busts? Can you build a highway through a neighborhood and leave the burden of tossed waste on the residents? Nomenclature guides the relationship with the bio-region and sets the parameters of its ethical code.

More recently, I have been steadily developing an archive in collaboration with the Florida Immigrant Coalition (F.L.I.C.). Migrant workers, labeled "undocumented aliens," are intrinsically tied to the second largest industry in the state of Florida, agriculture. These "immigrants" are often disempowered politically, invisible socially and working under challenging conditions in the fields. Yet, as a society, we maintain a detachment between nourishment and these hardworking "foreign" people. The F.L.I.C. records reflect the ongoing conflicting relationship of our country with immigration and the exploitative nature of our food production and consumption. Higher education research centers are impoverished without these perspectives. By including these voices in the archives, students and scholars have found creative ways to enter into dialogue with these communities. They have identified the above mentioned groups as pertinent, completed oral history projects with real people, and written papers and graduate thesis inspired by these community issues. This creative work is born out of unforeseen new narratives and has emerged out of a desire to belong to and truly inhabit a space.

There are presently many university programs that work to connect the insights of the humanities to agency in civic and community engagement. These institutions have identified civic engagement as an essential component to a university education. I remember S.A.F.E. visits to Italian recycling plants, animal shelters, and co-operatives. These excursions were coupled with lectures, seminars, and discussions on human existence vis-à-vis other life systems on the planet. As we face environmental challenges, I realize how the experience in Assisi went even further by daring to speak of the sacred dimension of the wild and to identify the power of internalized belief systems and their creative potential.

REFERENCES

Berry, T. 1990. *The Dream of the Earth*. San Francisco, California: Sierra Club Books.

---. 1993a. Typescript. "The meadow across the creek."

---. 1993b. "The wild and the sacred." Paper presented at the Sacred Arts Festival, Cathedral Saint John the Divine, New York.

Corte, N. 1957. *La vie et l'âme de Teilhard de Chardin*, France: Arthème Fayard.

19

AN ASSISI OF THE MIND

STEVE SNIDER

This personal essay describes traveling with a group of college students to the historic city of Assisi, Italy, in the summer of 1991 to study with Thomas Berry, the renowned theologian and cultural historian. In addition, this essay outlines Berry's thinking around the human sensitivity or "deep change in mind" that is required by the human community, both individually and collectively, if we are to succeed in creating a sustainable, human-Earth relationship.

Rising steeply out of the endless miles of beautiful green and yellow pastures in the Umbrian valley of central Italy, about a hundred miles north of Rome, stands a stunning, tidal wave of mountain known as Monte Subasio. Perched on its northwestern foothill sits the ancient town of Assisi. It was in this town, surrounded by fertile farmlands and olive orchards, where I first deeply encountered the hearts and minds of two extraordinary men of global significance: Giovanni di Pietro Bernardone, also known as Saint Francis of Assisi (1181-1226), and Thomas Berry (1914-2009).

I was a 22-year-old college student in the summer of 1991, about the same age as Giovanni (aka "Francesco") when he was captured almost 800 years earlier during a battle with the neighboring town of Perugia. I was also about the same age as Thomas when he entered a Catholic monastery in 1934 to begin his lifelong journey of intense learning, contemplation and reflection about the state of the modern world. As a Study Abroad for Earth (S.A.F.E.) participant, I was part of a small group of college students and adult learners, who were lucky enough to travel to Assisi to study with Berry, a man considered by many as one of the greatest minds of the 20th century.

The buildings of Assisi were constructed over many centuries out of the pinkish-white stones from the very mountain upon which it rests. These beautiful buildings stand in stark contrast against the sloping, green backdrop of the giant mountain behind them.

Assisi is a city of steep hills, narrow, zigzagging cobblestone streets and tight alleyways that climb up and down between buildings. Walking Assisi's maze of endless pathways and shortcuts in the summer is a workout that left us students short of breath and drenched in sweat. In many ways, daily life may have changed little since the time of Saint Francis. Around every twist and turn you find Italian homemakers sitting quietly in their second floor windows, sweeping their front stoops, or hanging their laundry out to dry.

Assisi in the summer bustles with locals and tourists alike and is filled with great, family-run businesses such as the Hotel Posta Panoramic where we stayed. The inn provided delicious home cooked Italian meals, breathtaking views of the verdant valley below – and no air conditioning. For Thomas and I, both North Carolina natives, the lush green meadows, woodlands and mountains of Umbria felt familiar and made us feel at home.

I first encountered Tom's work in 1987 when I was a senior in high school in my hometown of Chapel Hill. By chance, I randomly discovered Brian Swimme's book *The Universe is a Green Dragon*, based on Berry's work, at The Intimate Bookshop in Chapel Hill. Coincidently, Thomas was born in 1914 in Greensboro, fifty miles down the road. Over the course of the next four years, I became a big fan and reasonably well-versed in Berry's work. I had been also been lucky enough to meet Thomas and hear him speak a few times at a conference in Seattle the previous year. This trip to Assisi was to be the first of three consecutive summers I spent traveling to Assisi with my lifelong friend and collaborator, Drew Dellinger, to study with our hero and future mentor. The summer of 1993 was our last trip to Assisi and also included a very memorable journey with Thomas to Ecuador. Studying with Berry in Assisi that first summer initiated what was to become a deep personal transformation of my understanding of history, the universe and human role in the universe.

Our classes were held in the *Sacro Convento*, a Franciscan monastery that is part of *the Basilica di San Francesco di Assisi*. This massive building complex had been the spiritual center of the Franciscan order since it was completed in the year 1263. The *Basilica*'s location on the steep side of Mt. Subasio – part of the ancient, 870-mile Apennine mountain chain – served to make its dimension even more dramatic. Your mind first absorbs the beauty of the exterior, with its whitewashed facade, ornate carvings and intricate stonework. Entering the interior of the Upper and Lower churches (the latter housing the tomb of Saint Francis) the vaulted ceilings, stained glass and colorful frescos, and dramatic architecture awakens a sense of wonder. Listening to Berry share his wisdom in this historic and sacred environment was exhilarating and awe-inspiring.

The Romans first constructed the 30-foot walls that encircle Assisi when they took control of central Italy in 295 BCE. The walls are a powerful reminder of the long history of brutality and violence that permeated the "invade and conquer" mentality of the medieval European culture that Saint Francis himself was born into. As a young man, Assisi's patron saint fell victim to the brutality of this culture prior to his well-documented moral and spiritual transformation in the early 13th century.

To understand the spiritual and cultural context of Assisi, one must understand the story of Saint Francis. In Assisi, this story could be found everywhere. It was told in books in the local gift shops, by the presence of the Franciscan friars in the main *piazza*, the art in the churches, and the statues and memorials around the city. It was also in the bustling *Piazza del Comune* where we spent most of our free time, hanging with Thomas and our other teachers, and getting to know each other over a glass of wine, a *cappuccino* or a *gelato*; and that this exact spot, the heart of Assisi's social, cultural and political life, was the same ground on which Saint Francis once walked was not lost on me. Along with the teachings of Thomas Berry and immersing myself in the cultural life of Italy, the story of Saint Francis would become a core part of my studies during my first Assisi summer.

Legend tells us that in his youth Francis enjoyed a life of luxury, living his teenage years with reckless abandon, the benefit of having a successful and wealthy silk-merchant father. It was a life filled with parties, music, women and drinking – not too different from many 20th century American kids, myself included.

In 1202, when he was 21 years of age, Francis was captured during a brutal battle with the neighboring town of Perugia. His life was spared because, like other wealthy young men from Assisi, rather than being left to die on the battlefield, he could be held for ransom. While in captivity he fell extremely ill and continued to be nearly bedridden for a year after his father's ransom allowed him to return home to Assisi. During this time, Saint Francis experienced a life-changing spiritual transformation, or what is sometimes called: "*metanoia*," meaning "a total change of heart and mind."

Much more than a clichéd religious conversion, this experience profoundly and permanently changed the way Francis chose to live in the world. As a result, he adopted a radical stance against the excessive greed and misguided capitalist pursuits of the dominant culture. These newly awakened spiritual and political beliefs came at a great personal sacrifice, resulting in the loss of childhood friendships and tragically, even his own family.

Francis was known to give away his father's expensive merchandise and money to those less fortunate. This was a source of constant frustration for his father, Pietro, who in 1206 demanded that the local bishop convene a trial about the behavior of his misguided son. At the trial, Francis surprised everyone by publically denouncing his father and his inheritance. History tells of the young Francis dramatically stripping off his expensive clothes, handing them to Pietro and announcing that from that day forward he would no longer call him "father." Vowing to live only as a child of "Our Father, who Art in Heaven" (ETWN 2014), he declared his commitment to a new life dedicated to the way of God and justice, rather than materialism, greed and exploitation.

Publicly scorned, Francis chose to live as a wandering beggar and mystic. A vision to rebuild the dilapidated church of San Damiano, just outside of the fortified walls of Assisi, was made a reality by begging for building stones in the streets, recruiting masons and working alongside them. This act, among others, began to inspire local disciples who donned Francis' simple habit and joined a growing fraternal order who adopted the Franciscan vows of poverty and simplicity.

Greatly influenced by the story of Jesus, these early Franciscans chose to be in solidarity with the poor, disadvantaged and marginalized. This was not merely a spiritual calling, but a radical moral and political stance. Rejecting the dominant culture of capitalism and materialism, Francis turned his compassionate heart toward loving the poor and downtrodden, the animals and the natural world. He was said to worship and celebrate the divine in nature and through nature. Francis' universal, even cosmological, perspective is deeply evident in his writings.

Remarkably in 1210, this scrappy band of Franciscan acolytes sought and received Pope Innocent III's blessing to continue promoting their emerging Order of Friar Minors. After this papal endorsement, knowledge of Francis grew rapidly in the Italian world and he amassed followers and influence until his death and canonization in 1226 and beyond. Over centuries, Francis of Assisi became one of history's most venerated religious figures, crossing boundaries of denomination, faith and tradition and demonstrating a receptiveness to the message of divine immanence in global mainstream culture.

For Francis, *all things were connected; all things were sacred*. He developed a unique sensitivity towards the natural world and for his fellow human beings. Francis saw what Berry understood eight centuries later, that the "universe is the primary revelation of the divine" (Berry 1991). He poetically expressed reverence and praise for "Brother Sun, Sister Moon, Brothers Wind and Air, Sister Water, Brother Fire and Sister Mother Earth" as sustaining, governing life forces in his work, "The Canticle of the Sun," also known as "The Canticle for the Creatures"(*Custodia Terrae Sanctae* 2011). This special awareness would, 800 years later, be identified by Berry as the gift of "sympathetic presence" (Berry 2006): a blueprint of sorts for creating a just and sustainable world.

Carl Sagan and a group of twenty-two of the world's most prominent scientists famously endorsed the very same concept in 1990 in Moscow at the Global Forum of Spiritual and Parliamentary Leaders on Human Survival. Prophetically, Sagan and his colleagues listed the dangers of global warming, the depletion of the ozone layer, the extinction of plant and animal species, the destruction of rain forests and the threat of nuclear war as the most pressing issues of the twentieth century. Their warning also came with an important prescription for a deeper, cosmological awareness, "as scientists, many of us have had profound experiences of awe and reverence for the universe. We understand that what is regarded as sacred is more likely to be treated with care and respect. Our planetary home should be so regarded. Efforts to safeguard and cherish the environment need to be infused with a vision of the sacred" (Suzuki and Knudtson 1992, 227). The scientists went even further, "Problems of such magnitude and solutions demanding so broad a perspective, must be recognized from the outset as having a religious as well as a scientific dimension" (Steinfels 1990).

Berry himself could have easily made this statement, and his cosmological focus provides the broadest possible perspective to address these important ecological issues. "What I am proposing, " says Berry, "is a deep change in mind – a meta-religious orientation with three conditions: 1) The universe is a communion of subjects, not a collection of objects; 2) the Earth exists and can survive only in its integral functioning. We cannot save the Earth in fragments, and 3) the Earth is a onetime endowment" (Berry 1991). The concept that a "deep change in mind" is required to sustain a "mutually enhancing, human-earth relationship" (Berry 1991), formed the core of Berry's teaching that summer.

My front row seat to the great mind and generosity of this extraordinary teacher was also infused with the constant presence of Assisi's character and beauty. My daily intellectual journeys with Tom would begin by waking up early each morning, sometimes leaning out my hotel window that faced out upon the beautiful, green Umbrian valley below and catching the sunrise over Assisi (or sometimes even the waning morning moon over the valley). I remember being awestruck watching the morning swallows engaged in their daily diving and soaring ritual, moved by the possibility that Saint Francis himself might have had the very same experience.

Over breakfast before our first class, I asked if Tom Berry was familiar with a well-known writer in the field of Transpersonal Psychology, Ken Wilber, whose work I had studied at Prescott College. He said yes, but surprised me slightly by not showing more interest in the topic. Sensing this, he said, "my work is not psychological or sociological, it's cosmological and ecological," adding, "ecology is a functional cosmology" (Berry 1991). Berry always brought the conversation back to the comprehensive story of the universe, stressing its importance for the sustainability of our planet.

As Tom introduced himself to the class for the first time, and he often did this when meeting with new groups, he mentioned, with a shy grin on his face, that he was a not a theologian exactly, he was a "geologian -- a theologian of the Earth." It was clear that he was making a joke and a serious point at the same time. Tom had great charm and a youthful sweetness, even though he was three-quarters of a century old. Although polite and respectful, Berry was by no means a passive intellectual. Engaged and passionate, he spoke in a soft, quivering and slightly strained voice. Yet this voice always had precision and clarity, conveying Berry's powerful message about a world that, disconnected from a cosmological dimension, had lost its sense of direction and purpose.

During our classes, this frail but energetic 76-year old explored all aspects of not only human history, but the history of the earth and the universe itself from every angle imaginable. From Greek philosophy, to indigenous cultures, from classical religious traditions to modern science, Berry danced back and forth, effortlessly. His daily musings frequently ventured deep into prehistoric time, before human eyesight, even before the existence of our solar system. He brought the class in contact with intimate moments of cosmic unfolding, moments of "cosmogenesis," as he described in detail the birth of stars, galaxies and planets over millennia. In fact, nearly every talk included a sweeping presentation of cosmic history in its broadest, most profound sense. This perspective was drawn from the breadth of his understanding as a cultural historian, philosopher, religious scholar and practitioner -- and importantly, from his personal experience.

As a child Berry began to recognize, "the beginnings of biocide and geocide" (Berry 1991, 144) inherent in the emerging industrial process. In his book, *The Great Work*, Thomas describes his own transformational experience as an 11-year-old boy,

> It was an early afternoon in late May when I first wandered down the incline, crossed the creek, and looked out over the scene. The field was covered with white lilies rising above the thick grass. A magic moment, this experience gave to my life something that seems to explain my thinking at a more profound level than almost any other experience I can remember. It was not only the lilies. It was the singing of the crickets and the woodlands in the distance and the clouds in a clear sky... this early experience, it seems, has become normative for me throughout the entire range of my thinking. Whatever enhances this meadow in the natural cycles of its transformation is good; whatever opposes this meadow or negates it is not good. My life orientation is that simple. It is also that pervasive. It applies in economics and political orientation as well as education and religion. (Berry 1999, 12-13)

Thomas grew up knowing the modern world was not working. His frustrations mounted over time as he realized that our cultural, political and religious institutions, including his own Catholic tradition, were "assuming no responsibility for the state of the earth or the fate of the earth" (Berry 1991, 143). In the tradition of St. Francis, Tom Berry dedicated his life to cultivating in others a sense of the sacred, traveling and teaching as many people as possible in order to shift our collective consciousness. This was nothing less than a battle for the mind and hearts of the human community in order to save the planet from desolation. "We are a pathological generation. We have become autistic, psychologically locked into ourselves, with no feeling towards the natural world, no rapport with the larger universe" (Snider 1993). "Though we cannot make a blade of grass," Berry would say, "there will not be a blade of grass if we do not accept it, protect it and foster it" (Snider 1991).

For Thomas, cosmology told and taught as a story was a way deep into the human heart and mind because story is "our primary mode of understanding" (Berry 1991). By delivering a sense of meaning, and purpose and value, cosmology can affect real and lasting change in our world. In fact, for Berry, the universe could only adequately be understood within the context of a cosmological story. "All things find their place within the context of the universe, which forms one integral, sacred whole" (Berry 1991).

I was attracted to this cosmological dimension of Berry's work from the moment I first discovered in 1987 Swimme's book, *The Universe Is A Green Dragon* (1985). Then, a few years later in 1990, when I was a student at Prescott College, I discovered Berry's book, *The Dream of the Earth*, (1988), and was deeply moved and inspired by his thoughts and perspectives. I was captivated in particular by his articulation of the "discovery of a new origin story". He conveyed that this discovery of an evolving universe was the "supreme historical event of recent times" with a revolutionary sense that this new-found awareness should act as a guide for "every phase of human activity" (Berry 1988, 111). Berry's powerful and precise language and his comprehensive perspective resonated deeply with what I knew to be true about the world. As we students sat with him in the Sacro Convento in the summer of 1991, immersed in his mesmerizing style of teaching, I felt it in my bones. Thomas would often deliver his ideas in elaborate, multi-part sentences, like a jazz musician riffing off concepts he had spent a lifetime crafting. He would say, "the historical mission of our times, is to reinvent the human, at a species level, in a time-developmental context, with critical reflection within the community of life systems of planet Earth, by means of story, and shared dream experience" (Snider 1991).

In fact, as Tom would recite these complex sentences he would often lose his place, going off on fascinating tangents for long stretches and then needing to start over again. My friend Drew and I would joke that we should make him huge cue cards, but that was definitely not Berry's style. No slides, no visual aids, it was simple and very straightforward: just him sitting or standing in front of us, thoroughly enjoying teaching and sharing.

To understand his inordinate grasp of the breadth of ancient and modern history and religion one must look to Berry's own extraordinary history as a scholar. In the decade Berry spent as a monk between 1934 and '43, alongside daily prayer and vespers, he studied nine hours each day, immersing himself in world history, including the histories of cultures, religion, philosophy and science. He was ordained as a Catholic priest in 1942 and left the monastery in 1943 to pursue his doctorate in history from Catholic University in Washington, D.C.

Over the course of the next two decades, from the mid-1940s through the mid-1960s, this Catholic priest and cultural historian mastered Italian for the purpose of writing his doctoral dissertation on the work of Italian philosopher and historian, Giambattista Vico. He later learned the ancient language of Sanskrit, and the pictorial language of Chinese, exclusively to study the sacred texts of Asia in their original languages. As a testament to Berry's commitment and genius, he mastered multiple other languages to mine their hidden truths and sought to apply this wisdom to the most pressing issues of our times: the survival of the planet Earth.

With this academic and intellectual pedigree, it is not surprising that by the time he founded *The Riverdale Center of Religious Research* in Riverdale, New York in 1969 – the year I was born – he had become one of the world's greatest living cultural historians and religious scholars. By 1991, Tom had been studying and teaching for nearly 57 years.

In Assisi, Tom's classes never ended and each class drew deeply from this wellspring of study. Literally an all-day affair, classes went from dawn to dusk, and sometimes late into the evening. Like children around a campfire, we students basked in the glow of Berry's mind, soaking in as much heat and light as we could. We sat with him at breakfast in the hotel, walked with him to the monastery for morning class, and followed him to the hotel for lunch. After a short break for lunch and homework, we would join him again for our afternoon class followed by dinner and frequent informal meetings at the *Piazza* to continue our conversation over wine or ice cream.

On one memorable morning he was explaining his position on the ecological crisis and his perspective on spiritual limitations of the conservative, mainstream leadership within the Catholic Church. Decrying the church's lack of response to the crisis, his voice rose slightly as he said, "I am more orthodox than the Pope!" (Snider 1991). Berry was very blunt and deadly serious when he said, "we must recover the cosmological or we will die" (Snider 1991). He went on to stress the absurdity of the church's historic suppression of creation-centered mystics like Saint Francis, Hildegard von Bingen, and Julian of Norwich, to name a few and joked that the only reason he had not been excommunicated by the Catholic Church was simply that they didn't understand his work.

The irony of Tom making this statement in the heart of the Sacro Convento was not lost on me. Growing up in the bible belt of the south, I was familiar with the problems and limitations of fundamentalism and biblical literalism within mainstream Christianity. Berry's views validated my experience in a way that was deeply satisfying and challenged me to question how a Catholic tradition that celebrates the cosmological vision of Saint Francis could push an agenda that was so profoundly disconnected from the natural world and to the major sociological and ecological issues of our times.

Throughout his life, Berry conveyed a sense of urgency about the global environmental crisis that we cannot ignore. "We are working with what is perhaps the most precious reality in the universe -- the earth -- and we are spoiling it" (Berry 1991). To remedy this cultural pathology, Berry emphasized the profound and unique achievement in the development of human conscious awareness as it is manifested in the universe through the emergence of the human.

According to Berry and Swimme, "the story of the human is the story of the emergence and development of ... self-awareness and its role in the universe." They speak of a "new faculty of understanding" that exploded into existence in the form of human consciousness, which created a special power where "the Earth and the universe itself as a whole," developed the ability to "turn back and reflect on itself" (Swimme and Berry 1992, 143). As Teilhard de Chardin, one of Berry's greatest influencers famously said, "the human is the sum total of 15 billion years of unbroken evolution now thinking about itself" (Kenney 2010, 60).

The universal significance of this achievement cannot be underestimated. This is not just a basic, human awareness, but "a special mode of conscious self-reflection" combined with Berry's concept of "sympathetic presence," or an "understanding heart" (Berry 2003, 96). This heightened sensitivity is not unlike the gift exhibited by St. Francis. Sympathetic presence is the conscious recognition of that reciprocal relationship or "mutual presence" between the universe and the human. "Understanding heart" arises when we gain insight into the non-dual, inner nature of the universe itself. This is what it means to infuse the world with a vision of the sacred. We are creatures that stand before creation, rapt in awe by the great mystery that envelops us all. Berry says that, "awareness of an all pervading mysterious energy articulated in the infinite variety of natural forms seems to be the primary experience of human consciousness" (Berry 1988, 24). Swimme adds that, "the universe [literally] shivers with wonder in the depth of the human" (Swimme 1985, 32).

Berry would often point out that if you were born on the moon, your mind would be as barren and colorless as the lunar landscape. As humans, we are born out of the Earth, with the vast diversity of life and colors, of smells and tastes. According to Berry, our poetry, our art, and our music, emerge out of an experience of the diversity of our natural world. This incredible diversity facilitates the development of the human psyche, of the human mind, and, most importantly, sympathetic presence. It is the gift that makes us most human and the primary gift that we, as humans, bring to the universe. It is our destiny as a species to recover, celebrate and utilize this gift, and, if we do not cultivate it, our children will live in a profoundly diminished world.

Though perhaps not a true "*metanoia*" in the sense that Saint Francis experienced, my first summer spent with Thomas Berry in Assisi was both extraordinary and seminal, shaping many of the core values I cherish and inspiring me to this day. These include poetic and precious gifts in the form of a simple phrase or a complex and detailed historical perspective. In any form Berry's thoughts hold a timeless relevance.

One late afternoon after our studies at the Sacro Convento, I was walking slowly with Thomas through the Piazza del Comune as we returned to our hotel for dinner. I found myself both moved, and somewhat stunned by Berry's wisdom and the depth of his inquiry over the course of more than five decades of study. I was also freshly inspired by my recent encounter with of the story of Saint Francis. I tried to articulate the power of my experience to Tom, but in my exuberance, I stumbled over my words as I tried to convey the profound impact of studying with him in beautiful Assisi, absorbing the assigned readings and engaging in in-depth, thought-provoking discussions with my teachers and fellow students. In my joy and excitement, I urged that we find a way to expand our small summer program so that students worldwide could share the same, extraordinary experience. As we continued to walk slowly together through the *piazza*, he said matter-of-factly, in his soft, quavering voice, "You know, Steve, we don't need Assisi. We need an Assisi of the mind."

REFERENCES

Berry, Thomas. 1991. *Befriending the Earth*. Mystic: Twenty-Third Publications.

---. 1988. *The Dream of the Earth*. San Francisco: Sierra Club.

---. 1999. *The Great Work*. New York: Bell Tower.

---. 2006. *Evening Thoughts*. San Francisco: Sierra Club.

---. 2003. "Affectivity in Classical Confucian Tradition & Confucian Spirituality" vol. 1: 96.

Custodia Terrae Sanctae. 2011. "The Canticle of the Creatures." Last modified 2011. http://www.custodia.org/default.asp?id=1454.

EWTN. 2014. "Saint Francis of Assisi, Founder of the Friars Minor". https://www.ewtn.com/library/MARY/FRANCIS.htm.

Kenny, Jim. 2010. *Thriving in the Crosscurrent*. Wheaton: Quest Books.

Passionist Missionaries. 2013. "Thomas Berry". Last modified 2014. http://thepassionists.org/passionist-spirituality-and-charism/thomas-berry/.

Snider, Steve. "Thomas Berry." (notes from Assisi 1991).

---. "Thomas Berry." (notes from Ecuador 1993).

Stienfels, Peter. 1990. *The New York Times*. (January 16, 1990, accessed March 2014.)

Suzuki, David and Peter Knudtson. 1992. *Wisdom of the Elders*. New York: Bantam.

Swimme, Brian and Thomas Berry. 1992. *The Universe Story*. New York: Harper Collins.

Swimme, Brian. 1985. *The Universe is a Green Dragon*. Santa Fe: Bear & Company.

PART IV

SACREDNESS & INTERCONNECTION WITH THE NATURAL WORLD

Cosmologies and spiritual practices that acknowledge and integrate the sacredness of the natural world which is the source of our wellbeing and our spirituality with the awareness that the current problems we face stem from a crisis of values.

20

MYSTICAL PROPHET FOR THE POSTMODERN GLOBAL ECOLOGICAL ERA

JOE HOLLAND

This essay traces the roots of Thomas Berry's mystical-prophetic vision of an authentically postmodern global ecological era to the noetic-artistic evolutionary understanding of the Universe first articulated by Pierre Teilhard de Chardin. It then explores how Thomas Berry, together with his co-visionary Brian Swimme, developed the Teilhardian legacy into a philosophical-scientific "New Cosmology." Finally, the essay reflects on the philosophical, theological, and societal significance of this "New Cosmology."

The writings and person of late Thomas Berry have been a major influence on my intellectual worldview. For that reason, I am deeply grateful to Dr. Elisabeth Ferrero for inviting me to write about memories of Tom in Italy, and about what I learned from him. In this essay, I will first share my experiences with Tom in Italy, then summarize what I learned from him, and finally reflect on what I consider the significance of Tom's thought.

Experiences

Thanks to Elisabeth, I was able to be with Tom in Italy during one of her Study Abroad for Earth (S.A.F.E.) programs. Years later, Tom joined Elisabeth, my wife Paquita, and myself for another trip to Italy. This time the trip was for the presentation of Elisabeth's and my book, *The Earth Charter: A Study Book of Reflection for Action*, for which Tom had written the Preface. Both events were a great privilege for me – being able to learn first-hand from Tom's vast wisdom.

Earlier, I had the honor of working closely with one of Tom's siblings, the late Jim Berry, who was equally committed to ecology, though with a different style. Jim had been a bomber pilot in World War II and continued his career in the Air Force as an intelligence officer. Later, in his retirement, Jim developed an intellectual center where he promoted Tom's thought. While Tom's approach was lyrical and seductive, Jim's was militant and campaigning. They were both wonderful people and complemented each other.

The S.A.F.E. program in Assisi took place during the summer months in Italy's lush green province of Umbria. During that summer, as had been the case in earlier summers, Tom was the featured teacher. Actually, he was far more than a teacher. He became sage, mentor, and companion to just about everyone there.

As mentioned, my wife Paquita and I again had the pleasure of accompanying Elisabeth and Tom to a trip to Italy, this time to celebrate the presentation of the Italian edition of the book on the Earth Charter. Tom was then ninety-one years of age. Different that the Assisi experience, however, the Rome weather was cold. I was grateful to have brought warm clothes.

Soon after we arrived, Elisabeth asked me to pick up Tom at Rome's airport, which I happily did. Greeting Tom as he exited from security area, I noticed that he was wearing only a light jacket. When I asked if he had a warm coat, Tom said the jacket would be sufficient.

Then I noticed that he was carrying a small paper bag that looked like a lunch bag. So I asked him to what baggage area his luggage was being delivered. He looked at his little "lunch bag" and said quietly, "This is all I have." Tom thus personified the simplicity promoted by Saint Francis of Assisi, patron of the city where we had last met.

During this second Italy trip with Tom, we first travelled to presentation ceremonies for the book at Milan in the north, then to Rome in the center, and finally down to the south in the province of Puglia. All the while, Tom scarcely showed uncomfortableness with the cold and, despite his ninety-one years of age, he maintained boundless energy. I thought to myself, what an extraordinary human being.

Influences

As mentioned, Tom's thought and person have had a profound intellectual influence on my worldview. Many decades ago, during a mid-life career as a public intellectual and beginning to study Tom's writings, I unexpectedly came to a turning point. A quiet thought began to haunt me that I should be working more closely with young people. Of course, the place to ensure extended conversation with young people is the university, where they cannot escape from their teachers! I soon began to explore the possibility of a university-based teaching position.

At the time, while several possibilities presented themselves, the most attractive was St. Thomas University, today in Miami Gardens, Florida. Two faculty members there, Elisabeth and Dr. Joseph Iannone, had been working for some time with Tom (and with Brian Swimme). They had made the school a center for interest in Tom's and Brian's creative spiritual-ecological thought. That was of great interest to me. I had already known from my studies that, as the most important protégé of Pierre Teilhard de Chardin, Tom (with Brian) had been developing Teilhard's legacy into the "New Cosmology."

Taking a teaching position at St. Thomas University in the early 1990s, I grew amazed at the creative work that both Elisabeth and Joe Iannone had done with the insights of Tom Berry and Brian Swimme. Immediately, I plunged myself into support for their work, including becoming a member and for a while co-chair, of a new committee seeking to create an ecological university.

So effective was Elisabeth and Tom's work that in 1992 St. Thomas University received, in an impressive ceremony in the Washington D.C. area, the prestigious Renew America Award from a consortium of more than 20 leading U.S. environmental organizations. The consortium gave the award to St. Thomas University because of Elisabeth and Joe Iannone's pioneering work in creating a comprehensive ecological curriculum, heavily based on the ideas of Thomas Berry and Brian Swimme.

While this award was the highlight of my engagement with Tom's thought, please allow me now to trace my earlier intellectual development leading up to this engagement.

In my work on social analysis, I had become convinced that there was something fundamentally wrong with the philosophical foundations of what I call "modern Western industrial-colonial bourgeois civilization." I had long concluded that this civilization was not sustainable – not ecologically, not socially, and not spiritually. In response, I had initially studied critiques of capitalism and the alternative of socialism. While I learned much from those studies, before long it became clear that the problem was far deeper culturally than what proponents of either of these two modern ideologies could imagine

At that point, I explored critiques of the modern European Enlightenment. The Enlightenment had provided the bourgeois philosophical-scientific foundation for the materialist ideologies of both liberal capitalism and scientific socialism. Yet even those critiques still did not seem deep enough.

It was then that I began my study of Tom Berry. He went truly deep into the full story of the human journey, deeper into the underlying Earth story, and even deeper into the surrounding story of the Cosmos. By engaging with Tom's thought (again, enhanced by Brian), I concluded that the fundamental problems of modern Western industrial-colonial bourgeois civilization needed to be traced to their philosophical roots in the early modern Cartesian-Newtonian Cosmology (now the "Old Cosmology").

That Cosmology constituted the intellectual foundation of modern Western bourgeois philosophy and simultaneously of modern Western bourgeois science. After being developed in the seventeenth century by early modern "natural philosophers" (as scientists were called at the time), the Cartesian-Newtonian Cosmology was applied to society during the eighteenth century in the modern European Enlightenment (again, the origin of the modern social sciences). From that development, the modern materialist ideologies emerged to guide (or misguide) modern Western industrial-colonial bourgeois societies. Hence, I realized that the unsustainability of modern Western industrial-colonial bourgeois civilization had its deep root in the foundational Cartesian-Newtonian paradigm for modern Western philosophy and science.

Later, I explored how modern Western bourgeois philosophy and science were together grounded in the atomistic cosmology of the classical Greek materialist and antireligious philosopher Epicurus. But that insight would come later. For the moment, I was drawn to Tom and Brian's contribution to the emerging New Cosmology.

Again, by studying Tom's and Brian's articulation of the New Cosmology, I realized that it was at this truly deep level of analysis that we needed to develop a critique of the dysfunctionality of modern Western industrial-colonial bourgeois civilization. I also realized that it was at this level that we needed to search for the creation of a regenerative and authentically postmodern global ecological civilization.

The emerging postmodern New Cosmology provided important intellectual resources for exploring a regenerative and authentically postmodern cosmological future for philosophy and science, and within that framework for education, technology, religion, and all human institutions. I say "authentically postmodern," because what academics typically call "postmodernism" remains in my judgment simply late modern or, to use the language of Charlene Spretnak, only "hypermodern" (Spretnak 1999).

Implications

In the remainder of this essay, I would like to reflect on the intellectual significance of the work of Thomas Berry. I will divide the significance into three areas, first philosophical, second theological, and third sociological.

Philosophical Contribution

As mentioned, following a long intellectual journey I had concluded that the roots of the ecological, societal, and spiritual degeneration in late modern Western industrial-colonial bourgeois civilization (again, which I perceive to be in fundamental breakdown) were found in the philosophical assumptions embraced by early modern Western philosophy and science. Those early modern philosophical assumptions, retrieved from ancient Greek Epicurean atomism, led to an understanding of the universe in terms of time and space as fragmented into autonomous particles. According to that worldview, the particles bear no relationship to each other; they accidentally assemble themselves into artificial aggregates only by random chance; and they do so without intellectual purpose or spiritual meaning.

At the time, that neo-Epicurean cosmology was called the "mechanical philosophy" and became, as mentioned, the philosophical foundation of modern Western bourgeois science. Later, as also mentioned, in the Enlightenment another generation of philosophers applied that mechanical philosophy to human society. The cosmology had already become became canonized in the work of René Descartes and Isaac Newton, respectively considered "fathers" of modern Western philosophy and of modern Western science.

For anyone who has eyes to see, it is now clear that, despite the extraordinary achievements of modern science and technology, the Cartesian-Newtonian paradigm has ultimately proved an unwise and even misguided philosophical guide for civilization. Still worse, in its current political-economic forms of modern bourgeois neoliberal globalization, it is now proving an unwise philosophical guide for the entire human family. Following the Cartesian-Newtonian paradigm, global elites are the human family into ecological catastrophe, into social catastrophe, and into spiritual catastrophe.

For that reason, it is imperative for the human family to discover a fresh and regenerative philosophical path. Gratefully, the intellectual work of Tom Berry and Brian Swimme has already helped to open that path for us. Though Tom and Brian did not articulate the New Cosmology in strictly philosophical terms, they nonetheless have created for us a fresh philosophical vista. As we know from their work, the emerging new cosmology perceives the universe as relationally holistic, artistically evolutionary, and wondrously mystical.

Theological Contribution

The second great contribution of Tom Berry is theological. As the primary protégé of Teilhard, he advanced and deepened Teihard's work in linking Catholic theology with the scientific discovery of evolution.

From a Christian viewpoint, the New Cosmology represents an authentically postmodern retrieval of the classical Christian understanding of the natural world as the first book of revelation, long called the "Book of Nature" and which Tom called the "Primary Revelation." The "Book of Nature" stands as a revelatory partner with the "Book of the Bible." Classical theologians, more so in the East than in the West (though in the West Augustine celebrated the "two books"), long celebrated the fact that the Creator gave us these two complementary books of revelation. Christians can authentically read the "Book of the Bible" only with conscious awareness of the Divine revelation in the "Book of Nature." Unfortunately, modern Western theologians, both Protestant and Catholic, frequently have forgotten this deep and ancient Christian truth. Gratefully, Tom retrieved for us that ancient teaching in a fresh and authentically postmodern way.

The deep cultural transition from the modern Old Cosmology to the postmodern New Cosmology has also been explored by the Austrian physicist Fritjof Capra in his insightful books on physics, biology, and cognitive science. Drawing on the Santiago School, Capra proposes in his recent book *The Systems View of Life* that matter carries within itself a proto-cognitive and intentional capacity as artistic creator. This view means that the material world is full of creative cognitive energy (Capra 2014).

This deep understanding resonates closely with the primal spiritualities of all the ancient spiritual cultures of Earth's peoples, though the ancient members of those cultures of course did not know about evolution. This understanding of matter as cognitively creative also resonates with several schools of classical philosophy – for example, in the East with Daoism and in the West with Stoicism, and with its earlier antecedent in the *Logos* of Heraclitus. Further, it resonates today with the work of spiritual feminists in the school of ecophilosophy, particularly with the creative work of Charlene Spretnak.

This understanding of the material world as holistic, creative, and even mystical, then leads to an understanding of the human as a more complex and advanced form of the consciousness of matter itself, and ultimately as the self-conscious (yet hopefully humble) guide of planet Earth's artistically cognitive ecological unfolding.

Sociological Contribution

Tom repeatedly made clear that all human institutions – economic, political, cultural, religious, and educational – need to refond themselves on the wisdom of this fresh ecological, evolutionary, and mystical paradigm. Presently, practically all institutions on planet Earth, still grounded in the limited and misguided bourgeois philosophy and science of the Cartesian-Newtonian paradigm, have now become dysfunctional.

Such is the deep root of the alienation of so many young people from contemporary institutions. For some young people, this alienation leads to cynicism or even despair, but for others it gratefully leads to hope and transformation.

Tom and Brian's contribution here is not simply a critique. It is at the same time, and even more powerfully, a creative vision to guide us into the future. It is this vision that can nourish fresh generations of young leaders in all fields. Helping young leaders to become truly regenerative is the great task before the authentically postmodern University.

To support these young future leaders, the late modern university now needs to move beyond its current state of intellectual dysfunctionality, beyond the limits and misguidance of its still intellectually foundational Cartesian-Newtonian paradigm. The late modern university needs to explore the healing and regenerative vision of the New Cosmology across the creative communion of ecological, social, and spiritual life.

Conclusion

I feel blessed to have known personally, and to have spent rich time in the company of, such a visionary and mystical figure as Tom Berry. I feel equally blessed to have shared in the company of those who learned from him, and who contributed their own insights to opening the new path. Here, I think especially of Brian Swimme and my own colleagues from St. Thomas University, Elisabeth Ferrero and Joe Iannone.

From Tom and from these colleagues, I have learned that the task before us is clear, namely, to build a regenerative and authentically postmodern global ecological civilization. This new global ecological civilization needs to ground itself in the New Cosmology, and at the same time to remain rooted in the rich wisdom of the ancient spiritual traditions of Earth's human family.

REFERENCES

Berry, Thomas & Brian Swimme. 1994. *The Universe Story: From the Primordial Flaring Forth to the Ecozoic Era – A Celebration of the Unfolding of the Cosmos*. Reprint Edition. New York: Harper One.

Capra, Fritjof. 1984. *The Turning Point: Science, Society, and the Rising Culture*. New York: Bantam.

---. 1997. *The Web of Life: A New Understanding of Living Systems*. Anchor.

---. 2004. *The Hidden Connection: A Science for Sustainable Living*. Anchor.

--- & Pier Luigi Luisi. 2014. *The Systems View of Life: A Unifying Vision*. New York: Cambridge University Press.

Ferrero, Elisabeth & Joe Holland. 2005. *The Earth Charter: A Study Book of Reflection for Action.* Miami: Redwoods Press.

Holland, Joe. 2013. "Pacem in Terris & Philosophy." In *Pacem in Terris: Its Continuing Relevance for the Twenty-First Century,* ed. Francis Dubois and Josef Klee, 71-98. Washington DC: Pacem in Terris Press.

Spretnak, Charlene. 1999. *The Resurgence of the Real: Body, Nature, and Place in a Hypermodern World.* New York: Routledge.

21

BEYOND THE BIRD BATHS[1]

PETER DAMIAN MASSENGILL

We begin many adventures in life by external stimuli that touch the heart. It is only after these begin to internalize and integrate within the brain that they really become life-changing experiences.

Saint Francis has been named the Patron Saint of Ecology by the Roman Catholic Church. St. Clare could be regarded as the Patroness of Eco-feminism. These are popular attributes given to these Saints as can be witnessed by the large number of garden birdbaths with statues of St. Francis standing in the middle surrounded by birds and sometimes other animals. But as people who are seriously interested in what historical figures like Francis and Clare of Assisi bring to a dialogue on ecology, and specifically sustainability, we must move beyond the birdbaths.

Let us begin by looking at what was happening in the 1200s in the world of Francis and Clare. Towns were beginning to become interdependent through the development of commerce. Francis was part of a successful commercial family and the new wealth that came with that, while Clare was challenged from another side, being part of the

---

[1] A version of this essay was published in *Earth Ethics*. 1997-98. Vol. 9.1&2: 18-19.

noble family, whose power lay in name and old money. The conflict of rising social issues had a direct influence upon both Francis and Clare.

Religious life was enwrapped in dualism. There were popular heresies concerning the distinction between Christ's divine and human nature. Religion was called "sacred," and the world was called "profane." Spiritual traditions were turned into special rituals instead of principles for daily living. A whole body of literature developed around the "lives of the Saints," which was intended to demonstrate how heroic figures successfully overcame the dichotomy of the "sacred" and the "profane." This was the religious atmosphere into which Francis and Clare lived, and to which they reacted by their very lifestyle, which was intentionally contrary to the prevailing dualism.

Communications were very limited, but travel was expanding, so people were able to learn the technological developments made by other cities and countries. The way of looking at the "universe," a concept with a much more limited definition than we have today, was still dependent upon the immediately observable.

We can begin to appreciate the unique perspective that Francis of Assisi brought to the world of his time by looking at his "Canticle of the Creatures." The idea of writing a poem or hymn that calls upon all of Creation to give praise to its Maker is not at all unique, given that the sermons and liturgical direction at the time of Francis and Clare laid heavy accent upon the almost "science fiction" images of the Book of Daniel and the extensive use of the Psalms of Cosmic Praise. Neither do we find the structure of his work unique. He laid out his poem strictly following the world view of his time: Creator, Sun and Moon, the four elements, and humanity. It had the classic proportions of the 1200s.

So what is innovative about it? What Francis recalls in his Canticle is the familial relationship of all Creation. Francis uses the terminology of "brother" and "sister" for the elements, which is unique in the literature of his time. He also uses descriptions of particularity attributing specific qualities and characteristics to each creature.

Let us look at the Canticle itself. The Invocation could have been taken almost directly from the Psalms. It is classic,

> *Most High, all-powerful, all good, Lord!*
> *All praise is yours, all glory, all honor, and all blessing.*
> *To you, alone, Most High, do they belong.*
> *No mortal lips are worthy to pronounce your name.*
> *All praise be yours My Lord, though all that you have made.*
> (Francis 1-8)

We move directly to the Sun and Moon, receiving both a place in the family as a brother and sister, as well as qualities and characteristics,

> *And first my lord, Brother Sun,*
> *Who brings the day;*
> *and light you give to us through him.*
> *How beautiful is he!*
> *How radiant in all his splendor!*
> *Of you, Most High, he bears the likeness.*
> *All praise be yours My Lord,*
> *through Sister Moon and Stars;*
> *In the heavens you have made them,*
> *bright and precious and fair.*
> (Francis 9-17)

There follows, now, the four basic elements Wind, Water, Fire, and Earth. Again, we see their sibling relationship with us, and the attributes that make them unique. Note that Francis speaks of both the positive and the negative aspects that make them real for us,

> *All praise be yours, My Lord,*
> *through brothers Wind and Air,*
> *And fair and stormy, all the weather's moods,*

> *By which you cherish all that you have made.*
> *All praise be yours My Lord, through sister Water,*
> *So useful, lowly, precious, and pure.*
> *All praise be yours My Lord, through brother Fire,*
> *Through whom you brighten up the night,*
> *How beautiful is he, how gay! Full*
> *of power and strength.*
> *All praise to you, My Lord, through sister Earth, our Mother,*
> *Who feeds us in her sovereignty*
> *and produces various fruits with colored flowers and herbs.*
> (Francis 18-32)

And last we come to humanity and the virtues necessary for common life,

> *All praise be yours, my Lord,*
> *through those who grant pardon for love of You,*
> *through those who endure sickness and trial*
> *Happy are those who endure in Peace,*
> *by you, Most High, they will be crowned.*
> (Francis 33-37)

The final strophe brings home the reality that those who live within the context of the created order, and respect that sacred relationship, have nothing to fear,

> *All praise be yours My Lord, through sister Death,*
> *from whose embrace no mortal can escape.*
> *Woe to those who die in mortal sin!*
> *Happy those she finds doing your will!*
> *The second death can do no harm to them.*
> *Praise and bless my Lord and give him thanks,*
> *And serve him with great humility.*
> (Francis 38-44)

Both Francis and Clare bring to us a profound affection for the world. In other writings in the form of admonitions to their followers they state that, "touching the world is a physical encounter with the body of Christ itself." In the early lives written of these two saints, the structure and elements laid down by the Church for the writing of hagiography were closely followed. But even so, the unique relationship of Francis to creation is brought out in these writings. There were all kinds of stories of holy people commanding the animals, and even the elements, but in Francis, we are offered once again an innovation. In the early lives, we find the biographers almost embarrassed to relate the affection with which he took up and protected the animals, the reverence with which he walked upon the earth, and how he often led the animals into prayer indicating a relationship of not just service, but of shared response to the Creator.

These are the innovative elements that Francis and Clare brought to the 1200s; it is our task to look at the innovations appropriate to our time. This will require that we engage our own complex realities of social context, religious context, and worldview, and find a "canticle" which will bring into harmony our own intimate relationship to the whole universe. Since the United Nations Conference on the Environment and Development held in Rio de Janeiro in June of 1992, a concrete expression of this relationship has taken the form of a document called *The Earth Charter*. The examples of Francis and Clare of Assisi, who established innovative and consistent principles of environmental ethics, can be tested against our current structures and translated into significant application for our day. Engaging the complex reality of our day demands that we apply a consistent ethic in a number of areas: religion, anthropology, science, technology, economics, society, law and institutional structures, to name just a few. Francis and Clare of Assisi have already passed on our road of dialogue, but they continue to overtake us and keep us attentive to what must lie ahead.

REFERENCES

Francis of Assisi. "The Canticle of the Creatures." *St. Francis of Assisi, Lover of All Creation.* Accessed March 12, 2015. http://www.appleseeds.org/canticle.htm

22

EARTH AT RISK REDUX:
SUSTAINABILITY GROUNDED IN SPIRITUALITY

RODNEY L. PETERSEN

As the twenty-first century unfolds, humanity faces the threat of an unmitigated ecological disaster. This essay discusses how science and religion find themselves drawn together in dialogue in our present context with implications for spirituality and civic life.

The connection between spirituality and sustainability is central to the work of Thomas Berry. His environmental ethics has served to awaken those sensitive to the life of the spirit to environmental consciousness every bit as much as Rachel Carson alerted us to a threatened sustainability manifest in a silent spring. Berry stood committed to an integration of a spirituality grounded in an evolutionary perspective of science very much in the way of a Teilhard de Chardin but which drew Berry to envision and to articulate a deep ecological commitment (Conroy and Petersen 2000).

A suggestive baseline for linking spirituality with sustainability is with the World Council of Churches' "Conference on Faith, Science and the Future" in 1979, a conference held at the Massachusetts Institute of Technology in Boston.[1] Its premises concerning creation were brought into alignment with the breadth of the known universe. Paul Albrecht writes,

> *By the term 'creation' we mean the entire universe in relation to God. It includes therefore both humanity and nature and the disciplines which study them, whether the natural or social sciences or the humanities. God remains free in relation to his creation. In his faithfulness he grants its continuity and permanence. He is always at work in creation, enters it in Jesus Christ, and purposes to complete and perfect his communion with it. This cannot be deduced from a scientific view of nature but only from our knowledge of God in the history of Israel and through Jesus Christ. But it gives the work of science and technology a basis, meaning and direction.* (Albrecht 1980, 32)

---

[1] The emerging conceptual framework, "Justice, Peace, and the Integrity of Creation," itself was grounded in thinking that extends back to the Conference on Church and Society (Geneva: 1966), which had the theme "Christians in the Technical and Social Revolutions of our Time." The Fourth Assembly of the WCC (Uppsala, Sweden: 1968) had urged further work in this area at a time when many physical and social scientists were beginning to alert the human community of the danger of resource depletion and environmental collapse. A series of Working Committees on Church and Society in the early 1970s began to link concern for social justice with an awareness of growing ecological problems. The conference "Science and Technology for Human Development: An Ambiguous Future – and Christian Hope," held in Bucharest, Romania (1974), was a result of this thinking. The Fifth Assembly of the WCC (Nairobi, Kenya: 1975) received this work and, stimulated by the able thinking of the Australian biologist Charles Birch, adopted through its Central Committee in the following year, the program area "The Struggle for the Just, Participatory and Sustainable Society." The Committee authorized work for a conference in 1979 which was eventually held at the Massachusetts Institute of Technology (MIT), occurring during Nash's tenure as executive director of the Massachusetts Council of Churches.

As the twenty-first century continues to unfold, this conference and its conclusions will be increasingly seen as a part of the background to Berry's work and prophetic of the unmitigated ecological disaster facing humanity apart from the earth consciousness fostered by Berry. At MIT science and religion found themselves drawn together in dialogue in our present context with implications for spirituality and civic life. This is the work that Thomas Berry went on to do after 1979 (Berry 2006; Berry and Tucker 2009). It is work toward building a sacred community that many have gone on to do into the present (Hart 2006).

In his remarks at the MIT conference "Nature, Humanity and God in Ecological Perspective," Charles Birch (1918-2009), geneticist and early ecologist, laid a foundation for environmental ethics by contending that we have created a mechanistic cosmology of science out of what was once perhaps a useful tool in severing the cord for science and religion from a worldview suffused with superstition and magic, but that this cosmology is now threatening to redefine who we are. Birch argued for a more integrative approach, suffused with subjectivity, in our relations with nature as informed by process theology.

The MIT conference continues to stand as a watershed in contemporary ethical environmental thinking. Perhaps the most important insight it raised had to do with the relationship between ecology and worldview, as this one issue helps to shape the conception of so many other issues. We can credit persons like Thomas Berry, Brian Swimme and James Nash for giving us these insights and awakening us to the importance of understanding the contributions of the spiritual and historical stories of all peoples, as partners at a table set by contemporary mechanistic science and the older western Jewish and Christian theologies.

Berry alerted us to the fact that our system of public belief is in need of radical revision if we are to survive as a species. Such an argument, coming from the social or natural sciences, draws us to reflect on religion in relation to values. In these reflections we will dwell on Judaism and Christianity, but recognize that we might do this for an array of religious traditions (Tucker 1997 *et pass.*). Berry himself was particularly influenced by traditions of Buddhism.

It is from Judaism that western culture has largely inherited its vision of a creator in relation to the cosmos. According to Michal Smart, former director of education for the Coalition on the Environment and Jewish Life (COEJL), this conception begins with the phrase, "God created the earth," implying a purposeful, creation shaping, environmental concern. The care for creation shapes Jewish ritual whereas its destruction is tantamount to blasphemy. The weekly cycle of time with its focus on the Sabbath acknowledges the goodness of creation. This divine stamp on space and time shapes the Jewish view of social justice and ecojustice in the acknowledgment of the Sabbath or Jubilee Year. Such "macro" events replicate the concern found in everyday life seen in the blessing required every time something is taken from the earth. God's compassion extends to all species, and their ordering in creation is expressive of God's will as further articulated in the covenant between creator and creation. This covenant tempers individualism and establishes an intergenerational responsibility (Smart 2000).

Christian Scripture scholar Richard Clifford argues that while Christianity and Judaism are religions centered in a Book, each has developed an interpretive tradition for reading Scripture. Augustine of Hippo (354-430 C.E.) helped to shape the dominant tradition for Roman Catholics and Protestants. This tradition tended toward anthropomorphism, finding redemption in Jesus Christ. It was characterized by a moderate dualism, giving priority to questions of spirituality. Without challenging this tradition, Clifford writes that the idea of the process of creation does not imply a dichotomy between nature and human beings. Rather, the world that emerges reveals a human race that is embedded in emergent materiality (Clifford 2000).

Early in this drama the *locus classicus* (Genesis 1) for "dominion" theories of human oversight or stewardship of nature appears. The literary structure of the text presents humans as fully a part of the web of creation, while only they directly encounter God. Their rule images God's rule: it is to foster the continuity and fruitfulness of all life according to God's order. Any latent anthropomorphism is subject to a withering critique in the book of Job. The ancient world depicted by Genesis 2-11 shows an earth that shares in the consequences of humanity's sin. Death, the ultimate effect of this alienation, is mitigated by a foreshadowing of restoration, first through Eve and then, in the post-diluvian world, in the covenantal blessing given to all sentient and vegetative life. Clifford concludes: there is a relative, not absolute, anthropomorphism in the Jewish and Christian Bibles; God is the power behind fertility and infertility in the natural world; the cosmogony found in the Bible connects patterns in human society and the natural environment. God's work – creation out of chaos, and new creation out of sinful human history – is inextricably intertwined with the state of the earth.[2]

Beyond classical Jewish and Christian conceptions, the question of religion's partnership with environmental concern (Gottleib 2005) receives added attention through deepening aspects of mysticism in our developing global culture (Dalby 1949). For Berry there was an attempt to view the entire universe in relation to God, the universe as the only self-referential reality. The story of the universe is not only the story as ultimate reality, but it is the story all sentient and non-sentient forms put into their own language. However, just as anthropomorphic religion can become characterized by self-deception and

---

[2] As Brueggemann(1977) and Wright (1993) both show, the biblical book of Leviticus is a rich source for reflection on the interrelationship between spirituality and materiality for both the Hebraic and Christian traditions.

escapism, so also can the deep ecology of environmental spirituality. For example, the mysticism of deep ecology seeks to emphasize our capacity to love beings across space and time. Deep ecology asks us to see ourselves as a part of the web of life, for example as a part of the rainforest trying to save itself. Herein lay the advantages and liabilities of deep ecology. Like other forms of mysticism, it can slide into an attempt to escape society. If we really love nature, ethicist and philosopher Roger Gottlieb adds, we are called to love people and to seek justice.

Together with Smart and Clifford, Gottlieb challenges us not to abandon nature but to see it as another lens along with that of the lens of history. It is in this context that we find transcendence and ethics, the twin axes along which an authentic social self develops. Gottlieb continues a theme we have seen in Thomas Berry and other contemporary authors such as Leonardo Boff: Environmentalism needs to embrace environmental justice (Boff 1997). As such, a chastened deep ecology can serve to deepen our spiritual temperament as we work for a just social transformation. It can also remind us that Christian theology has been so focused on the second article of the creed, redemption through Jesus Christ, that the first and third articles, dealing with God and creation as well as the Holy Spirit and sanctification, have often been overlooked. An inter-religious dialogue that draws upon the faith perspectives and worldviews of others can help to shape a more inclusive and nuanced perspective for an earth at risk (Burrell and Malits 1997; Lash 1993; McDade 1990).

Religious traditions are read through certain lenses. This enables some things to be seen while others are overlooked.[3] The fact that

---

[3] H. Paul Santmire (1985) distinguishes two thrusts in the history of Christianity out of its Hebraic and Hellenistic contexts, a spiritual and an ecological motif in continuing tension with one another. Robert Booth Fowler (1995) traces in broad strokes the increasing influence of environmentalism on American Protestantism since the first Earth Day in 1970.

there are different ways of reading and "seeing" has been important in contemporary discussions of shifting paradigms for understanding. For example, Eastern Orthodox expressions of Christianity have remained less dualistic than some Western spiritualities, more centered on pre-Scholastic schools of mysticism. The Orthodox Christian approaches God's creation with thanks (eucharist) and is characterized by asceticism in spiritual life.[4] The variety of perspectives among Roman Catholics includes but is wider than Augustine's "spiritualizing" of the Bible (Bührig 1989).[5] Among Protestants the interpretive spread is also wide, with Evangelicals, for example, found in an array of positions from the "Wise Use" Movement on the extreme right to quite activist and communitarian views among post-conservative Evangelicals.[6]

A critique of inherited patterns of Jewish and Christian interpretation can only be done here schematically. Already mentioned is the influence of process theology as a way of discerning the evolving pattern of life and co-creative work of humanity. The moderate dualism found in Augustine has been criticized by theologies of embodiment which have tended to emphasize more immanent conceptions of God, as in the work of Sallie McFague and her successors, who find

---

[4] The ascetic nature of Orthodoxy suggests the need for a God-centered prayerful self-discipline to curb our appetitive desires, particularly significant in light of population and consumptive patterns as they bear upon the carrying capacity of the earth. That Orthodoxy is awakening to its global ecological role was seen pointedly in 1989 when His Holiness Ecumenical Patriarch Dimitrios of Constantinople declared September 1, the first day of the Byzantine Ecclesiastical Year, as Environmental Protection Day (Limouris 1990).

[5] The concept of the integrity of creation is found in paragraph 26 of Pope John Paul II's 1987 encyclical *Sollicitudo Rei Socialis* (Catholic Church 1988).

[6] Francis S. Schaeffer (1970) issued an early Evangelical call to ecological responsibility; later, J. Mark Thomas (1993) cited leading Evangelical voices on environmental stewardship. Shaw (1993) linked personal Christian discipleship to environmental ethics as did Granberg-Michaelson (1984).

the universe or world as God's body to be an organic model from which to consider every major theological topic. Feminist and Womanist perspectives might also be cited (Peck and Gallo 1989; Reuther 1972, 1992). Speaking out with one voice against an older theology conceived of in terms of the metaphor of male dominance,[7] feminist theologies form an array of positions from reference to "Mother Earth" and Gaia as poetic metaphors to new forms of dualism that find in Gaia a parallel to Isis, Astarte, and all of the "Great Mothers" of Antiquity.[8]

Indigenous and Native American spiritualities should be singled out for special attention. Vine Deloria Jr. describes the appeal of such spirituality in a time of collapsing values in Euro-American culture, the disillusionment with Civil Rights and power movements and, earlier, over Vietnam and more recent wars, of an escape into drugs and return to Mother Earth.[9] Sadly, he and other Native writers score negatively a romantic and often fraudulent turn to Native American spirituality as part of this search for authenticity. Native people have been typed as exemplary "stewards" of the land but also as pillagers of nature, eco-terrorists out to exterminate animal life for the sake of

---

[7] Contrary to the cautious attitude toward nature as a realm of immense mystery in medieval Europe, the seventeenth-century English philosopher Thomas Hobbes regarded nature as existing solely for human usage, "She is no mystery, for she worketh by motion and geometry .... [We] can chart these motions. Feel then as if you lived in a world which can be measured, weighed and mastered and confront it with audacity." (Wiley 1950).

[8] Judith Plaskow and Carol P. Christ (1989) presented helpful essays in understanding the nature of and motivation for goddess spirituality. Wilkinson (1993) expressed an alternative view.

[9] Vine Deloria (1973) holds that Christianity has forsaken nature and that an ecological era requires the spiritual resources of Native American religions for spiritual guidance. His book's second (1992) edition sets the recovery of Native spirituality more clearly in the context of the collapse of values in contemporary society.

the fur trade. In the lens of contemporary ecological concern, Native peoples have been viewed as the first American "bio-regionalists," as sensitive to the web of life through reciprocity, and as reflecting environmental ethics in ritual and mythology. In assessing such ideas, Jace Weaver (1996) writes in his introduction that Native peoples are "neither saints nor sinners in environmental matters. They are human beings."

Valuable characteristics are exhibited despite wide Native diversity: (1) the practice of reciprocity and natural conservation so that ample resources exist for themselves and their progeny, (2) an emphasis upon community for purposes of collective survival, and (3) a sense of nature as an organic whole. Thomas Berry (1991) has demonstrated that the [Rousseauian] belief that indigenous peoples have a special contribution to make to environmental consciousness transcends native experience in North America and includes, for example, the Celtic and Sammi peoples of Europe, the Maori of the South Pacific, tribal groups in Africa or South Asia, and indigenous peoples of Central and South America (Berry and Clarke 1991; and McDaniel 1990).[10]

A diffuse New Age spirituality runs through environmental concern. As defined in relation to deep ecology, a pattern of deepening commitment might run as follows: (1) a "shallow" perspective which favors land conservation, stewardship, and the preservation of endangered species (Passmore 1974);[11] (2) an intermediate collection of approaches, including the land ethic of "ecosaint" Aldo Leopold

---

[10] These writers' interest in indigenous peoples' contributions to this approach is evident in the World Council of Churches' programming, especially in Unit III of its *Theology of Life* study (Geneva: 1991).

[11] Passmore's work was criticized for an anthropocentric framework and instrumentalist perspective on the natural world.

(1949)[12] and the animal-liberation movement of Peter Singer (1975), denying exclusive supremacy to human interests but acknowledging human responsibility for the ecosphere; (3) Deep Ecology, formulated by Arne Naess (1976, 1990), and by William Devall and George Sessions (1985),[13] calling for a nonhuman ethic which would provide ecospheric equalitarianism and biodiversity; and (4) Deep Green Ecology, a deepening of Deep Ecology to a more critical and inductive style with an added dimension of metaphysical naturalism (Sessions 1981).

Reflection on Scripture and alternative theologies has inevitably led to discussion about other worldviews or living religious traditions in relation to ecology, a topic of increasing study. As a part of contemporary postmodernism, a deepening interest has developed into what wisdom other religions have to offer about how to live in harmony with nature. There is a manifest consensus that our environmental crisis is so complex that no one religious tradition or philosophical perspective has the solution to it. Buddhist philosopher Tu Wei-ming argues for a post-Enlightenment mentality that mobilizes the spiritual resources of the ethico-religious traditions (Greek philosophy, Judaism, Christianity), non-Western axial-age civilizations (Hinduism, Jainism, Buddhism, Confucianism, Taoism, Islam), and the spiritual resources of primal traditions.[14] There is a wide field for

---

[12] For example, see the land ethic of Aldo Leopold (1949) or the work of historian Lynn White (1967). Leopold claims that a biblically inspired Abrahamic ethic underlies our misuse of the land, and claims that John Muir took Judeo-Christianity to task before the turn of the century, arguing that narrow-minded religionists could not conceive the idea that God cared for the rest of creation as well as humankind.

[13] Naess' work stresses life-forms' self-realization, developed from Spinoza into a cosmology of biotic *Bildung*.

[14] Tu Wei-ming, "Beyond the Enlightenment Mentality," in Mary Evelyn Tucker and John A. Grim, *Worldviews and Ecology: Religion, Philosophy, and the Environment* (Maryknoll: Orbis Books, 1994): 19-29.

discussion here that includes how we live together in one world holding different worldviews.[15]

But the question of environmental consciousness is even more profound. To put it in terms that reach to the heart of Berry's work, the environmental crisis presents us with the question of a "green grace," nature (i.e., the universe) as mediator of God's goodness and salvation, or a "red grace," the sacrifice of Jesus Christ as revelation of God's goodness and agent of salvation. Another way to put this division is the extent to which religion itself is a product of culture or of nature (Burkert 1998). This way of putting the question draws us to Berry's vocation and work as a Roman Catholic priest and Passionist Father.

The universality of religion in historical time and geographical space seems evident today from anthropology. But is religion a subset of culture or of nature? Or does religion stand in tension between the two, a natural impulse made manifest in culture?[16] If the answer to the first question is on the side of culture, then positing the existence of religion is to affirm a dualism such that the phenomenon of religion cannot be treated as an aspect of nature. This opens up a set of questions with respect to environmental issues and how they are approached. If the answer to the second question is in the affirmative, however, then epistemology is more foundational and cultures less

---

[15] George H. Williams (1996) explores the term "mercy" and its linguistic roots in a number of different cultures with the view of finding a cross-cultural basis for environmental ethics. The works of Paul Knitter (1985), and Gavin D'Costa (1986, 2005) mark out different positions in the debate about the unique nature of Christian salvation. Special attention should also be given to the ongoing discussion on Gospel and culture facilitated by the World Council of Churches in Ariarajah (1994).

[16] Unresolved here is whether religious symbols are instrumental, with the implication of transcendence, or pragmatic with respect to divinity (Charles Peirce) or to religious forms of life (Ludwig Wittgenstein and Derrida). See Neville (1996), chaps. 2-3.

subject to reification. When dealing with environmental issues the phenomenon of religion is more embedded and areas for discussion clearly cross-cultural. A breach has been made for such debate as revolves around the place of natural and revealed theology. However, it is not the purpose of this essay to answer this question. It is sufficient here to have raised the issue of nature and nurture as it applies to religion.

We might conclude with three points that relate to the Seoul Affirmation (1990), "Creation as Beloved of God," which also stands in line from the WCC/MIT conference in 1979. First, it appears that the environmental crisis is causing us to reflect more deeply upon relationships, how we interpret our relationship to God and to community in the widest sense as inclusive of all sentient and non-sentient beings, Berry's universal story. Douglas John Hall (1990) asks us to consider whether we are above nature, in nature, or with nature; Hall himself opts for the third.[17] Christian theology will hold this interconnectedness in tension with the distinction that God is the "Ground" of Being (Tillich) but yet distinct (Sittler 1970, Hall 1986). Second, how we live out these relationships becomes a matter of ecojustice: "Religion caring for creation" cannot mean an environmentalism simply defined as wilderness preservation or the maintenance of biodiversity. People are natural. We are a part of nature. The concern for social and human health is as important as the general health of the planet. This interrelationship is taken up by Leonardo Boff (2009) as an extension of Liberation Theology.[18] Finally, we do come back to the na-

---

[17] Sensitivity to the interconnectedness of all things has been an attractive feature of some religions, e.g., see the Buddhist scholar Masao Abe (1985).

[18] Earlier (1995), Boff wrote, "The dominant trend of Christian reflection has not taken ... creation to any profound level of consideration. For historical and institutional reasons, there has been much more consideration of redemption" (pp. 45, 47). See also Gottlieb, (1993).

ture or nurture question: certainly for the Christian, and also for adherents of many other faiths, the issue of salvation in light of the environmental crisis is neither red grace nor green grace alone. Indeed, it is to learn to live, metaphorically, "between the flood and the rainbow."[19]

REFERENCES

Abrecht, P. ed. 1980. *Faith and Science in an Unjust World: Report of the WCC Conference on Faith. Science and the Future, Cambridge, MA, 12-24 July, 1979.* Vol. 2: Reports and Recommendations. Geneva: WCC.

Ariarajah, S.W. 1994. *Gospel and Culture: An Ongoing Discussion within the Ecumenical Movement.* Geneva: WCC.

Berry, T. 2006. *The Dream of the Earth.* New York: Sierra Club Books.

---. and M. E. Tucker. 2009. *The Sacred Universe: Earth, Spirituality, and Religion in the Twenty-first Century.* New York: Columbia University Press.

---. with T. Clarke. 1991. *Befriending the Earth: A Theology of Reconciliation Between Humans and the Earth.* Mystic, CN.: Twenty-Third Publications.

Boff, L. 1995. *Ecology and Liberation: A New Paradigm.* Maryknoll: Orbis Books.

---. 1997. *Cry of the Earth, Cry of the Poor.* Maryknoll: Orbis Books.

---. 2009. *The Tao of Liberation: Exploring the Ecology of Transformation.*

---

[19] This is the title of Niles' 1992 compilation, *Between the Flood and the Rainbow: Interpreting the Conciliar Process of Mutual Commitment (Covenant) to Justice, Peace, and the Integrity of Creation.* See also (Nash 1991).

Maryknoll: Orbis Books.

Burkert, W. 1998. *Creation of the Sacred: Tracks of Biology in Early Religions*. Cambridge: Harvard University Press.

Burrell, D. and E. Malits. 1997. *Original Peace: Restoring God's Creation*. New York: Paulist Press.

Brueggemann, W. 1977. *The Land*. Philadelphia: Fortress Press.

Bührig, M., ed. 1989. "The JPIC Process: A Catholic Contribution," *The Ecumenical Review* 41, (4): 591-602.

Catholic Church and John Paul II. 1988. *Encyclical Letter Sollicitudo Rei Socialis of the Supreme Pontiff, John Paul II, to the Bishops, Priests, Religious Families, Sons and Daughters of the Church and All People of Good Will for the Twentieth Anniversary of Populorum Progressio*. Washington, D.C.: Office of Publishing and Promotion Services, United States Catholic Conference.

Clifford, R. 2000. "Biblical Sources: Witness to the Interpretive Value of the Earth," in Don Conroy and Rodney Petersen, eds., *Earth at Risk: An Environmental Dialogue between Religion and Science*. (147-164) Amherst: Humanity Books.

Conroy, D., and R. Petersen, eds. 2000. *Earth at Risk: An Environmental Dialogue between Religion and Science*. Amherst: Humanity Books.

Dalby, J.1949. *Christian Mysticism and the Natural World*. Greenwood, S.G.: Attic Press.

D'Costa, G.1986. *Theology and Religious Pluralism*. Oxford: Blackwell.

---. 2005. *Theology in the Public Square*. Oxford: Blackwell.

Deloria, Jr., V. 1973. *God is Red*. New York: Grosset and Dunlap.

---. 1992. *God is Red*, 2d ed. Golden, Colo.: Fulcrum.

Fowler, R. B. 1995. *The Greening of Protestant Thought*. Chapel Hill: University of North Carolina.

Gottlieb, R. 1993. *Forcing the Spring: The Transformation of the American Environmental Movement*. Washington, DC: Island Press.

---. 2005. *Forcing the Spring: The Transformation of the American Environment Movement*. Washington, DC: Island Press.

Granberg-Michaelson, W. 1984. *A Worldly Spirituality: The Call to Take Care of the Earth*. San Francisco: Harper & Row.

Hall, D. J. 1990. *The Steward: A Biblical Symbol Come of Age*. Grand Rapids: Eerdmans.

---.1986. "The Ontology of Communion," in *Imaging God: Dominion As Stewardship*. Grand Rapids: Eerdmans.

Hart, J. 2006. *Sacramental Commons: Christian Ecological Ethics*. New York: Rowman & Littlefield Publishers.

Knitter, P. F. 1985. *No Other Name? A Critical Survey of Christian Attitudes toward World Religions*. Maryknoll: Orbis Books.

Lafleur, William R. ed. 1985. *Zen and Western Thought*. Honolulu: University of Hawaii Press.

Lash, N. 1993. *Believing Three Ways in One God*. Notre Dame: University of Notre Dame.

Leopold, A. 1949. *Sand County Almanac*. Oxford: Oxford University Press.

Limouris, G. ed. 1990. *Justice, Peace, and the Integrity of Creation: Insights from Orthodoxy*. Geneva: WCC Publications.

McDade, J. 1990. "Creation and Salvation: Green Faith and Christian Themes," *The Month* 23.

Naess, A. 1976. *Ecology, Community, and Life-Style*. Cambridge: Cambridge University Press.

--- with Rothberg, D., trans. 1990. *Ecology, Community, and Life-Style* .Cambridge: Cambridge University Press.

Nash, J. A. 1991. *Loving Nature: Ecological Integrity and Christian Responsibilit*. Nashville: Abingdon.

Neville, R. C. 1996. *The Truth of Broken Symbols*. Albany: State University of New York Press.

Niles, D. P. 1992. *Between the Flood and the Rainbow: Interpreting the Conciliar Process of Mutual Commitment (Covenant) to Justice, Peace, and the Integrity of Creation*. Geneva: WCC.

Passmore, J. 1974. *Man's Responsibility for Nature*. London: Duckworth.

Peck, J.C. and Gallo, J. 1989. "JPIC: A Critique from a Feminist Perspective," *The Ecumenical Review* 41, (4):573-81.

Plaskow, J., and C. P. Christ. 1989. *Weaving the Visions: New Patterns in Feminist Spirituality*. San Francisco: Harper & Row.

Reuther, R. R.1972. *Liberation Theology: Human Hope Confronts Christian History and American Power*. New York: Paulist Press.

---. 1992. *Gaia and God: An Ecofeminist Theology of Earth Healing*. San Francisco: HarperCollins.

Santmire, H. P. 1985. *The Travail of Nature: The Ambiguous Ecological Promise of Christian Theology*. Minneapolis: Fortress.

Schaeffer, F. S. 1970. *Pollution and the Death of Man: The Christian View of Ecology*. Wheaton: Tyndale House Publishers.

Sessions, G. 1981. "Shallow and Deep Ecology: A Review of the Philosophical Literature," *Ecological Consciousness: Essays from the Earthday X Colloquium*, ed. Robert C. Schultz Jr. and Donald Hughes Washington, DC: University Press of America.

Shaw, V. C. 1993. *Thorns in the Garden Planet: Meditations on the Creator's Care*. Nashville: Thomas Nelson.

Singer, P. 1975. *Animal Liberation: A New Ethics for Our Treatment of Animals*. New York: Avon.

Sittler, J. 1970."Ecological Commitment as Theological Responsibility," *Zygon: Journal of Religion and Science* 5.

Smart, M. F. 2000. "The Earth Matters: Foundations for an Environmental Ethic," in Conroy, D., and R. Petersen, eds., *Earth at Risk: An Environmental Dialogue between Religion and Science*. Amherst: Humanity Books.

Thomas, J. M., ed. 1993. *Evangelicals and the Environment: Theological Foundations for Christian Environmental Stewardship*, a dedicated edition of the *Evangelical Review of Theology* 17, (2).

Tucker, M. E. ed. 1997-2004. *Religions of the World and Ecology*. Center for the Study of World Religions. Cambridge: Harvard University Press.

Weaver, J., ed. 1996. *Defending Mother Earth: Native American Perspectives on Environmental Justice*. Maryknoll: Orbis Books.

White, Jr, L. T. 1967. "The Historical Roots of Our Ecologic Crisis," *Science* 155 (1203–1207).

Wiley, B. 1950. *The Seventeenth Century Background*. Garden City, NY: Doubleday-Anchor.

Wilkinson, L. 1993."Gaia Spirituality: A Christian Critique," *Evangelicals and the Environment: Theological Foundations for Christian Environmental Stewardship*, ed. J. Mark Thomas, *Evangelical Review of Theology* 17, (2): 176-89.

Williams G. H. 1996. "Mercy in the Grounding of a Non-Elitist Ecological Ethic," in *Festschrift in Honor of Charles Speel*, ed. J.

Sienkiwicz and James Betts Monmouth, Ill.: Monmouth College.

World Council of Churches. 1966. "Christians in the Technical and Social Revolutions of our Time," *Conference on Church and Society*. Geneva: WCC.

World Council of Churches. 1991. *Theology of Life*. Geneva: WCC

Wright, C. 1993. "Biblical Reflections on Land," *Evangelicals and the Environment: Theological Foundations for Christian Environmental Stewardship*, ed. J. Mark Thomas, *Evangelical Review of Theology* 17, (2): 153-75.

23

ECOLOGICAL REFLECTIONS IN THEOLOGY

Roberto Tagliaferri

When religious rites are seen in their ecological dimension, they keep the biological, social, individual and religious levels separate and yet in communication with one another. Moreover, these rites say no to a reconciliation dictated only by the desire to maintain an established order and to resolve into a reassuring sense of identity.

In March 2003 I had the privilege of meeting Thomas Berry during his trip to Italy for the book publication of a commentary on the Earth Charter, by Elisabeth Ferrero and Joe Holland. Tom had written the book's Preface and was accompanying Elisabeth and Joe. I still have my copy of that book which Tom gave me and which he autographed with his telephone number and his email address. His gift showed that he had intended to continue our dialogue in the years to come. Instead, the dialogue was cut short by his death. In memory of Tom and his prophetic work, I would now like to share a few reflections about the ecological consciousness in Italy in relation to the theology of ritual.

One of the major questions that we need to ask ourselves today is what is the theological content of rituals and how do they function. Are rituals only a mimetical mechanism that tends to keep a definite order of the world? Or can they become innovative?

Today, I propose, that we need to understand rituals as an organization of experience seeking a meaningful direction in the mist of complexity. We need to reconceptualize rituals as phenomena that interface creativity and necessity by incorporating completely the anthropological even in its adaptive traits, and especially by re-elaborating their process ecologically in service of a transformed and sustainable way of life.

Ecological Transformation of Rituals

This reconceptualized symbolic condensation of rituals needs to go beyond the currently fragmented social consciousness by connecting and integrating our much needed contemporary social, ecological and religious adaptations. By so doing, these rituals could lead us to a holistic perspective of deep ecology, and one ultimately resonating with a theological ground.

The similarity of ecological and theological knowledge seems evident. Both disciplines, from a functional point of view, were born to reduce "the complexity of contingency"(Luhmann 1997). It is not accidental that today ecology feels the duty to offer a "function of exoneration" similar to the one that religion has exercised (Turner 1992). In the past, theology provided the same function, and now ecology faces a similar challenge. In other words, ecology needs to embrace all knowledge and go beyond the specialization of the sciences. It needs to go beyond the various interests of every particular knowledge, and it must become a true and comprehensive *encyclopedia* – not in the sense of a quantitative accumulation of knowledge but in the original sense of a holistic *enkyklios paideia* that places all knowledge within a comprehensive whole beyond separate and disconnected points of view (Morin 1989). Yet, while classical epistemology was based on the individual as the correlated subject of knowledge, the emerging ecological epistemology presses theology toward a continual confrontation between the inside and the outside, between observable systems, and without any guarantee from above.

The key point for a holistic perspective of an ecological theology of ritual is the fact that ritual is a phenomenon which exchanges systematically life with death in such a way to create a constant equilibrium with continual lacerations towards a progressive acceptance of the finite as the human condition in front of life and death. Therefore, ritual is not so much an escape mechanism from the finite, from danger, from loneliness or ultimately from death, but rather a homeostatic mechanism which facilitates the exchange of life and death within a dynamic order and disorder. Ritual is a sacred measure because it releases continuously the conflict between chaos and canon, not in the repetitive sense of that which is identical returning, but in the creative sense of producing new orders. Thus, we humans can face the disorder underneath a ritual because the ritual is orderly and reassuring, and at the same time we can do so without feelings of panic as we become aware of the secret of the world and of the relentless exposure to no-thing.

Faced with this secret we humans instinctively defend ourselves, yet in ritual we humans can learn to expose ourselves by risking an act of freedom, which is also called faith. However, in this symbolic procedure between life and death the exchange is not linear but traumatic as the totally human act of freedom risks in front of no-thing. Thus, ritual makes an important contribution to life which is never a given but goes through turns and traumas that need to be re-absorbed in the larger context. The ritual modality of the symbolic disconnection of the various systems places together different orders of reality by introducing alarming elements which produce a "ritual jump" in the sense of life. Bataille says that the sacred is, "that prodigious excitement of life which keeps us in chains and that chaining then changes into violence" (Bataille 1997, 49).

Much has been said about this aspect of ritual to access the sacred. The sacred fire of rituals is the human act of separating oneself from the trivial to commune with the sovereignty of life and with the totality of the human experience.

We could interpret this ecological perspective of ritual as a sacrifice which tampers, at times violently, with the order of the world in order to establish an order which goes back to its origins, to a sacred order which needs constantly to be re-discovered. Thus, ritual in eco-philosophy demolishes the technical logic of the 'useful' and replaces it with grace as gratuitousness. In Christological terms ritual allows the faithful to enter into the *kenosis* of the Son, whom the Father answers with exaltation (Phil. 2: 5-11). Sacramental initiation rituals share in his death (Rom. 6.3). Bataille is right when he places the sacrificial ritual at the origin of sovereignty, in other words it is the reconciliation of life with death. Sacrificing the useful is the condition to access the non-useful, grace and playfulness.

In sum, ritual reveals itself to be a homeostatic mechanism capable of keeping the tensions, the variations, the tearing and the violence of nature without exploding the system; in fact, it allows the system -- the human in creation -- to accept her/his death as the pulsation of life.

Conclusion

As we have tried to illustrate, a transformed ritual can unify within an ecological framework the biological, the social, the individual, and the religious levels across their separate dimensions yet in communication with one another. Ritual in this sense does not allow easy solutions from one level to the next. It rather de-stabilizes in order to open new horizons, and not only religious ones. At the same time, it re-establishes a paradigmatic measure which gives the sensation of the stability and the sacred equilibrium of the world.

Translation by Elisabeth M. Ferrero

REFERENCES

Bataille, George. 1977. *La limite de l'utile*. Paris: Gallimard.

---. 1973. *Teoria della religione*. Milan: SE Conoscenza Religiosa.

Deleuze, Gilles. 1997. *Differenza e ripetizione*. Milan: Raffaello Cortina Editore.

Firth, Raymond I. 1977. *I simboli e le mode*. Bari: Laterza.

Luhmann, Niklas. 1977. *Funktion der Religion*. Frankfurt: Suhrkamp.

Mandelbrot, Benoit B. 1988. *La bellezza dei frattali*. Torino: Bollati Basic Book.

Morin, Edgar. 1989. *Il metodo. Ordine, disordine, organizzazione*. Milan: Feltrinelli.

Naess, Arne. 1994. *Ecosofia*. Como: Red Edizioni.

Piaget, Jean. 1979. *La costruzione del mondo nel bambino*. Firenze: La Nuova Italia.

Rappaport, Roy A. 1980. *Maiali per gli antenati*. Milan: Franco Angeli Editore.

Smolin, Lee. 1997. *La vita del cosmo*. Torino: Biblioteca Einaudi.

Turner, Victor. 1993. *Antropologia della performance*. Bologna: Mulino.

---. 1986. *Dal rito al teatro*. Bologna: Mulino.

Varela, Francisco J., Evan T. Thompson, and Eleanor Rosch. 1979. *La via di mezzo della conoscenza*. Milan: Feltrinelli.

PART V
ECONOMICS & SUSTAINABLE DEVELOPMENT

Ecologically sustainable models and practices of livelihoods that do not abuse Earth's resources but enhance and work towards paradigms centered on natural, social, and spiritual wealth.

24

GEN, GAIA EDUCATION, AND GAIA ECONOMICS AS THE NEW STORY

HILDUR JACKSON

GEN is a network of eco-villages dreaming a new story for Gaia and making it happen all over the planet. This essay will discuss how Gaia Education has collected the experiences from these villages and is teaching that information in thirty-six countries both in villages and virtually with the same curriculum in ten languages. A new economy is needed to make this transition happen on a large scale.

With Thomas Berry & Rashmi Mayur in Assisi

In 1998 my husband, Ross Jackson, and I were invited to the conference on *Spirituality and Sustainability* in Assisi. In prior years we had initiated a global network of sustainable settlements, GEN, the Global Ecovillage Network. We encouraged projects that had a spiritual practice to join the movement, as we found that to be of major importance. To go to Assisi was a chance for us to spread the good news and to test our ideas in an interesting forum. And we loved Assisi from an earlier visit. Most of the participants in Assisi were American professors. We invited Rashmi Mayur from the International Institute for Sustainable Future (IISF) in Mumbai to join us in order to have a strong voice from the Global South. Also we brought our youngest son, Frej, 18, named after the Nordic god of fertility and peace, as a last chance of influencing him before leaving home. It was an unforgettable week.

The first day we were received at a reception by the Franciscans and the warmth of Father Max on a terrace overlooking all of Assisi. Steven Rockefeller explained the importance of the *Earth Charter* and later we went to the church of San Damiano where a young priest talked about the famous cross which talked to Francis. When I filmed Rashmi in the cloister yard, he was whispering to Thomas Berry about his mother, who never spoke but gathered things and food and would bring these items to the villages to help the people there. How strange that these two persons who had never met before had become so close in just a few minutes. They looked like old chums!

We met Rashmi at the UN Social Summit in Copenhagen in 1995 under most unusual circumstances. My husband, Ross, was part of a group organized by Hazel Henderson to find ways to fund the UN, so we invited the group -- which turned out to be 47 persons -- to an informal dinner in our home. Rashmi was one of them. We subsequently developed a close relationship with him. I had started meditating with him. In Assisi, Thomas and Rashmi dined together and talked whenever possible. They must have been old souls meeting again.

When Thomas Berry spoke at the *Spirituality and Sustainability* conference I was deeply touched as he had the answers to everything and I felt totally overwhelmed. What I remember the most was the time alone with Tom, Rashmi and Ross. It was a time so intense, so full of love, so full of joy and ideas. Several times after dinner we were sitting under the stars at night, chatting. One evening I remember giving Thomas a massage on his neck and back as I could feel how his old body (85?) was suffering from the uncomfortable antique benches and chairs of Assisi's Town Hall and sitting in them for long hours.

GEN, the Global Ecovillage Network

In Assisi, our presentation at the Conference about Ecovillages all over the planet was received very positively. People in the member communities of GEN already live what the participants were discussing about at the conference: a new ecological and spiritual lifestyle. By linking the ecovillages in GEN since the first meeting in 1993 we hoped to make them stronger and models for society at large to replicate. And ecovillagers loved learning from each other. Recently we celebrated 25 years of Gaia Trust, which we had founded in 1987. There are networks of ecovillages all over the world today, and new projects are being built in spite of a total lack of public interest and difficulties in getting permissions to build. What is happening in Eco villages is that people "reinvent themselves at a species level" as Thomas claimed was necessary (Berry 1999). It is happening all over. They redefine how to live with each other and the natural world in a way built upon harmony and respect. They heal themselves and help others by teaching their principles. In Findhorn, Scotland, they have been communicating with nature spirits. They honor and listen to nature in many different ways. In Italy, they built an underground temple where they can communicate via energy lines with the whole world and create world class artwork. In many places they develop new food systems, ecological building, biological waste treatment and renewable energy systems. They learn to solve conflicts and create a truly participatory democracy. The "integral practice" defined by Ken Wilber has been their daily life for years. They are not "a collection of objects, but a communion of subjects" (Berry 1999) -- another concept of Thomas which expresses our movement. Ecovillages demonstrate that people want to take responsibility for their lives and act -- to be a *communion of subjects*. They are capable of building a new culture even with very small means. Ecovillagers are full of creativity, purpose and will. It is a whole new paradigm in science and planning: people can and will. They are not the helpless objects of studies of social scientists, politicians and planners. They are "shakers and movers," they can create whole settlements, art and beauty. They know how they want to live. They live a new paradigm, a new culture. And that is what we need to see happening at a large scale all over the Earth.

Gaia education

In 2002, Karen Svensson and I gathered the experiences from Ecovillages all over the planet in a book with five hundred color photos. It was a colorful, enthusiastic project which shows the incredible courage, imagination and diversity of people all over the world who are driven by the same values (Svensson and Jackson 2002). Thomas Berry inspired my introduction, and gave us the courage to be bold.

Actually, writing the book on Ecovillage living was the basis for inviting twenty-four educators from all over the planet to develop an educational program in sustainable living. After seven years of hard work by thirty teachers from Eco-villages across the planet, Gaia Education was born in Findhorn in October 2005. The first program was called EDE, Ecovillage Design Education. It is a four week course, covering four sustainability dimensions: Social, Ecological, Economic and Worldview. Each of these four dimensions is subdivided into five modules, so that all together we teach twenty modules. This is a holistic vision of a new culture. It has now been taught over one-hundred-forty times in thirty-five countries. The teachers call themselves GEESE, (Global Ecovillage Educators for a Sustainable Earth). They come from all continents. The EDE curriculum is available for free in ten languages including Chinese and Japanese. The immersion experience of actually living what you learn has been a major component for the students to be very active "shakers."

GEDS, the virtual version

In 2008 we started a virtual version of the EDE, the second program of Gaia Education, in cooperation with The Open University of Catalonia (OUC) in Spain. It is an eight months course. May East, our Mother Goose since 2004, called me and asked if I would write the Worldview text for the education, to be known as GEDS (Gaia Education Design for Sustainability). Was I capable of doing that, I asked myself? It is different from writing a normal text, and it also needs a lot of illustrations and pictures. It had to be acceptable to students from all over the planet, without cultural biases! Was that possible? Would the rest of the GEESE accept that I, as the founder, took on this job? I was unsure, so I decided to sleep on it.

The next morning I woke up with a beautiful dream about Thomas Berry. I felt so close to him. I was so happy. It is the only dream I have ever had about our dear, Thomas Berry. I immediately accepted the job and spent three months writing it with the help of my husband.

Reflections

After twenty years of work with Eco villages and ten with Gaia Education we realized that change cannot happen only from the bottom up. Grassroots activists need allies from within the system. In particular, we need changes in the global economic and political system for the desired cultural transformation to happen on a global scale. This was the motivation for Ross, with his unusual background in both international finance and grassroots organizations, to write *Occupy World Street: A Global Roadmap for Radical Economic and Political Reform*. In this book, he puts forward a concrete design for a new supra-national organization based on only two centralized principles -- serious sustainability and human rights, with everything else delegated to local democracies in the form of diverse sovereign nation states, each in sole charge of its economy and priorities. He envisages that these reforms could come about if only a few small countries -- he concedes that the largest economies, including the USA and EU are not prepared to take the lead -- were to reject neoliberal economics and break away from the suffocating WTO/IMF/World Bank institutions, and then form eight new institutions that will "serve the planet and serve the people" in a new "Gaian League," while inviting other countries to join when they are ready.

The struggle to fulfill the vision that Thomas Berry so eloquently put into words continues and will continue, indefinitely. A new, young generation is already picking up the torch.

Thank you, Thomas!

REFERENCES

Berry, Thomas. 1999. *The Great Work: Our Way into the Future.* New York: Bell Tower.

Jackson, Hildur, and Karen Svensson. 2002. *Ecovillage Living: Restoring the Earth and Her People.* Dartington, Totnes, Devon: Green Books.

Wilber, Ken. 2007. *Integral Life Practice: A 21st-Century Blueprint for Physical Health, Emotional 'Balance, Mental Clarity, and Spiritual Awakening,* 1st ed. Boston, MA: Shambhala

25

CAN WE ACHIEVE THOMAS BERRY'S DREAM OF THE EARTH?

Martin S. Kaplan

The human community must "come to appreciate the gifts that the Earth has given us" (Berry) which will enable us to ensure a future on Earth for many generations of all species.

I first met Thomas Berry at the Harvard Center for the Study of World Religions in May 1996. The occasion was the first in the series of *Religion and Ecology* conferences, on Confucianism, which I had read about in the Harvard Gazette. Each conference was to present scholarly and practical analyses of the relationship of one religion, its theology, traditions, values and practices to the natural world and the environment. I was managing a foundation interested in connecting values to environmental issues and policies, and I thought that Berry and the conferences might serve as important guides to the field. I called John Grim at the Center, who encouraged me to attend and also agreed to send me a copy of Berry's prepared speech in advance, since I explained that it would help me understand his presentation.

John sent it and I read it in advance. On the first day of the conference, I began to follow Berry's text as he spoke. Berry stuck to it for about one and a half pages, at which point he deviated and riffed on the subject, returning regularly to the text, and adding commentary throughout his presentation. At first, I was perplexed – why would he not follow this fine draft? Why was it necessary for him to explain and analyze – almost thinking out loud as he went along? But after a while, I settled into his rhythm of teaching, finding his approach refreshing and engaging, challenging and provocative. By the end of the session, I realized that I was in the presence of an intellectual and moral master.

Mary Evelyn Tucker and John Grim, the organizers of the conference series, encouraged my wife Wendy and me to participate the following year in the *Spirituality and Sustainability* conference (1997) in Assisi, sponsored by Saint Thomas University in Miami and the Center for Respect of Life and the Environment. In Assisi, Berry opened the conference with a prepared speech, and true to form, left the text at whim, going off in tangents fascinating and rewarding for all of us. His open, conversational approach encouraged us to join in his thinking process, and to appreciate his wry comments and probing questions, all designed to challenge the orthodoxy of materialism, unending economic growth and short-term thinking.

Berry inspired us with an optimistic vision that we could change the dominant mindset of economic growth over all other values. He states that our goal must be to develop awareness that we, human beings, are part of the larger Earth community; that it is our responsibility to preserve the Earth as a biosphere for all species; and that the Earth and all other living things do not exist just for the benefit of human beings. This is a moral imperative, as set forth in *The Dream of the Earth* (Berry 1998), which calls for a new intellectual and ethical framework by placing the well-being of the Earth, the biosphere, all species, at the center of human responsibility (Berry 1998).

This awareness also recognizes our own self-interest: all species are interconnected in a living web, and we humans cannot destroy the world of other species without destroying ourselves too. Now, many years later, there is far greater acknowledgement of the existential environmental crises we humans and all other species confront. Societies increasingly understand the destructive role our species plays in creating the conditions we face. This is a time of crisis on Earth, with the threat of climate change accelerating and the human response hanging in the balance.

This is therefore also a time to reflect on the need for scientific, religious, economic, academic, government and civic leaders to attain a new unity of thinking and action in order to address the threat of climate change to all species. Berry's vision has had a significant impact on my thinking and my own work on environmental issues, as scientific evidence causes us to challenge the economic and social values that have driven the human experience for the past two hundred years commencing with the industrial revolution.

The Challenge from the Scientific Community

The challenge from the science community has become clear. Twenty-six years ago, James Hansen, the Director of NASA's Goddard Institute for Space Studies, testified before Congress (Senate Committee, June 23, 1988) and delivered the first well-publicized warning of the threat of climate change. In a profile of Hansen, "The Catastrophist," in the *New Yorker*, June 29, 2009, Elizabeth Kolbert quoted Hansen stating that he, "has now concluded, partly on the basis of his latest modeling efforts and partly on the basis of observations made by other scientists, that the threat of global warming is far greater than even he had suspected" (Kolbert 2009). Kolbert also quoted Hansen's 2004 letter to John Holdren, Science Advisor to President Obama, insisting that, "a stark scientific conclusion that we must reduce greenhouse gases below present amounts to preserve nature and humanity, has become clear. It is still feasible to avert climate disasters, but only if policies are consistent with what science indicates to be required" (Kolbert 2004).

The overwhelming majority of scientists who understand the climate field have reiterated these warnings and strengthened them as the situation has deteriorated well beyond the rate of Hansen's original expectations and warnings. Kolbert also quoted in the same article Hans Joachim Schellnhuber, the head of Germany's Potsdam Institute for Climate Impact Research, who observed, "we are on our way to a destabilization of the world climate that has advanced much further than most people or their governments realize" (Kolbert 2009).

The internationally recognized Intergovernmental Panel on Climate Change (IPCC) released The Fourth Assessment Report in 2009, analyzing the scientific reality of global warming during the period 2001 to 2007. The IPCC constitutes the largest collaborative science project ever undertaken, involving 4000 scientists who are specialists in the applicable sciences. R. K. Pachauri, Director General of The Energy and Resources Institute in India and now Director of Yale's new Climate and Energy Institute, received the 2008 Nobel Peace Prize on behalf of all of the participating scientists.

Established by the United Nations in 1988, the IPCC has been instrumental in providing comprehensive, rigorously documented assessment reports every five to six years, summarizing the current knowledge and future projections of climate change. The IPCC has provided irrefutable data and analysis informing public opinion as well as policy-makers of the scientific reality of climate change. The IPCC left no doubt, as scientific fact, that the causation of this immense climate change rests squarely with the billions of human beings on this Earth, and that the risks to the planet are immense (IPCC 1988).

The IPCC released its most recent report (IPCC 2014) in connection with the 19th annual meeting of the United Nations Framework Convention on Climate Change held in Warsaw in November 2013, shortly after the devastating Philippine typhoon drew great attention to climate issues. Delegates agreed to broad outlines of a proposed system to reduce emissions and deal with the costs and suffering expected from climate change impacts. While no binding commitments were made, the 10,000 delegates hope that progress will be made at the 2015 Paris conference to replace the moribund Kyoto Protocol and at the climate summit to be held at the United Nations in September 2015. While there is much hope, I have little confidence that world policy makers and political leaders of nations have the will power and the ability to address climate issues effectively. Meanwhile, the warnings and desire to take action are not limited to scientists and those who understand the risks to human life. As an example, the United States Department of Defense published a warning in August 2009 that climate change would become a major issue of national security with potential large-scale drought, starvation, flooding of coastal areas, massive refugee movements, and wars over rights to water and land (DOD 2009).

Edward O. Wilson of Harvard University, among other prominent scientists, has made clear that we are in the midst of a sixth extinction of species on our planet, and that this is the first for which human activities are predominantly responsible, as opposed to the prior extinctions that took place over millions of years as planet Earth evolved. Wilson has also commented that humans cannot expect that we will be immune from that same ultimate fate (Wilson 1992).

Jim Robbins in his November 24, 2013 *New York Times* essay "The Year the Monarch Didn't Appear," reported that climate change and human behavior are also having immense negative effects on many species of insects, including the Monarch butterfly and the wild bee. Robbins quoted scientists to the effect that eighty percent of our food crops are pollinated by insects, primarily the 4000 species of bees, and their disappearance will cause a huge problem for most of the foods on which humans depend (Robbins 2013).

We live in a world we did not create and that we must not destroy. Environmental issues respect no borders, and the future of human life on our planet is interdependent with other living organisms. Global warming will significantly change the world as we know it, accelerating the ongoing crash of biodiversity, diminishing all life.

The Vision of Thomas Berry

Thomas Berry's extensive writings provide guidance for us in this time of crisis. Building on The *Dream of the Earth*, Berry published *The Great Work: Our Way Into the Future* (1999), and expressed the hope on the eve of this new millennium, "that we see these early years of the 21st century as the period when we discover the great community of the Earth, a comprehensive community of all the living and non-living components of the planet. We are just discovering that the human project is itself a component of the Earth project" (Berry 1999). Berry expressed the fervent belief that recognition of these truths is the foundation of our journey into the future.

As an influential cultural historian, Berry articulated his belief that in earlier times people were profoundly concerned with divine-human relations, and in more recent centuries, people have become increasingly involved with inter-human relations. But Berry believed that the natural world is our primary revelatory experience, and that world religions in recent times have neglected the manifestation of the Divine in the natural world. He said, "our future destiny rests even more decisively on our capacity for intimacy in our human-Earth relations" (Berry 1999). Berry criticized universities and other institutions for their emphasis on how humans can use and exploit the Earth through the systems and standards of the professions: science, engineering, law, education and economics. He believed that we humans have an inadequate recognition that it is this planet that brings us into being, sustains us in life, and delights us with its wonders (Berry 1999). Berry posited that,

> The Great Work before us (is) the task of moving modern industrial civilization from its present devastating influence on the Earth to a more benign mode of presence....(it) is not a role that we have chosen. We were chosen by some power beyond ourselves for this historical task. We do not choose the moment of our birth, who our parents will be, our particular culture or the historical moment when we will be born. We do not choose the status of spiritual insight or political or economic conditions that will be the context of our lives. We are, as it were, thrown into existence with a challenge and a role that is beyond any personal choice. The nobility of our lives, however, depends upon the manner in which we come to understand and fulfill our assigned role. (Berry 1999, 7)

Berry believed that we must expand the scope of religious and humanist concerns to embrace the larger life systems and all species of the planet. As a lawyer, I am intrigued by Berry's call for a broader vision of rights. Berry stated, "as regards *law*, the basic orientation of American jurisprudence is toward personal human rights and toward the natural world as existing for human possession and use. To the industrial-commercial world the natural world has no inherent rights to existence, habitat or freedom to fulfill its role in the vast community of existence. Yet there can be no sustainable future, even for the modern industrial world, unless these inherent rights of the natural world are recognized as having legal status" (Berry 1999, 60).

Berry extended this thinking to the economy as well, stating that, "we must recognize that a human economy can only exist as a subsystem of the Earth economy" (Berry 1999, 132). Thus, Berry proposes a radical shift in our world view, leading to the question of whether we can change our value systems in order to meet the challenge of the future. His *Dream of the Earth* envisions human responsibility for planetary renewal, for the survival of all species as well as a recognition that Earth does not exist just for human benefit and exploitation (Berry 1998).

How Can We Meet the Challenge of the Future?

Scientists can create numerous solutions to address the climate change challenge, but nothing will happen unless governments and societies acknowledge their responsibility to do so. Fifteen years ago the American Academy of Arts and Sciences published the proceedings of two conferences held at the Academy as the issue of *Daedalus* entitled *Religion and Ecology: Can the Climate Change?* (McElroy 2001). These followed the ten World Religion and Ecology Conferences at Harvard (CSWR 1996-1998) and the culminating conferences held at the United Nations and the American Museum of Natural History (UM/AMNH 1999).

The *Daedalus* issue includes the eloquent and powerful challenge of Professor Michael B. McElroy, then Chairman of the Earth and Planetary Sciences Department at Harvard and Director of the Harvard Center for the Environment. McElroy stated that,

> *We live at a unique point in the history of planet Earth. After almost four billion years of evolution, a single species ... has evolved with the capacity to think, to contemplate not only its place in the universe but also potentially to control its own destiny and that of other species as well ... We have we developed the capacity to alter the environment on a global scale"* (McElroy 2001, 31, 33).

McElroy went on to quote the late Roger Revelle, one of the first scientists to study global warming,

> *We have embarked on an unplanned global experiment and our ability to predict the consequences is deficient ... We need a moral compass ... to chart a responsible course to the future.* (McElroy 2001, 32)

McElroy challenged us on a basis other than science, adding,

> *If our actions lead to elimination of entire ecosystems on the planet, tropical rainforests for example, should our children have the right to hold us accountable? ... What is our proper place in nature? ... Science alone cannot provide answers to these questions. Nor can we expect a definitive response from our colleagues in economics.* (McElroy 2001, 32)

McElroy invoked both the Old and New Testament in response to the argument that the United States need not do anything about greenhouse gas emissions until developing countries act as well, and warned, "is there not an ethical imperative for the rich to take the first step? The New Testament extols the responsibility of the rich to help the *poor*" (McElroy 2001, 53). McElroy concluded,

> *We need a global vision to recognize that there is a unity to life on Earth, that we are part of nature, not independent ... drawing on insights not only from science but also from the intellectual heritage codified in the world's great philosophical and religious traditions.* (McElroy 2001, 56)

Berry quoted Brian Swimme, a distinguished cosmologist, who had stated in *The Hidden Heart of the Cosmos*,

> *Humans, through our scientific insight and our technological skills, have become a macro-phase power, something on the level of the glaciations or the forces that have caused the great extinctions of the past. Yet we have only a micro-phase sense of responsibility or ethical judgment. We need to develop a completely different range of responsibility.* (Swimme 1996)

The hope that humanity can, and indeed will, sustain life on this planet rests with those governments and institutions that will marshal the intellectual and political resources to address the central environmental challenges that will determine the human future. Those scientists and economists who have studied climate change believe that the dangers can be abated, but the missing ingredient has been the willpower of government leaders and the public to recognize the gravity of the risks, to understand the applicable science, and to attack the problem, all of which are necessary to implement the solutions that can be developed.

The Response to the Challenge

Thoughtful institutions -- governments, universities, corporations and world religions -- must address issues that relate to climate and the environment with a deep awareness of their relevance to the very maintenance of human life and the life of many other species on Earth. There has been a meaningful response to this challenge from many leaders in the scientific community, as shown above.

Important religious leaders have also recognized the danger we face. In July, 2009, Pope Benedict XVI referred to and drew on "the great visions (of) Teilhard de Chardin," the French Jesuit scientist and philosopher who died in 1955 in expressing the hope that "at the end we will have a true cosmic liturgy, where the cosmos becomes a living host." Pope Benedict also issued an encyclical entitled "Caritas in Veritate" ("Charity in Truth" 2009) in which he critiques our current economic system and how it harms both people and the planet (Pope Benedict XVI 2009).

This follows in the tradition of Pope John Paul II, whose New Year's message in 1990 stated,

> *Theology, philosophy and science all speak of a harmonious universe, of a cosmos endowed with its own integrity, its own internal, dynamic nature. This order must be respected. The human race is called to explore this order, to examine it with due care and to make use of it while safeguarding its integrity.* (Pope John Paul II 1990)

Ecumenical Patriarch Bartholomew II, the leader of the Greek Orthodox Church, has repeatedly emphasized human responsibility for the environment, and has sponsored several symposia on Religion, Science and the Environment. Archbishop Rowan Williams, leader of the Anglican Church, has made strong appeals to care for creation. And the Episcopal Church in the United States adopted a resolution endorsing the Earth Charter, a resolution proposed by the Dioceses of New York and Newark (August 2009). The mission of the Earth Charter Initiative is to promote the transition to sustainable ways of living and a global society based on a shared ethical framework that includes respect and care for the community of life, ecological integrity, universal human rights, respect for diversity, economic justice, democracy, and a culture of peace (Ferrero and Holland, 2005).

The Dalai Lama and numerous other leaders of world religions similarly urge increased attention to the issues of climate change and the preservation of biodiversity. The role of religion is crucial; for many people, religion is the most powerful force in their lives, not community or nation. Some governmental leaders are clearly aware of the dangers of climate change, and to the ongoing destruction of the intricately-balanced biosphere which we share with other species. Prime Minister Anders Fogh Rasmussen of Denmark, speaking at the United Nations General Assembly referred to the "grinding catastrophe of global warming" (September 2008).

The Global Humanitarian Forum released a report, *The Anatomy of a Silent Crisis*, documenting the impact of climate change as the most severe, ongoing, silent, unrecognized, crisis of human history (September 2009). Its president, Kofi Annan, former Secretary General of the United Nations, states in his introduction, "if we do not reverse current trends by close to 2020, we may have failed. If political leaders cannot assume responsibility for (success at the COP-15 conference in Copenhagen in December 2009), they choose instead responsibility for failing humanity. In 2009, national leadership goes beyond the next elections and far beyond national borders" (Annan, 2009, Introduction). In spite of the overwhelming evidence of climate change, little was achieved at the COP-15 conference – a failure of leadership by all major countries, particularly the United States and China.

On the economic and business side, increasingly, economists are aware of the potential significant economic impact of Climate Change, both the costs of mitigation and the costs of doing nothing. The Stern Review's *Economics of Climate Change* concluded that not taking action in response to climate change will cost more than taking action. At the corporate and investment level, CERES and the Global Reporting Initiative are leading the movement for investors and corporations to understand the impact of climate change on each corporation (Stern 2007).

At the Investor Summit on Climate Risk sponsored by the United Nations and CERES, the Boston-based coalition of investors, industries and environmental groups, there were calls for immense investment by the corporate world to retool our world-wide economies for climate change. And, this effort is being led by banks and insurance companies, which have been in the forefront of analyzing and planning for the impact of climate change and the related climate volatility (January 2014).

But we live in an age dominated by short-term thinking – two and four year electoral cycles, quarterly and annual financial results, and also dominated by values that reflect material consumption and instant gratification. People find it difficult to consider the long term – a future beyond their own lives and perhaps those of their children. Analysts of population growth generally conclude their estimates around the year 2100, as if we either cannot project further or have no responsibility beyond that date. But 2100 is within the lives of our children and grandchildren. What do we expect their lives to be like at the end of this century? And what will their expectations be in 2100 for their children and grandchildren? Are not future generations an imperative for action by the human community now?

I would note also that for most of the policymakers of the world, "development" only means economic development. However, we really should be emphasizing a more comprehensive definition of human development, with a commitment to social and moral values along with improvement in standards of living for all people.

We all share this planet, and perhaps are trapped in it, as Earth shows the strains of climate change, the result of our human actions. Is Earth suffering a stroke, or cardiac arrest? We are experiencing a dance of the Earth, and we humans have in fact become the choreographers of our planet. We are not dancers controlled by fate. There is no escaping from this planet, and unless we address the existential threat of climate change, we may be choreographing a dance of destruction, at least for the human species and many other species as well. Will we have the will and the wisdom to work our way out of our trap?

John Holdren stated at the annual conference of the Consultative Group on Biological Diversity in June 2006 that, "the human response to climate change will be three-fold: mitigation, adaptation and suffering; and we will have a great deal of all three. The only question is how much we will have of each" (Holdren 2006).

Connecting Values & Science

Thomas Berry has taught us that we must connect both science and values to the reality that we live totally immersed in the Earth community. Neither science nor religion has as great an impact as they should on public policy relating to global warming, which I believe is the most serious global challenge of our time. The world's policymakers are wrestling with scientific imperatives that are not susceptible to political compromise. As our political leaders seek a "solution" that will strike a "balance" between those who recognize the problem and those who do not, nature scoffs. Or, in the words of the ancient proverb, "Man plans; God laughs."

Berry presented the case that in the modern world, the dominant intellectual framework since Descartes and Newton has made human societies as independent as possible from the natural world, and made the natural world as subservient as possible to human decisions. However, he did not contend that the application of our scientific-technological powers in this direction derived solely from the scientific tradition, although that is a common accusation. He stated,

> It was an early afternoon in late May when I first wandered down the incline, crossed the creek, and looked out over the scene. The field was covered with white lilies rising above the thick grass. A magic moment, this experience gave to my life something that seems to explain my thinking at a more profound level than almost any other experience I can remember. It was not only the lilies. It was the singing of the crickets and the woodlands in the distance and the clouds in a clear sky… this early experience, it seems, has become normative for me throughout the entire range of my thinking. Whatever enhances this meadow in the natural cycles of its transformation is good; whatever opposes this meadow or negates it is not good. My life orientation is that simple. It is also that pervasive. It applies in economics and political orientation as well as education and religion. (Berry 1999, 12-13)

Perhaps the success of the human species has blinded us to the threat of climate change due to our human-centered arrogance.

Berry considered the challenge of our time as similar to a geological shift.

So now in this transition period into the twenty-first century, we are experiencing a moment of grace, but a moment in its significance that is different from any previous moment. For the first time the planet is being disturbed by humans in its geological structure and its biological functioning in a manner like the great cosmic forces that alter the geological and biological structures of the planet. (Berry 1999, 198)

Berry saw a "moment of grace" as having both destructive power and creative potential. Referring to the potential impact of climate change and global warming, Berry concluded, "so severe and so irreversible is this deterioration that we might well believe those who tell us that we have only a brief period in which to reverse the devastation that is settling over the Earth" (Berry 1999). Berry expressed the profound hope that we human beings would rise to this challenge and develop a way of life on and in this Earth that is not destructive (Berry 1999).

Berry called the expectation of modern human beings that everything can be solved by technology, a "technological trance." He disdained the blind faith that many have that technology will solve all problems. We all know that technological advances not accompanied by application of the "precautionary principle" have led to the unregulated use of chemicals in agriculture and industry, resulting in significant harm to the health of people as well as the environment. Faith in technological solutions must be matched with a healthy respect for both foreseeable and unintended consequences (Berry 1999).

Elizabeth Kolbert, commenting on her book *The Sixth Extinction: An Unnatural History* in the Natural Resources Defense Council's *onEarth* magazine, shares Berry's belief that technology will not provide magic solutions to our problems, "and the notion that we're going to come up with some fix that will allow people (and, unfortunately, only people) to transcend geophysics sounds a lot like wishful thinking, and I'm afraid, will turn out to *be* wishful thinking" (Kolbert 2013/2014, 27).

Nevertheless, the moral imperative of mitigating the impact of climate change and adapting to it requires us to embrace the potential in innovative technologies. No one could have foreseen the unbelievable technological progress in virtually all fields of human endeavor since Sputnik was launched half a century ago. Immense sums have been invested in the exploration of space, the development of medical advances, military technology, and the internet. We must make the same deep commitment to investing in research and innovation in all directions that might hold promise for mitigating the impact of climate change, and adapting to it.

The present estimate of the potential impact on Earth of unchecked climate change is calamitous, and we do have, in geological time, only a brief period in which to mitigate and adapt. We must use technology as effectively as possible, but technology alone cannot achieve the avoidance of the destructive power of climate change. This is the "moment of grace" described by Berry, the brief period in which we human beings must undergo a moral transformation in our habits and our lives, in order to fulfill the role that Berry saw as the challenge of our historical moment (Berry 1999). We cannot rely on science and technology to miraculously save our Earth. With an understanding and acceptance of scientific reality human beings must attain the moral and political will to preserve our planet for our children, grandchildren, and further generations. Religion and science see the long-term problem; it is time that all of society take action.

Conclusion

Thomas Berry is the preeminent inspirational leader in the field of moral and ethical ecology which he based on the cosmology of Teilhard de Chardin. Berry stated in *The Great Work, Our Way into the Future*, "it is tragic to see all those entrancing forms of life expressions imperiled so wantonly, forms that came into being during the past 65 million years, the lyric moment of Earth development. Yet, as so often in the past, the catastrophic moments are also creative moments. We come to appreciate the gifts that the Earth has given us" (Berry 1999, 199).

Thomas Berry's dedication in *The Great Work* is to all the children,

> *To the children*
> *To all the children*
> *To the children who swim beneath*
> *The waves of the sea, to those who live in*
> *The soils of the Earth, to the children of the flowers*
> *In the meadows and the trees in the forest, to*
> *All those children who roam over the land*
>
> *And the winged ones who fly with the winds,*
> *To the human children too, that all the children*
> *May go together into the future in the full*
> *Diversity of their regional communities* (Berry 1999, v).

This is Thomas Berry's *Dream of the Earth*. Can we achieve it?

REFERENCES

Annan, Kofi. 2009. "Introduction," in *The Anatomy of a Silent Crisis.* Geneva, Switzerland: Global Humanitarian Forum.

Benedict, Pope XVI. 2009. "Caritas in Veritate." *United States Conference of Catholic Bishops.*

Berry, Thomas. 1998. *The Dream of the Earth*. San Francisco, CA: Sierra Club Books.

---. 1999. *The Great Work: Our Way into the Future*. New York, NY: Tower Press.

Ferrero, Elisabeth M. & Joe Holland. 2005. *The Earth Charter: A Study Book of Reflection for Action*. Miami, FL: Redwoods Press.

Kolbert, Elizabeth. 2013. "The Sixth Extinction: An Unnatural History," in *Natural Resources Defense Council's OnEarth Magazine*.

---."The Catastrophist". *The New Yorker*. June 29, 2009. Accessed March 11, 2015.

McElroy, Michael B. 2001. "Perspectives on Environmental Change: A Basis for Action," in *Daedalus, the Journal of the American Academy of Arts and Sciences*. Issue entitled "Religion and Ecology: Can the Climate Change?" Volume 130, 31-59. Cambridge, MA: American Academy of Arts and Sciences.

Paul, Pope John II. 1990. "New Year Message". Message for World day of Peace.

Robbins, Jim."The Year the Monarch Didn't Appear". The New York Times. November 23, 2013. *http://www.nytimes.com/2013/11/24/sunday-review/the-year-the-monarch-didnt-appear.html?_r=*

Accessed March 11, 2015.

Stern, Nicholas. 2007. "Stern review on the Economics of Climate Change". Cambridge, MA: Cambridge University Press.

Swimme, Brian. 1996. *The Hidden Heart of the Cosmos: Humanity and the New Story*. Maryknoll, NY: Orbis Books.

Wilson, Edward O. 1992. "The Human Impact", in *The Diversity of Life*. Cambridge, Mass: Harvard University Press.

CHICAGO WILDERNESS:
NEW ALLIES FOR URBAN SUSTAINABILITY

LAUREL M. ROSS

A bold vision of people and nature thriving side-by-side in a major metropolitan region was imagined in 1996 by a diverse group of conservationists, scientists, and educators. This essay traces the roots of that vision and describes, using real life examples, how a large and diverse partnership is moving the Chicago metropolitan region toward a more sustainable future.

We have hopes that the Chicago Wilderness initiative will become a model both for citizen participation and for inter-agency cooperation in conservation. This effort has been described as having the elements of a new environmental ethic, one that recognizes the role of human beings in a metropolitan area as important and necessary components of a thriving natural system. We envision the work in Chicago moving like a prairie fire igniting the spirits of people in other places and inviting others to take, like sacred fire, this idea home to their own communities. (Ross 1997)

Introduction

At the time that I participated in the *Spirituality and Sustainability* conference, Assisi 1996, a group of us in Chicago were immersed in an intensely collaborative creative process that, in order to succeed, demanded that we stretch our minds to new possibilities. We couldn't find good solutions among existing choices for the very real problems we faced and were forced to come up with new approaches. It was painful and frustrating at the same time that it was exciting and fun. I am not sure why I decided to make the trip to Assisi at that time since I am not an academic. I am a conservation practitioner, and conferences are not the venue I typically choose to ask questions and find answers or to refresh and express myself. But something about the framing of the theme called to me. It promised that participants would explore some of the same questions we were grappling with at home: how to work toward achieving a vision for ways that people and the rest of nature could live in true harmony, striving not for mere co-existence, but for the flourishing of all. I had at that time only a little familiarity with Thomas Berry's writings, but did have a lifelong affinity with the teachings of St. Francis whom I was exposed to along with Emerson and others in my Unitarian upbringing in NE Ohio. The project we were working on at the time came to be called Chicago Wilderness and in retrospect I can honestly say that that project owes some of its originality of approach to the insights I brought back from the experience that summer in Assisi. I was influenced by the process of sharing ideas and fellowship through formal sessions, long intimate conversations with new friends, and spectacular meals with bottomless wine glasses. I was also influenced by the challenging conclusions we reached that pushed us all to find ways to make real change in this world through whatever work we were leading. This short essay is about living in Chicago and about the city's relationship with nature. It's about what is left of wild nature in the metropolitan region and what Chicagoans are doing to preserve it, to restore it to health, and in some cases expand and connect its small and large remnants. We are doing good work in Chicago and Tom Berry's presence, his writings and his convening of like-minded people contributed to our success.

Chicago Wilderness

The unusual alliance of thirty-four conservation, research and cultural institutions that launched the Chicago Wilderness initiative began with the stated purpose of bringing to life a vision for the Chicago metropolitan region's landscape as a thriving mosaic of natural areas, connected by greenways and wildlife corridors and embedded in the nation's third largest metropolis. In creating this vision there was full attention paid to the need for the region's human communities to reclaim pieces of the cultural tradition of earlier inhabitants of the region who proactively managed their landscape. In almost twenty years Chicago Wilderness has grown to become in 2014 a vibrant coalition of over 300 organizations cooperating on four major regional initiatives: 1- connecting children with nature, 2- promoting green infrastructure, 3- restoring natural communities and 4- adapting to climate change.

The earliest organizers of Chicago Wilderness were land managers and scientists who knew from direct experience the ecological value of the natural resources in the 7.8 million acre metropolitan area -- the rare plants, animals and natural communities that were hanging on in the protected remnants of public land. Though they spoke from the beginning about the central role of people in conserving this landscape, the human dimension has continued to grow in prominence.

It is surprising to many, even those who live there, that some of the finest remaining prairies and oak woodlands on the planet are right in the Chicago metro area, and that in Illinois the highest concentration of rare and endangered species is near the city, not in the agricultural counties with low human populations. But that is, in fact, true and it is true because the city is where most of the people in the state live. Most of the rest of Illinois is wall-to-wall corn and soy beans, a virtual biodiversity desert. Chicagoans have preserved over 545,000 acres of public land in 38 counties for ourselves. We have shown by our actions that we want to live near nature and spend time there -- and we have been willing to pay the cost, which has been substantial. Most of the legal protection of the landscape took place in the first half of the twentieth century resulting in large part from the vision of the Plan of Chicago -- the famous "Burnham Plan." However, setting the land aside, as significant as it was, later proved to be not enough to truly conserve it and in the second half of the century many conservationists recognized that much of the public land was seriously degraded ecologically. Fire suppression, invasive species, altered hydrology and fragmentation were taking a biological toll on the iconic Midwest prairies and oak woodlands in our city and suburban forest preserves. Ecological restoration, a new discipline emerging in the conservation world at that time, seemed to many of us to be the perfect antidote, but it was a little known field still being invented and tested and every estimate of the cost of such an endeavor seemed daunting. The public loved and understood the concept of protecting land and repeatedly voted in favor of taxing themselves through bond referenda for land acquisition, but neither they nor elected officials were aware of the ecological problems plaguing the land. Preliminary polling showed that no one was interested in investing public dollars into the staff and equipment required to manage and restore the ailing land to health. The Chicago Wilderness consortium was born of the need to connect the organizations and agencies that own the protected public land to each other and to their constituents to accomplish this immense task. We needed to find ways to work together to build political will and to find significant new funding for nature conservation in a big American city. No one quite knew how to do that at the beginning, but the important first step of talking to each other to identify shared interests eventually led to shared solutions.

Perhaps the single most important early success factor in Chicago Wilderness was the fostering of collaboration across disciplines, institutions and agencies. Nontraditional partnerships have infused this work with enormous strength. A prime example was the collaboration by the region's scientists, land managers, educators, community-based organizations and policy-makers that culminated in the creation of the Chicago Wilderness *Biodiversity Recovery Plan* in 1999 (Chicago Wilderness 1999). The *Plan's* recommendations were developed by consensus and adopted internally by member organizations, i.e. this was NOT a top down process. This road map has guided both conservation and communication efforts of member organizations and has led to the restoration of thousands of acres, the development of new tools for management of those areas, the adoption of important conservation practices by local communities and coordinated outreach to tens of thousands of residents to make them aware of their rich and diverse natural heritage and to involve them directly in its management.

This last component of the plan's recommendations continues to be key to its successful implementation. As Thomas Berry has expressed in many of his writings over the last thirty years, "the natural world is a communion of objects rather than a collection of objects. This has been recognized from an early time by the indigenous peoples of the world" (Berry 1996). He challenges us to recognize that there is no discontinuity between the human and the non-human world. Acting on that understanding in a large, culturally diverse urban area for the mutual benefit of the human and non-human world has been instructive. We are learning to reconnect on a large scale. One compelling message in the CW outreach to the public has been the vision of what this land once was. "The land of the Potawatomi Ottawa, and Chippewa, the land that was to become Chicago was once a tapestry of rolling savanna and prairie, clear streams and noble groves of ancient oaks. These provided habitat for elk, buffalo, parakeets, swans, cranes, turkeys, beavers and mountain lions, as well as vast beds of mussels and clams. Beneath it was a rich black soil that European settlers soon turned into the basis for the Midwestern economy. In the process they came to see Chicago as 'the City in the Garden' fashioning a good life from the wilderness" (Ross 1997). A glossy magazine, *Chicago Wilderness*, published quarterly from 1997 to 2009, was filled with gorgeous photography of regional plants and animals, as well as information about how to visit these places to learn more. People responded enthusiastically to that message.

The next part of the story we tell is what happened to that land. The 19th and 20th century almost spelled the doom of many of the charismatic species in our region. An inventory of the natural areas in Illinois in the 1970s showed that *less than a tenth of one percent of the original landscape* remained (White 1978). "But," we said, "take heart!" The message to both the public and the decision makers was, and still is, that we can turn this around if we, the people, decide to do that. With our actions we can create a narrative in which people are not the enemy of nature, but in fact potentially an important part of nature's recovery. The 21st century can see a thrilling revival of nature in and around the City, readily available for our spiritual, physical and emotional refreshment. It helps our cause that the results of early efforts of ecological restoration are beginning to be more apparent. In 2014 the Carolina parakeets are gone forever, but beavers are now everywhere, Sandhill Cranes and Wild Turkeys are nesting successfully, and even cougars are being regularly reported nearby. Thousands of species of native plants and animals, some of which are found nowhere else on Earth, are making a measurable comeback in the places where restoration investments have been made -- in forest preserves, parks, and even back yards, living among the millions of people who also call the Chicago region home.

This restoration of public land has proceeded on two fronts: professional land managers and citizen volunteers. The increasing investment by landowners comes as elected officials and the voting public put an increasingly high value on the results and is an extremely important part of the future success of the vision. However, here I want to focus on the second front. The strategy to involve the public directly in the actual work of healing the land may prove to be the best strategy of all if we can do it on a large scale and find ways to include people of all ages, cultures, and backgrounds. Thomas Berry talked compellingly about the autism of humans in our culture -- our inability to communicate with the rest of life on earth (Berry 1999). Participating in ecological restoration is one powerful way for people to engage in an ongoing two-way conversation with their natural landscape and the Chicago metro area has been a perfect place for this conversation to begin to play out. The result seems to be mutually beneficial -- healing of the land and healing of the people. As Berry reminds us often this general approach is tapping into views and wisdom held by many world religions such as Buddhism, "self and other heal together" (Leighton 2003).

Every weekend, twelve months a year, there are scores of opportunities in the Chicago metro area for people to join the effort of restoring their public land to health. And join they do! The work includes such tasks as cutting invasive brush, removing choking weeds, and collecting and planting seeds of native flowers and grasses. As one stewardship volunteer put it, "This is the best free outdoor recreation experience there is, year round! And you feel great because you are not just getting exercise, you are doing something important." Volunteer stewardship, as it has come to be called, has attracted people with many different skills and passions. Some people have become citizen scientists, learning the technical skills to monitor plants, birds, mammals, mussels, reptiles and amphibians and providing valuable data on the progress of the restoration work. Others have taken on the job of bringing children into the restoration work through new programs created for this express purpose, such as the Mighty Acorns through which over 8,000 city children a year do land stewardship. Still others have worked hard to diversify the ranks of the restoration corps by reaching out and involving friends and neighbors in their own communities -- African Americans, Latinos, communities of faith, even corporate leaders. It is a growing movement which is currently being looked at by some federal agencies and national organizations as a model for other urban regions.

In the early days of Chicago Wilderness ethics had not been an explicit concern, though arguably, every aspect of this work has ethical dimensions. However, in the fall of 2007 Chicago Wilderness was invited to be the experimental first case study for discussions convened by the Center for Humans and Nature (CHN) in their effort to develop a "code of ethics for biodiversity conservation" through the Biosphere Ethics Initiative (BEI) of the International Union for the Conservation of Nature (IUCN). The two day convening, called a *Relato*, was reminiscent of the Assisi meeting ten years before. It featured good food and drink, long intimate hours together in a beautiful setting, and a series of rambling and exciting facilitated conversations among a diverse selection of international experts on ethics and a number of interested Chicago Wilderness leaders. We from CW had been so focused on doing our work that we had spent very little time reflecting on it before then. Insights gained through this process have been summarized and published by CHN, "Chicago Wilderness showed us the ability of a powerful story told passionately to change minds and open hearts" (Mackey et al, 2008).

Subsequently CW representatives were invited to participate in several other *Relatos* to bring the Chicago story to South Africa, Rio de Janeiro, and Amman, Jordan and to hear the stories of the people working there. All of these stories informed the evolving ethics document. If we look at environmental rights through the work of Thomas Berry we see that the emphasis is placed on the fact that the human community must accept "the Earth as a single integral community, with every being having inherent value and corresponding rights according to its mode of being" (Berry 1997-1998, 29). This, in a nutshell, expresses well the concept that emerged from the CHN international environmental discussions. And while that is not the language we would use in Chicago, it is certainly an important part of the message that is conveyed when we tell our story. Within the environmental movement, the great spiritual traditions of the world have emphasized some significant points: that the natural world has value in itself; that there is no discontinuity between the human and the non-human; that greed and destructiveness of the natural world is condemned; and "the most difficult transition to make is from the anthropocentric to the bio-centric norm of progress ... Any progress of the human at the expense of the larger life community must ultimately lead to a diminishment of human life itself. A degraded habitat will produce degraded humans" (Berry 1988). In the more often quoted words of Aldo Leopold, "we abuse the land because we regard it as a commodity belonging to us. When we see land as a community to which we belong, we may begin to use it with love and respect" (Leopold 1949).

We are proud of what we have accomplished in Chicago, though we are far from finished with our work. From thirty-four founding organizations Chicago Wilderness has grown to a current membership of more than three hundred. Biodiversity has been newly prominent at the table in a number of recent regional planning efforts further demonstrating that it is not possible to plan successfully for nature without considering people, and vice versa. Important links with the region's business community were forged through the formation of a Corporate Council further making this conservation agenda a part of the mainstream regional agenda. Because of the effectiveness of this approach Chicago Wilderness has been recognized outside of the region as an outstanding model for urban conservation. Numerous efforts throughout country and the world have benefited from the lessons learned. This model of collaboration and connection has fostered working relationships such that working collaboratively has become simply the way to do business in this part of the nation.

REFERENCES

Berry, Thomas. 1988. *Dream of the Earth*. San Francisco: Sierra Club Books.

---. "Ethics and Ecology." Paper presented at the Harvard Seminar on Environmental Values. Cambridge, Massachusetts, 1996.

---. Fall/Winter 1997-98. "The Challenge of Our Times." *Earth Ethics*, Volume 1 and 2, 29.

---. 1999. *The Great Work*. New York: Three Rivers Press.

Chicago Wilderness, (formerly known as the Chicago Region Biodiversity Council). 1999. *Biodiversity Recovery Plan* Chicago: Chicago Wilderness.

Leighton, Taigen Daniel. 2003. *Faces of Compassion*. Somerville: Wisdom Publications.

Leopold, Aldo. 1949. *A Sand County Almanac*. New York: Oxford University Press.

Brendan Mackey, Kahryn Kinzele et al. 2008. *Keeping Nature Alive: Toward a Code of Ethics for Biodiversity Conservation*. Gland, Switzerland: IUCN, vii + 27.

Ross, Laurel M. 1997. "The Chicago Wilderness, A Coalition For Urban Conservation." *Restoration and Management Notes*. 15:1 18 – 24

White, John and Corbin, Calvin C. 1978. *Illinois Natural Areas Inventory*, Volume 1 and 2. Urbana-Champaign: University of Illinois

27

IS AN ECOLOGICAL SOCIETY STILL BELIEVABLE?

KARL-LUDWIG SCHIBEL

A sustainable society cannot be based exclusively on rational thought and even less so when it takes the reductive form of instrumental rationality. Ecological conversion has to be founded in reason that knows its limits and is clear about its roots that reach beyond its realm.

Our "masters" have left us, and it is up to us to explain to ourselves and to those who might listen, how to understand, interpret and live in a world full of contradictions, impending disasters and some hope. The founder of social ecology was Murray Bookchin. For decades I followed his thoughts, sharing and discussing them, but not always agreeing. When I presented my ideas, very much inspired by this anarchist thinker in 1996 with a contribution on the "Politics of Ecological Conversion" in one of the seminars with Thomas Berry in the *Spirituality and Sustainability* conference in Assisi, Italy, I felt outside of my intellectual world. Spirituality, the search for the spiritual dimension of our present ecological crisis seemed more part of the problem than part of the solution. To me, then and still today, the Earth is not a mother, not even a stepmother; and the most I am willing to say is that in one of the innumerable solar systems, our planet saw the transition from the inorganic to the organic about two and a half billion years ago. Since then an evolution of life has taken place that produced our own species, a particular kind of life that the idealistic philosopher Fichte describes as a necessary manifestation of consciousness in nature,

> *Nature rises gradually in the determinate order of its productions. In raw matter it is simple being; in organized matter it returns into itself to work upon itself there inside itself, to form itself in the plant, and to move itself in the animal. In man, its greatest masterpiece, it returns into itself to look at itself and observe itself: it duplicates itself in man as it were, and its mere being becomes being and consciousness in union.* (Preuss 1987, 15)

For both Thomas Berry and Murray Bookchin, the emergence of self-reflexivity in human as a result of the evolution of life, is a crucial point of departure for their thought. Berry puts this process into a much wider context, invoking the whole universe,

> *We must feel that we are supported by the same power that brought the Earth into being, that power that spun the galaxies into space, that lit the sun and brought the moon into its orbit. That is the power by which living forms grew up out of the Earth and came to a special mode of reflexive consciousness in the human.* (Berry 1999, 173)

Bookchin's time frame is more contained starting with life on planet earth, "human consciousness, in effect, is placed in the service of both human needs and ecological diversity. Inasmuch as human beings are themselves products of the natural world, human self-consciousness could be described in philosophical terms as nature rendered 'self-conscious,' a natural world guided by human rationality toward balanced or harmonious ecological as well as social ends"

(1980, 109). On this point both Berry, the Catholic eco-theologian, and Bookchin, the anarchist social ecologist, converge on a crucial line of thought for ecological discourse: there is a logic to the evolution of life on this planet which can be reconstructed on empirical grounds and in which life exhibits a growing differentiation, an exuberant variety, a multiplying complexity and continuous spontaneity. This unfolding logic of life's evolution ties us insolubly to the natural world and forms the spiritual dimension of the relationship between humans and nature.

At the beginning of the modern ecology movement – what today could be called the transcendental dimension of thinking ecologically – was not the point of departure for me or the general debate. The modern ecological discourse got off to a dramatic start in the early 1960s with urgent alarms sounding for the future of humankind. Rachel Carson saw a *Silent Spring* looming; Murray Bookchin foresaw a *Synthetic Environment,* and Paul Ehrlich invoked a *Population Bomb.* The differences in their thinking notwithstanding, what united these three and many others was a stark alternative: ecology or catastrophe. Not only would the birds stop singing but all of human's destructive relationship with nature – the rampant extraction of natural resources, the ignoring of *Limits to Growth*, the use of earth's atmosphere as a dump for greenhouse gases – would lead inexorably to the destruction of the natural base of human life on earth and to our species' self-extinction.

The alternative that these visionaries saw to our own suicide was an ecological society that stopped destroying nature and found a way of living in harmony with nature and with each other. To Thomas Berry, "the transition from a period of human devastation of the Earth to a period when humans would be present to the planet in a mutually beneficial manner" is *The Great Work* (1999, 2). Bookchin writes, "a balanced community, a face-to-face democracy, a humanistic technology and a decentralized society … belong not only to the great visions of man's future, they now constitute the precondition for human survival" (1972, 69). The creation of an ecological society is seen as the only possibility for the survival of humankind and the final breakthrough into the realm of freedom. With Bookchin it is part of a larger project that would also abolish class rule, economic exploitation, rampant inequality, gender discrimination and racism. With this new society he foresaw the ultimate end of hierarchy and domination, because the false idea that humans can dominate nature arises according to him from the very real domination of human by human.

The first mass mobilizations of the ecology movement got under way in the west, driven by the fear of an end of human life on earth. Huge "no nukes" demonstrations against nuclear power plants were motivated by an eschatological outlook and fears of catastrophic outcomes. Every ecological disaster – Three Mile Island and Seveso in the 1970s, the Exxon Valdez and Chernobyl in the 1980s – was seen as a sinister forbearer of an end to the world lurking right around the corner. This eschatological consciousness hid (and continues to hide) the true character of our ecological crisis. However horrific the disasters are, it is the normal way in which we produce things, distribute things, and dispose of things that is destroying the natural basis of life – day by day, every day. The Fukushima nuclear plant disaster and the Deepwater Horizon well-head blow-out are only the visible tip of a mostly-submerged iceberg. The attention that the environmental movement and the media give these spectacular events weakens public understanding of what the ecological crisis really is. Yes, the malfunctioning is a problem, but the developed world's economic system is most dangerous when it is functioning well. Industrial agriculture uses ever more land for cultivating genetically modified plants. Oil is extracted from ever greater depths. Fracking shocks the earth to get gases to the surface.

Problems arise when humans' interventions into nature are too deep, like nuclear technologies and genetic engineering, with possibly far-reaching and irreversible side-effects no one can anticipate. "The trends in our times," to quote from the *Ecology of Freedom* by Murray Bookchin,

> *are visibly directed against ecological diversity; in fact, they point toward brute simplification of the entire biosphere. Complex food chains in the soil and on the earth's surface are being ruthlessly undermined by the fatuous application of industrial techniques to agriculture; consequently, soil has been reduced in many areas to a mere sponge for absorbing simple chemical 'nutrients.' The cultivation of single crops over vast stretches of land is effacing natural, agricultural, and even physiographic variety. Immense urban belts are encroaching unrelentingly on the countryside, replacing flora and fauna with concrete, metal and glass, and enveloping large regions in a haze of atmospheric pollutants.* (1982, 40)

Most serious of the "too much" problems is the more than thirty billion tons of carbon dioxide rising into our planet's atmosphere every year. The main contributors are still the rich industrialized countries; but emerging countries increase their share every year, some of them dramatically. Power plants driven by fossil fuels; heating systems in homes, in stores, in schools, and everywhere; transportation, cars, trucks, buses, airplanes -- everything that is powered by fossil energy contributes to putting more than thirty trillion kilos of CO_2 into earth's atmosphere annually. So the ecological crisis emanates from the everyday functioning of industrialized societies. Climate change is the biggest single threat to life on earth. To all forms of life? Not really. Climate change does not threaten nature or the biosphere as much as it threatens the natural basis of complex life forms: most especially one species -- homo sapiens. As human has become the strongest geological force on earth, it is true we have entered a new era -- the Anthropocene. But it is also true that if humankind should succeed in its self-extinction, the biosphere will continue to exist. So, while the ecological crisis is concerned about the future of nature on this planet, the general public is mostly concerned with the preservation of one specific and rather fragile life form on this earth – us.

For humans to survive on this earth a drastic reduction of our consumption of energy and raw materials is required. Drastic here does not mean 30% or 40% it means a reduction in the magnitude of 80%-90%. Dramatic changes are required to attain a sustainable human society on earth. These changes will, indeed, require a whole new way of living in the world, which Alexander Langer tried to depict in a reversal of the Olympic motto: from *Citius, Altius, Fortius,* (faster, higher, stronger) our ideas and goals must change to *Lentius, Profundius, Suavius,* (slower, deeper, softer). Incisive technological changes that raise the efficiency of energy use and reduce consumption of raw materials must come; and will have to be accompanied by far-reaching changes in the way we live, the way we move from place to place, the way we work, and the way we spend our leisure time. Productive cycles will have to be closed; "cradle to cradle" will bring us into a co-productive relationship with nature.

The task is huge; the outcome uncertain. Since the enormous ecological problems -- global warming, the over-use of natural resources, the reduction of biodiversity, and desertification -- were first recognized and analyzed, none has brought a decisive step nearer to a solution. Energy saving is a top priority on the global agenda, as over half of the greenhouse effect is being created by the CO_2 emissions coming from processes of combustion of fossil energy sources. Scientists agree we must cut global CO_2 emissions by 80% by 2050 to avoid global warming's most catastrophic effects. Unfortunately, discouragingly, trends in the consumption of energy from fossil fuels are going in the opposite direction. Growing 2% every year, energy demand is expected to double by 2050.

A probable increase of 100% versus a required decrease by 80%? This stark discrepancy between the path to sustainability and continuing industrial growth has caused some outstanding ecologists to call for authoritarian solutions. In his book *The Logic of Salvation* the "necessity for survival" made Rudolph Bahro advocate a "healthy tyranny," an "ecological council" of outstanding persons (nominated, not elected), that has far-reaching powers to act for the common good. In *The Imperative of Responsibility* philosopher Hans Jonas suspected an ecological authoritarian rule might be required not to reach the greatest good but to avert the greatest evil -- the extinction of humankind (Jonas and Herr 1985, 36).

Calls to sacrifice democracy – as a way to solve the compelling urgency of the ecological crisis – puts survival before freedom on the basis of a seemingly objective scientific analysis. However, we are not dealing with a scientific question; and to believe that science could tell us what we must do to avoid extinction accurately enough to give up freedom is preposterous and historically has had only terrible results. Countless catastrophes' predictions (some based on very-well-argued theories) have proven wrong and become obsolete. Rosa Luxemburg saw an absolute limit to capitalist expansion from which, "the collapse of capitalism follows inevitably, as an objective historical necessity" (Luxemburg [1913] 2003, 398). A century later this has not yet happened. Paul Ehrlich argued cogently that overpopulation would bring mass starvation in the 1970s and 1980s (Lilley 2012). While I do believe that in the next years or decades the natural base of human life on this earth could be ruined, even our possible self-extinction cannot become, must not become, a basis for any kind of authoritarian tyranny controlling how we must live to survive. Authoritarian rule is in itself an extinction of the human spirit.

Excluding an authoritarian solution to the ecological crisis (even if green tyranny could really solve it) requires us to bring about an ecological conversion of the economy and society in a truly democratic fashion. Can it be done? The day-to-day functioning of the political systems in the USA, Western Europe and other industrial capitalist nations does not lend itself to optimism. A sustainable future is not part of the program of any major political force. The question of how to maintain and improve the achievements of human civilization while drastically reducing the consumption of resources is not on any government's agenda. The Green Economy will not bring the needed reductions, nor will green growth. It seems that *"Realpolitik"* today means avoiding the ecological crisis, ignoring its deep cultural causes, and forgetting any visions of a free, cooperative, and ecological society.

Environmental politics within the parliamentary institutions of Western democracies has led to a reformism that leaves the destructive tendencies of our society intact while trying to cure some of the most blatant symptoms. Environmental issues become pawns in a power game, and ecology is being reduced to environmental protection. This has little to do with character defects or incapacities of environmentally conscious politicians and everything to do with the logic of the political system. National and even more so international politics today can largely be characterized as crisis management, its priorities a result of the degree of urgency in the problems reaching the public's eye. In this context, value-oriented action and moral aims are indeed not *Realpolitik*; they are instead "unrealistic."

Things look better if we turn our attention to the local level. I have been active for the last two decades on the board of the "Climate Alliance of European Cities." Here, more than 1600 European cities and towns in 23 countries have committed themselves to reduce their carbon dioxide emissions by 10% every five years. Few succeed (which means some do) and many local administrators now base their actions on a clear understanding of the dimensions of the ecological crisis and the threat to the global climate. Many actions on the local level point in the right direction. In a number of European cities, new residential areas have been constructed for families who do not own a car. These families move around on foot, by public transport, by bicycle. If need be they use a car from a car-sharing organization. Again on the local level a growing number of communities are striving to become 100% self-sufficient in energy, and some have already reached this goal. Transition towns are experimenting to live without fossil fuels. These concrete utopias are exciting examples of the movement towards a solar era. They show that a life of high ecological well-being is possible without destroying its own natural basis. Unfortunately, these new utopias are marginal exercises. How, and even if, such places will enter into the dominant consciousness and the everyday life of large numbers of people remains to be seen.

Let it be understood, we are not talking about ecological fundamentalists that are sacrificing their lives for the "cause" but about "reformist" projects which solve, on a local level, real problems and satisfy existing needs. A neighborhood without cars not only makes a contribution to the reduction of the number of vehicles that circulate, but also creates a space where an ecological culture of life without the automobile can develop. Families satisfy their desire for mobility without owning a car and experience in their lives a reconciliation between individualism and collective necessity. In this sense neighborhoods without cars are a cultural phenomenon which transforms necessity into a practical and livable *Gestalt*.

Does living without owning a car, reducing meat consumption or becoming a vegetarian, being active in a divestment campaign against the fossil fuel industry, campaigning against fracking, or participating in an urban gardening group only add another way of living to the already numerous forms of lifestyle in our post-modern societies? We do not know. I would argue we cannot know, but we can hope these small changes are the beginnings of a deep and far-reaching evolution towards an ecological society.

At this point theoretical thought meets its limits. How much time will be needed for the ecological conversion of economy and society? It is an open question whether the powers of destruction or of creation will have the upper hand, and calls to immediate action because of catastrophes will not change that. To arrive at a comprehensive theory of the nature of the ecological crisis and its future -- in the tradition of our masters -- is impossible. This is not for lack of intellectual power but resides in the object itself. Theoretical thinking at some point must flow into action -- with an uncertain result. There is no evidence of a mass movement crying "ecologists of all countries unite." There is not a growing furor to end the ecological crisis in a revolutionary upheaval. Nor, fortunately, is there any evidence of plans to solve it by authoritarian measures. Meanwhile green politics works on curing symptoms. And local projects anticipate aspects of an ecological society.

So what are we left with? First of all with our own personal experience and commitment. In my case this includes the work with climate policies on the local level in the context of a city network and a personal commitment to living a more egalitarian life in an intentional community closer to nature. Encouragement comes at the same time from the overwhelming myriad of similar social and ecological initiatives, experiences, solutions, of practical utopias all around the world which Paul Hawken has described as "blessed unrest" (Hawken 2008). But the moment when we try to catapult our own work or the more general vision of a restless multitude into some theory detailing a process that will necessarily and absolutely bring us towards an ecological society, things start going wrong. To take flight into theory is tempting, because working in concrete situations with real people almost never brings spectacular results and easily lends itself to preoccupation with curing the symptoms without changing the underlying causes.

Having witnessed the astounding capacity of industrial capitalism to change and adapt, I will not exclude the possibility of a technocratic path towards sustainability that could succeed in securing the natural basis of human life for future generations. Such a solution might have little to do with an ecological society, where a creative and co-productive relationship with nature finds its social equivalent in the true equality of unequals. But there is no alternative: radical ecological politics must work on environmental reforms. We must deal with the concrete experiences of social groups and find practical solutions that lead to an ecological conversion. The history of labor teaches us our small steps can function as either elements to entrench an anti-ecological social order or as the first building stones for founding a new society. Reason as well as intuition, a thorough analysis as well as a clear understanding of our place in this world, must guide us in determining the direction of the steps we are taking, to understand their logic and to put them into relation with our aims for an ecological society.

It is here where spirituality comes in, understood in a wide sense as the attempt to reach an encompassing view and sensibility for the rootedness of humankind in the evolution of life as nature rendered self-conscious. Spirituality is a vital force for developing a sensitivity to the natural world that cuts through the mystifications of a technocratic outlook and resists a regressive individualistic outlook. Spirituality can give us important insights into the self-developmental and creative phenomena in natural and social evolution. Berry describes one way a higher vision can guide the ecological conversion. He compares it to that of an artist who, "in creating some significant work … first experiences something akin to dream awareness that becomes clarified in the creative process itself, so we must first have a vision of the future sufficiently entrancing that it will sustain us in the transformation of the human project that is now in process" (Berry 1999, Introduction). Without a vision we will not be able to keep alive the passion for an ecological society as we are immersed in piecemeal reforms where in a worst case scenario our efforts might only contribute to an ecological modernization of a forever unjust society.

It is not only that our masters are gone but that their form of thinking has died with them. The multitude of ecological initiatives, of communities working for the common good, of pioneers in a co-productive relationship with nature is overwhelming. At the same time there is an immense discrepancy between these numbers and the cultural, political and economic impact the restless multitude can have on the one hand and the powerful forces needed to bring about the ecological conversion on the other. Any attempt at developing an all-encompassing theory that pretends to analyze and explain the rich variety of organizations, initiatives, and movements engaged in creating a co-productive relationship between modern society and nature, melding them into a "global family" (Hawken 2008, 164), or reconducting them to some kind of overreaching principle, be it earth consciousness or libertarian municipalism, is fuzzy thinking.

After two world wars, the failure of a socialist revolution in the west, National Socialism in Germany, Stalinism in the Soviet Union, the genocide in Rwanda in the last century, the civil war in Syria and the blatant incapacity of the world community to come to terms with the threat of global warming in this century, the last vestiges of some kind of reason, spirit or logic that is expressing itself in the unfolding of world history seems preposterous. There is no room left for any kind of thought that tries to imbue history with the progress of reason, of a *Weltgeist*, of a Great Work whose fulfillment will unfold with necessity step by step in historical development. What can be seen and has been depicted by among others Murray Bookchin and Hans Jonas, Thomas Berry and Ilya Progogine, Ernst Bloch and Herbert

Marcuse, are the potentialities of a rational world society that lives, to use the concept of Bloch, in a "co-productive" relationship with nature (Plaice and Knight 1986, 686). We are not interested here in the important differences among these authors, in where they anchor this potentiality for a better world. Thomas Berry speaks of a genetic coding that "is more comprehensive than our cultural coding. Human genetic coding is integral with the whole complex of species codings whereby the Earth system remains coherent within itself and capable of continuing the evolutionary process" (1999, 105), Somehow, says Berry, "we must reach back to where our human genetic coding connects with the other species codings of the larger Earth community. Only then can we overcome the limitations of the anthropocentrism that binds us. Perhaps a new revelatory experience is taking place. ... In such a renewal lies our hope for the future for ourselves and for the entire planet on which we live" (1999, 106). In a similar vein Murray Bookchin says. "The separation of humanity from nature, its sweeping social trajectory into a history that produced a rich wealth of mind, personality, technical insight, culture, and self-reflective thought, marks the potential for mind in nature itself, the latent spirit in substance that comes to consciousness in a humanity that melds with the natural world. The time has come to integrate an ecological natural philosophy with an ecological social philosophy based on freedom and consciousness, a goal that has haunted western philosophy from the pre-Socratics onward" (1980, 27). Both are expressing a hope, speaking about a potential and by no means affirming certainty. Any attempt to translate these hopes into probable, let alone certain, material developments in our post-metaphysical era is preposterous.

An ecological society will not be the result of reason alone, the limits of which are all too obvious. Max Horkheimer has shown convincingly the perversions of instrumental reason which is ever more brilliant as far as its means are concerned and ever more obtuse in the choice of its ends. So what do we do, those of us who are "religiously tone-deaf," but very much aware of the limits of reason? Jürgen Habermas talks very cautiously about "a transcendent point of reference" and argues that, "without initially having any theological intention, the reason that becomes aware of its limitations thus transcends itself in the direction of something else. This can take the form of the mystical fusion with a consciousness that embraces the universe" (McNeil 2006, 40). This is the hope of a redeeming message, or the shape of solidarity with those who are oppressed.

So what we have are the visions our masters gave us of an ecological society which we share, and what we have is our own everyday involvement in concrete projects, dealing with climate or gender, or the rights of indigenous peoples far away, or the homeless in front of the door, or with urban gardening or raising children to become competent, self-directed human beings. We are involved in ecological politics and communitarian projects, in actions resisting the devastation of the environment and the violation of human rights, and in developing new forms of relating to nature and to one another. The challenge is to let vision and practice stand side by side, difficult as it may be to bear their un-reconciled coexistence, without ceding to the temptations to create any kind of forced connection between the two of them by way of some transcendental principle that works behind our backs or above our heads. As a hope, yes, as an intuition yes, as a dream, yes, as a belief, yes -- as a prefiguration no. We must do what we can today, we must do what we can tomorrow; no one can speak with certainty of what is yet to come.

Città di Castello, Italy,
with profound gratitude to John Calkins

REFERENCES

Bahro, Rudolf. 1987. *Logik der Rettung: Wer kann die Apokalypse aufhalten?* Stuttgart / Wien: Edition Weitbrecht in Thienemanns Verlag.

Berry, Thomas. 1999. *The Great Work, Our Way into the Future.* New York: Bell Tower.

Bloch, Ernst.1986. *The Principle of Hope.* Translated by Neville Plaice, Stephen Plaice and Paul Knight. Oxford: Blackwell.

Bookchin, Murray. 1975. *Our Synthetic Environment.* New York: Knopf.

---. 1980. *Toward an Ecological Society.* Montreal: Black Rose Books.

---. 1982. *The Ecology of Freedom: The Emergence and Dissolution of Hierarchy.* Palo Alto, CA: Cheshire Books.

Carson, Rachel. 1962. *Silent Spring.* Boston: Houghton Mifflin.

Ehrlich, Paul. 1968. *The Population Bomb.* San Francisco: Sierra Club/Ballantine Books.

Fichete, Johaan Gottlieb. 1987. *Theocation of Man.* Translated by Peter Preuss. Indianapolis: Hackett.

Haberman, Jürgen and Joseph Ratzinger. 2006. *The Dialectics of Secularization.* Translated by Brian McNeil, C.R.V., San Francisco: Ignatius Press.

Hawken, Paul. 2008. *Blessed Unrest.* New York: Penguin.

Horkheimer, Max. 2013. *Critique of Instrumental Reason.* Reprint, Brooklyn, NY: Verso.

Jonas, Hans and Herr, David. Trans. 1985. *The Imperative of Responsibility: In Search of Ethics for the Technological Age.* Chicago: University of Chicago Press.

Lazlo, Ervin and Allan Combs. 2011. *Thomas Berry, Dreamer of the Earth*. Rochester, VT: Inner Traditions.

Lilley, Sasha et al. 2012. *Catastrophism: The Apocalyptic Politics of Collapse and Rebirth*, Oakland, CA: PM Press.

Luxemburg, Rosa. 1913. *The Accumulation of Capital*. Reprint, New York: Routledge.

Meadows, Donella and Dennis, Jorgen Randers. 1972. *The Limits to Growth*. New York, Universe Books.

28

SUSTAINABILITY & EMOTIONAL EDUCATION

JACQUELINE WAGNER

This essay looks at urban life's disconnection from nature and the educational need to remedy that problem.

Going back to the 1990s there is still the fresh memory in me of these inspiring, intellect and heart nourishing *Spirituality and Sustainability* conferences initiated by Elisabeth Ferrero. The ideas of Eco theologian and cultural historian Tom Berry on our present-day economy, on how commercial values are threatening life on the planet, which is today even more relevant than ever before, made me think deeper. "We see quite clearly that what happens to the nonhuman happens to the human. What happens to the outer world happens to the inner world" (Berry 2000, 200). It encouraged me to launch projects for education & leadership and industrial projects on renewable energies.

Relations Between Emotions & Nature

Austria's Nobel Prize winner Konrad Lorenz had already noticed in the 1970s how feelings rapidly intensified by packing people in cities together; what Lorenz saw as dehumanization. (Lorenz 1974).

Experiencing nature's gorgeousness and abundance could encourage people to care for Earth, while realizing the deep connection of consumption and exploitation of nature; therefore developing compassion for this complex biosphere we are living in.

How can closeness to and responsibilities for nature grow, when necessary sensomotoric stimuli for the five senses, which support the emotional connection with earth, are missing in cities? Cities grow faster and create more stress, because of steady noise, which agitates and dulls the senses, with permanent advertisements and ongoing temptations for consumption. World health organizations state that there are already more people living in cities then on the countryside and up to 2050 this will increase up to seventy percent. Cities create painful solitude, marginalization, lack of communication, spatial narrowness and isolation, boosting mental illness and killing emotions. The nervous system needs certain attractions from nature to build the maturity of dendritic and synaptic architecture in the brain, which activates the senses in an elemental manner and brings essential information to our emotions, like the intoxicating smell of flowers, the touching of soft moss, listening to a bird's concert, tasting fresh picked raspberries and observing the harmonious shape of landscapes.

Jean Liedloff, a psychotherapist and one of the founders of the journal, *Ecologist,* described a tribe member in the Venezuelan jungle not willing to work. His relatives did not push the young man, but continued their work and provided a good example. After several years of passivity the man started his own vegetable garden and he was healed. Nowadays our fast-paced lives do not allow years to heal, but by becoming aware of the importance of emotions many problems could be prevented (Liedloff 1977). Emotions can handle more information than intellect and with less stress. Encouraging the flow of emotions to reconnect with ourselves, other people, fauna and flora, is something that can be learned and creates feelings of healthy links with nature and emotional stability.

Good & Bad Emotions

There are still millions of indigenous people living on Earth, like the native Yequana. Jean Liedloff, stayed with them in Venezuela where the tribe is not only living peacefully in the jungle, respectful and responsible for nature, but is also accepting comfortable and uncomfortable situations at times and not judging them as positive or negative, as good or bad. By accident one boy shot an arrow in the shoulder of another boy. The injured boy did not make a big deal of this. He accepted the pain as part of life and did not feel ashamed for his tears. After he was patched up, he continued playing with the other boy. No aggression from the injured boy and no revenge were observed (Liedloff 1977). Yequanas allow pain to come into their lives knowing that it will go away; while Konrad Lorenz noticed in western societies the opposite behavior was true by trying always to avoid unpleasant situations. In his opinion such avoidance weakens people's character and could even lead towards a downfall of a culture (Lorenz 1974).

Physical Effects by Emotions

Comprehensive scientific research shows impacts of emotional pain visible in the brain, heart and on DNA. Neurobiologist and psychiatrist Louann Brizendine explains about emotional pain triggering the same circuits in the brain like physical pain (2006), while cell biologist Glen Rein, and IHM Research Director, Rollin McCraty, examined the intentionally alter of DNA by emotions, even DNA external from the body (McCraty et al. 1993). The physician, neurologist and psychiatrist David Servan-Schreiber states that fifty to seventy-five percent of all sicknesses come from stress, which is an emotion and states that, "every emotional insult leaves a scar in the brain"

(Servan-Schreiber 2004, 49). Tom Berry has a reflective answer to reduce emotional stress, "in a special manner humans have not only a need for but a right of access to the natural world, not only to supply their physical needs but also to provide the wonder needed by human intelligence, the beauty needed by human imagination, and the intimacy needed by the human emotions" (Berry 2001, 10).

Emotional Pain – Changing the Perspective

Emotions are always with us and are seen through cultural lenses. During Jean Liedloff`s expedition in a Venezuela`s jungle, where westerners carried with the aborigines a canoe over a hilltop, because water rapids were too dangerous, she observed that the westerners cursed their efforts and their injuries, while tribe members made jokes and laughed at their stressful situations and because of their positive outlook they never became tired (Liedloff 1977).

What is Emotional Education?

"Above all we discover that every being has its own spontaneities that arise from the depths of its own being. These spontaneities express the inner value of each being in such a manner that we must say of the universe that it is a communion of subjects, not a collection of objects" (Berry 2000, 82).

If educational systems concentrate on accomplishments, then professional life might emphasize objects more than personal exchange and emotional balance. Activities based on intellectual and caring emotional commitments combine the benefit for ourselves with the benefit for others in any decision making process and contribute to both. Spontaneity appears as a lively expression of our individual character and is called soul-life, intuition, belly instinct and inner voice.

Emotional education provides self-leadership according to time, place and circumstances, it teaches detachment and the necessity to communicate emotional needs, it encourages a positive self-confidence and generates respect, whereby the combination with smooth movements indoor and outdoor facilitates the emotional and physical connection with Earth. Such an upbringing ingrains body, mind and emotions with the natural world. Respecting ourselves encourages respect to others. A rich and fulfilled emotional life creates feelings of success. As a new perceived responsibility for actions, words and thoughts increases, sympathy for humans, animals and nature evolves.

The implementation of Emotional Education

When the existing education system is linear and accomplishment-based one must add a cyclic emotional part to complement the other parts equally, balancing life energies, empowering everyone for reflection and recreation and by having sufficient time for intuitive evaluation and many-faceted understanding of each situation, while the intellect serves as an organizer, not as a controller.

Comprehensive knowledge in alliance with wisdom, which combines experience, realized knowledge and intuition, is quite a challenge today. Marie Curie -- the first female Nobel Prize winner in 1903 for physics and in 1911 for chemistry, mentioned that when she learnt about her having cancer, she tried to fully understand her own situation to reduce her fears. Her famous saying about rejoicing like a child when discovering new sights of nature built a beautiful bridge between emotional and intellectual learning (Curie 1923). Nature is first understood emotionally during childhood, later on intellectually, while a stable flow of emotions minimizes misunderstandings and misinterpretations. Living with appreciation for nature and being grateful for nature's gifts could give a deep satisfaction and meaning in life.

Remembering Tom Berry's devotion for the natural world and his incredible presence in Assisi, I feel great thankfulness and appreciation. The *Spirituality and Sustainability* conferences were very special occasions that transformed our consciousness, "Mother Nature & Mother Earth" and the Universe.

REFERENCES

Berry, Thomas. 1988. *The Dream of The Earth*. San Francisco: Sierra Club.

---. 2000. *The Great Work: Moments of Grace*. New York, New York: Bell Tower.

Brizendine, Louann. 2006. *The Female Brain*. London: Transworld Publishers.

Curie, Marie. 1923. *Pierre Curie. With Autobiographical Notes*. New York: Macmillan Co.

Ferrero, Elisabeth M., & Joe Holland. 2005. *The Earth Charter: A Study Book for Action*. Miami, Florida: Redwoods Press.

Liedloff, Jean. 1977. *The Continuum Concept*. New York: Alfred A. Knopf.

Lorenz, Konrad. 1974. *Civilized Man's Eigth Deadly Sins*. UK: Egmont Books.

McCraty, Rollin and Glen Rein. 1993. "Modulation of DNA by coherent heart frequencies." *Proceedings of the third Annual Conference of the International Society for the Study of Subtle Energy and Energy Medicine*, Monterey, California, 58-62.

McCraty, Rollin, Mike Atkinson, William Tiller, Glen Rein, and Alan D. Watkins. 1995. "The Effects of Emotions on Short-Term Power Spectrum Analysis of Heart Rate Variability." *The American Journal of Cardiology.* Vol. 76. No. 14. 1089-1093.

Servan-Schreiber, David. 2003. *Guerir le stress, l`anxiete' et la depression sans medicaments ni psychoanalyse.* Paris: Editions.

Robert Laffont Servan-Schreiber, David. 2004. *Neue Medizin der Emotionen* (New Medicine of Emotions), Munich: Antje Kunstmann GmbH.

Spitzer, Manfred. 2012. *Symposium ADD, Current Perceptions of Neuroscience: How do Children Learn?* Düsseldorf-Germany. http://www.youtube.com/watch?v=vujELzwcdpQ,quoted 1:27h.

Tucker, Mary Evelyn. 2012. *Biography of Thomas Berry.* http://www.thomasberry.org/Biography/tucker-bio.html

World Health Organization (WHO), "Global Health Observatory (GHO)." Last modified 2014. http://www.who.int/gho/urban_health/situation_trends/urban_population_growth_text/en/

PART VI

A NEW GLOBAL ETHIC: THE EARTH CHARTER

Moral and ethical implications of shifting from an anthropocentric to an eco/biocentric paradigm as we work towards creating legally-binding policies to care and protect Earth and all Beings. The Earth Charter is an important document proposing a new way of thinking, living and being as a paradigm based on a sustainable ecological vision of global ethics for all beings, institutions, governments and nations on Earth.

29

THE EARTH CHARTER:
AN ETHICAL FRAMEWORK OF
SPIRITUALITY AND SUSTAINABILITY

RICHARD CLUGSTON

> *Centers for transformative education using the Earth Charter adopt the teaching and learning approaches UNESCO defines as essential for ESD. These are interdisciplinary, holistic, and values-driven. They emphasize critical thinking and problem solving, multi-method, participatory decision making and local relevance. This essay explores the work of various educational centers utilizing the Earth Charter as a framework for strong sustainability, as an organizer of curriculum and as a guide to methods of teaching and learning.*

The annual *Spirituality and Sustainability* conferences provided a rich opportunity to gather for the drafting and launch of the Earth Charter. Drawing on the ecological vision of Thomas Berry, the creation spirituality of St. Francis, the sustainable practices of Umbria, we gave input into an integrated global ethic to guide sustainable development grounded in common spiritual values. This chapter describes the Earth Charter, its approach to spirituality and sustainability and its contribution to sustainable development policy.

The Earth Charter, as a document and the focus of a social movement, is making a catalytic contribution accelerating our transition to sustainable ways of living. Its integrated ethical vision increasingly serves as an inspiration as well as a "standard by which the conduct of all individuals, organizations, businesses, governments and transnational institutions are to be guided and assessed" (Earth Charter 2000, Preamble).

The Earth Charter guides us toward a deeper and fuller vision of what sustainability really requires. Its 16 main principles and 61 supporting principles provide a framework for sustainable development, or "good globalization," developed through a broadly inclusive and participatory consultation process.

The development of an Earth Charter originated in the call of the World Commission on Environment and Development in 1987 for the creation of "a universal declaration" that would "consolidate and extend relevant legal principles" creating "new norms needed to maintain livelihoods and life on our shared planet" and "to guide state behavior in the transition to sustainable development." (World Commission on Environment and Development 1987) Drafting an Earth Charter was part of the process leading to the Earth Summit in Rio de Janeiro in 1992, but the time for such a declaration was not right. The Rio Declaration expressed the common agreement on environment and development at the time. However, many felt a deeper vision of sustainable development was needed.

In 1994, Maurice Strong (Secretary-General of the Rio Summit) and Mikhail Gorbachev, working through organizations they each founded (Earth Council and Green Cross International respectively), launched an initiative (with the support from the Dutch Government) to develop an Earth Charter as a civil society initiative. From 1994 to 2000 the drafting and consultation process drew on hundreds of international documents and a worldwide participatory consultation process involving thousands of individuals and hundreds of organizations from all regions of the world, different cultures and diverse sectors of society.

The Earth Charter was approved by the earth Charter Commission at UNESCO in Paris in 2000. The Chair of the Drafting Committee, Steven Rockefeller, states,

> The Earth Charter is centrally concerned with the transition to sustainable ways of living and sustainable human development. The four major themes of the Earth Charter are expressed in its four parts: Part I, Respect and Care for the Community of Life; Part II, Ecological Integrity; Part III, Social and Economic Justice; and Part IV, Democracy, Nonviolence, and Peace. The Earth Charter vision reflects the conviction that caring for people and caring for Earth are two interrelated dimensions of one great task. It supports the view that economic institutions and activities should promote equitable human development and should value and protect Earth's ecological systems and the many services they provide. The Earth Charter is both a people-centered and ecosystem-centered document. Recognizing that our environmental, economic, social, political, and spiritual challenges are interdependent, the Earth Charter provides an integrated framework for thinking about and addressing these issues. The result is a fresh, broad conception of what constitutes a sustainable society and sustainable development. (Earth Charter International Website: History of the Earth Charter, n.d. pp. 1 and 2)

The Earth Charter affirms the three pillars of sustainable development -- social, environmental and economic well-being as well as commitment to future generations. But it articulates and refines what these pillars mean and shows their inextricable interconnections. It deepens the triple bottom line, strengthening the importance of people and planet. It also replaces our narrow and short-term anthropocentrism with a framework which draw us to "respect and care for the community of life." The Earth Charter states, "we must realize that when basic needs have been met, human development is primarily about being more, not having more" (Earth Charter 2000, Preamble).

To make development truly sustainable, our economic, scientific and technological accomplishments should assist the processes of individual psychological and spiritual development. We must reorient our economic bottom line to support this full human development in a flourishing Earth community. Strong sustainability is going beyond Eco efficiency and green growth to engage in the deep cultural shift that awakens our "Eco spiritual" selves and guides us to live in ways that all can live.

Strong sustainability requires a paradigm shift to an ecological/evolutionary orientation to life, and a restructuring of institutions accordingly (particularly economics). Many have been pointing to the need for a new worldview that moves us out of the mechanistic reductionism, anthropocentrism, utilitarianism of modernity, toward post secular societies. According to Peter Brown,

> *An overarching paradigm in this new and emerging understanding is an evolutionary and complex systems theory worldview (ECSWV) -- greatly enriched by developments in thermodynamics, genetics, systems theory, physics etc., especially since WWII. In this framework biological evolution is a special case which occurs within the context of an evolutionary universe ... The most fundamental truth in environmental science is that everything is connected to everything else, or that all activities in biological reality, including human activities, are embedded in, and interactive with the whole of the ecosphere.* (Brown, et al. 11)

The Earth Charter is an articulation of values and principles that recognize this ecological and evolutionary context. According to Klaus Bosselman, this document, *provides a strong definition of sustainable development, recognizing the three standard pillars [social, environmental and economic] but organizing them in a particular way. 'Environment' is not merely the resource base for human consumption, not just one of the three factors to be considered. Rather, it incorporates the greater community of life including human beings and the life-support systems on which we all depend. This shift to a broader life-centered perspective marks one key difference between 'weak' and 'strong' sustainability. Furthermore, the social dimension -- articulated in the Earth Charter in terms of principles for economic and social justice, democracy, non-violence and peace -- represents a set of pre-requisites and goals for sustainable development rather than negotiable or merely optional considerations.* (Bosselman and Engel 2010, 56)

The shift to a truly sustainable world will need to be informed and guided by frameworks like Brown's ECSWV, Earth Charter values and principles, the Great Transition scenario, and many other calls for new worldviews and for policy reform, and institutional and lifestyle changes, so that all can live well without undermining the life support systems of Earth.

There is a consensus today that there are three distinct but interrelated dimensions of sustainable development, namely, the social, economic and environmental. They are often described as the three pillars of sustainable development. This understanding is sound as far as it goes, but it does not go far enough or deep enough ... there is a fourth pillar -- the global ethical and spiritual consciousness that is awakening in civil society around the world and that finds expression in the Earth Charter. This global ethical consciousness is in truth the first pillar of a sustainable way of life, because it involves the internalization of the values of sustainable human development and provides the inspiration and motivation to act as well as essential guidance regarding the path to genuine sustainability. The lack of progress in the transition to sustainable development is often attributed to a lack of political will. What is not generally acknowledged is that the lack of political will reflects a lack of ethical vision and moral courage among our leaders and to some degree among most of us -- we, the people. The Earth Charter recognizes the ethical and spiritual as well as the environmental, social, and economic dimensions of the sustainable development challenge. (Rockefeller 2010, 2)

Ruud Lubbers, an Earth Charter commissioner, and former Prime Minister of The Netherlands, point to the universal spiritual values recognized in the Earth Charter. They are,

reverence for the mystery of being, gratitude for the gift of life, reverence for life, compassion, love, hope, humility, peace, appreciation of beauty, 'being more not having more' and the joyful celebration of life. Spirituality can blossom in a world in which people, planet and profits balance the importance of the market economy with corporate social responsibility, and where the Earth Charter complements the Universal Declaration of Human Rights. We might even begin to speak about the four P's: People, Planet, Profit and 'Pneuma.' (Lubbers, et al. 2008, 35).

The fundamental task of the Earth Charter process is to shape an ethical framework and identify those basic policy commitments necessary to ensure a viable future for the community of life on Earth. The impetus for this task is the recognition that dominant development paradigms and their associated economic and social structures are not bringing us down the path to justice and sustainability. Twenty-three years after the Rio Earth Summit the news is not good. Trends show accelerating increases in inequity, climate disruption, species loss, and environmental deterioration.

The Earth Charter Initiative 2000-2015

In the fifteen years since the Earth Charter was completed, Earth Charter International has focused on having the governments represented at the United Nations acknowledge the contribution of the Earth Charter and to translate its principles into action. Major efforts involved working with the Commission on Sustainable Development, The World Summit on Sustainable Development (2002), and with UN agencies (e.g., UNESCO, UNEP, UNDP) to endorse the Earth Charter and adopt policies consistent with its principles. UNESCO (and IUCN) did recognize the Earth Charter and some language in the Johannesburg Declaration was drawn from the Earth Charter.

However, until the preparatory process (2011-2012) for the United Nations Conference on Sustainable Development (Rio+20), governments and many NGOs were incapable or unwilling to recognize the need for fundamental, transformative change and to acknowledge the interconnectedness of our global challenges and the need to adopt a new development agenda with an integrated triple bottom line of sustainability at its center.

In preparation for Rio+20 Earth Charter International engaged the Earth Charter network in framing recommendations for the outcome document based on the Earth Charter principles. These recommendations are described in Appendix I. Three of the critical recommendations were to:

1. Create a green economy based on strong sustainability and adopt alternative economic indicators to GDP that include social well-being and ecological integrity.

2. Ensure that proposals for a new institutional framework for sustainable development, and related global governance reforms, include a mandate of trusteeship for global common goods on behalf of all peoples, the greater community of life, and future generations.

3. Ensure that all have access to quality education for sustainable ways of living. Clugston, R., et al, (2011) "Earth Charter International Recommendations for the Zero Draft of the UNCSD "Rio+20 Outcome Document."

While Rio+20 did not adopt these recommendations, it did solidify the recognition that "transformative change is needed" and "business as usual is not an option" and set up a plan for future work to establish the policy framework and governance structures to realize such change. This is epitomized by the following quote from the Earth Negotiations Bulletin (June 25, 2012), in its analysis of the 2012 United Nations Conference on Sustainable Development (Rio+20).

The Elders of the process and members of the Secretary-General's High Level Panel on Global Sustainability -- like prophets of old standing at the threshold between the old world and the new -- issued profound calls for a "great transformation" and a "new narrative" for the age of the Anthropocene. As the Nobel Laureates, scientific leaders and others reminded those in RioCentro, this is the era where humankind has become the dominant driver of geological change on earth, forcing a recognition that all activity must now be judged against its contribution to the creation of a civilization that can flourish within the "safe operating space for humanity" defined by social and ecological boundaries. This will be an era that some believe demands an unprecedented turn in our approaches to all three dimensions of sustainable development -- viewed not in isolation but as a "triple helix." Discussions on the green economy were also a pale reflection of current global research on a new political economy of sustainable development that would place new economics at the heart of macroeconomic decision making at this time when fresh thinking is required to respond to the systemic crises around traditional models of growth. (ENB, 20-23)

A major outcome of Rio+20 was the commitment by governments to develop and adopt a Post-2015 UN development agenda (in

September 2015) including new, universal sustainable development goals (SDGs) that would incorporate the unfinished business of the MDGs into a broader framework. SDGs are to be the guides, the dashboard for this transformative change. They are to be action-oriented goals, which are easy to communicate, while being universal and comprehensive. In July 2014, the Open Working Group completed its 13 sessions and submitted to the GA the Zero Draft of the SDGs. Since then a variety of UN offices have been analyzing these 17 goals and 169 targets and establishing a process for finalizing the SDGs by next September when the GA is to adopt the Post 2015 UN Development Agenda. On Jan 19-21, 2015, there was an intergovernmental meeting for reviewing the various inputs into the Zero Draft and finalizing the 2015 plans. The governmental representatives affirmed the need for transformative change guided by a new framework for development that would eliminate poverty, promote the breadth of human rights, and ensure equitable and inclusive economic growth-all within planetary boundaries (UN Sustainable Development Goals Report, 2014).

An Earth Charter Assessment of the SDGs

In a sense the Earth Charter was ahead of its time. The various actors involved in the UN deliberations on sustainable development were not ready to recognize the need for a deep shift in fundamental assumptions about the nature and purpose of development, nor see the interconnectedness of the economic, social and environmental challenges we face, and to create new goals and indicators for development grounded in a new narrative and a new bottom line that integrates these three dimensions and consideration for future generations. Now the time is ripe.

For the past two years, Earth Charter International has been co-convening a diversity of religious, spiritual and value-based organizations to shape input into the Post 2015 UN Development Agenda. One outcome of this process is a book titled, *Ethics, Spiritual Values, and the New UN Development Agenda.* The book emphasizes the need for transformative change and chapter authors describe their ethical and spiritual perspectives and use them to evaluate and strengthen the current proposals for sustainable development goals. Developing the book is an agenda setting and organizing tool to help shape goals for transformative change and to build a coalition and constituency to demand the adoption and implementation of these goals. The book is being edited by Mirian Vilela, the Executive Director of Earth Charter International and by Rick Clugston (the author of this essay). In it EC-Assess is used to evaluate the SDGs. Developed by Earth Charter International EC-Assess is an assessment tool for evaluating the sustainability of organizations, projects, initiatives and individuals. It is an ethical assessment tool that can be used by individuals or groups who want to evaluate and improve both their level of declared commitment and their level of performance in pursuit of a more just, sustainable, and peaceful world. EC-Assess is based on the ethical framework of the Earth Charter, and uses a simple worksheet based on the Earth Charter's 53 Supporting Principles in Parts II, III and IV. Evaluators first identify which Supporting Principles are relevant to the subject of the assessment. They then evaluate the extent to which each Supporting Principle is espoused publicly and the extent to which actual planning and performance reflect the implementation of that Supporting Principle in practice. The results allow the evaluator to identify areas where either the declared embrace of a Supporting Principle is strong or weak and where the actual practice of a specific Supporting Principle is strong or weak. By utilizing EC-Assess as a normative, systemic, and customizable assessment, individuals and organizations can stimulate discussion and inspire action to change lifestyles, goals, and operations to better reflect their espoused values. The results highlight those areas where declared commitment to a principle, and the practices of that initiative or organization, are not in harmony with one another. This enables the evaluator to identify priorities for improvement (Earth Charter International Secretariat 2008, EC-Assess booklet).

At the time of this essay's completion, the EC-Assess is not finished, nor is the book. However, ECI and its partners have done some preliminary analyses of the SDGs, and the following are the general findings. First, the Zero Draft of SDGs by the an UN intergovernmental working group is a major step forward in recognizing our global challenges, and coming up with a comprehensive, interconnected agenda for providing opportunities and building capacities, for full human development for all in a flourishing ecological system. Central to the document is providing social protection floors that meet the basic needs of all without crossing planetary boundaries.

The integrated ethical lens of the Earth Charter approaches the SDGs from a very different vantage point, grounding development in a different conception of the good life than economic growth and consumerism. While supportive of many of the OWG priorities, the Earth Charter framework would shift their focus away from a too narrow and overly materialistic emphasis on increasing income, education for success in the current labor market, high tech health care, etc. Instead the Earth Charter affirms a more Eco-centric, even Eco-spiritual, approach to the SDGs, which emphasizes the following four priorities:

1. Enabling sustainable livelihoods for all. Eradicating absolute poverty is not primarily about increasing income, i.e., access to money to buy goods and services. It is primarily about providing rich social and ecological environments in which individuals and communities can thrive, which requires respecting human rights, preserving cultural and ecological diversity and accepting common, but differentiated, responsibilities. Eradicating poverty requires eradicating greed, corruption, violence and oppression, in

part by changing policies and institutional structures that promote intolerance and short term gain for the few. We all must choose to live in ways that all can live, recognizing, as the Earth Charter states, that after basic needs are met, human development is about being more, not having more. As we set floors for how much is too little, we need also to explore ceilings on how much is too much.

2. Providing decent employment, social security, and health care for all. Here too it is essential that we do not define good jobs, social security, and adequate health care as primarily the result of having more money available for each individual to spend. Finding one's vocation, satisfying work, may mean a simple life of service. Social security is primarily social-being embedded in a caring community. Effective health care should help us to embrace necessary suffering and prepare us for the labor of conscious dying, as well as reducing disease, untimely death, and unnecessary suffering. In developed countries a large percentage of health care services (and costs) are used in the last years of life. High tech, drug and surgery based interventions are used to prolong life for a short and often miserable time. Drugs are prescribed (or taken) to eliminate every discomfort. The model we are pursuing is much lower tech, palliative and includes a quite different approach to death and suffering.

3. Adopting a new bottom line for economic development which provides necessary goods and services, builds opportunities and capacities, within planetary boundaries. The Earth Charter affirms the need to reorient the dominant global development paradigm toward an economics of full human development in a flourishing Earth community. Our failure to place our economic policies in the broader context of the environment and humanity's social and spiritual existence has led to a corrosive materialism in the world's more economically advantaged region and has

exacerbated conditions and perceptions of deprivation among the masses of the world's peoples. It has also accelerated the destruction of many species and the ecological systems essential for our well-being. Drawing together the variety of alternative frameworks and indicators for genuine progress, happiness, human development, life satisfaction, personal and planetary wellbeing into a viable alternative to GNP is a bottom line task for transformative change.

4. Providing quality education for sustainable development for all. Earth Charter education for sustainable development is the major focus of ECI. Ironically, it is the most educated who have created and are benefitting most from unsustainable practices. Our formal and informal education institutions all too often promote intolerant social projects, or the excessive pursuit of individual consumption and gratification. We want access for all to quality education, but a specific kind of education for sustainable development, one that enhances our capacities and motivation to:

   a. Engage deeply and effectively in contemplative and transformative practices that awaken and orient us toward a deeper self or source and to our vocations.

   b. Experience our interconnectedness and interdependence with the whole living world embracing diverse cultures of people and animals, agriculture and wilderness, the cycles of life and the seasons, as well as the unfolding cosmos.

   c. Feel and act from compassionate concern for others, doing no harm, reaching out to assist all beings.

   d. Live in ways that all can live, consuming no more than one's fair share of Earth's bounty-choosing products and services (e.g., food, energy, transportation, housing) that are ecologically sound, socially just and economically viable (e.g., local, fair trade, organic, carbon and pollution neutral, humane).

e. Ensure that our decision making and conflict resolution processes are open, enabling all to participate and clarify their preferences and grievances. Our process capacities -- to be humble, honest and respectful; to not blame and to forgive; and to compromise for the good of all -- are foundational for arriving at structures and solutions that further everyone's development.

f. Act to shift policies to support a just and sustainable future by voting, lobbying, and participating in political decision making at all levels to promote policies to better care for future generations and the whole community of life, e.g., creating better measures of genuine progress than GDP, internalizing social and environmental costs in pricing goods and services, eliminating perverse subsidies, and creating ethical assessment and trusteeship structures at all governmental levels.

Conclusion
Common Ground for Emerging Earth Ethics

The main goal of the Earth Charter, with the core theme of eight years of the Spirituality and Sustainability conferences in Italy, was to bring into the ethical center the recognition that existence is a living community of diverse subjects who deserve our respect and care.

Sustainable development must be grounded in an appreciation of the beauty, integrity, and interconnectedness of natural systems and the recognition of an inherent value, even a subjective interiority, in each living being. Animals, plants, rivers, stars -- all beings and natural systems are enlivened by a mysterious presence. All partake, in different ways, of this life and feeling. Evolution and development are processes which must be understood in their psychic and spiritual as well as material/physical dimensions.

Most importantly, diversity is lifted up as a central value. Protecting the diversity of life forms, cultures and languages, as well as rights and opportunities for each individual is fundamental. When we lose these different expressions of life, we lose sources of essential knowledge, wisdom, and technologies, we also lose the richness of our souls, for at some deep level our ecological and ethical selves require the enhancement of diversity against both the violence of exploitation and the efficiency of monoculture.

Our world is a community of subjects, not a collection of objects. It is filled with a rich diversity of life, cultures, and knowledge sustained by the struggles of countless generations. Our prevailing ethos is based on the desire for unlimited growth, fear of the other, and the urge to dominate and exploit. Willingly or not, we are agents of this violence and injustice. All of this is rooted in our inability to recognize our common humanity and role as a co-evolving species. We are called to creative partnerships with one another and with the evolutionary process. Despite the fact that many societies are filled with coercive violence and restrictions of basic freedoms, a global ethical consensus is emerging on human rights in general, with particular emphasis on the needs and rights of women and indigenous peoples. Also, nonhuman nature deserves moral standing.

We must also accept a world of material limits. A correlate of extending rights to others is recognizing the limits of human technological and intellectual capacities. This new world view demands that we humans accept a set of restraints on our exploitation of the natural world, based on respect for the integrity of the life community, as well as healthy skepticism about human ability to control and manage extraordinarily complex natural systems benignly. Human humility is essential.

It is essential to create a new "bottom line" for economics and development that differentiates between constructive and destructive economic activities. The globalized market focuses on increasing financial transactions through fostering material production and consumption. All religions and philosophies recognize qualitative ends beyond enhancing quantitative, material wellbeing -- these should also be our key measures of progress and development. The non-monetized human exchanges in the social economy, the contributions of the natural economy and the fundamental spiritual ends of human life all need to be factored into our calculations of the costs and benefits of economic development.

APPENDIX

Excerpts from
"Earth Charter International Recommendations for the Zero Draft of the UNCSD "Rio+20 Outcome Document

Recalling the recommendation by the 1987 report of the World Commission on Environment and Development (the Brundtland Commission report) for creation of a "Universal Declaration on Environmental Protection and Sustainable Development" in the form of a "new charter" with principles to guide nations in the transition to sustainable development, and the promotion of values that encourage consumption standards to which all can aspire within Earth's carrying capacity. Recognizing that the adoption of such an ethical Charter was a goal of the preparatory process for the 1992 Rio Earth Summit and that, since then, too little progress has been made in implementing governments' commitments to sustainable development. Realizing that the need for a stronger global ethical framework to guide sustainable development has only increased.

Mindful that the Earth Charter was drafted and launched by a global civil society initiative under the leadership of the Earth Charter Commission, and that the Earth Charter has been endorsed and recognized by thousands of organizations including UNESCO and the IUCN.

We recommend that the outcome document:

1. Express responsibility to future generations by implementing the precautionary principle and establishing Ombudspersons for Future Generations at global, national and local levels.

1. Create a green economy based on strong sustainability and adopt alternative economic indicators to GDP that include social well-being and ecological integrity.

2. Acknowledge the fundamental importance of shared ethical and spiritual values in making the transition to a sustainable way of life.

3. Adopt a sustainable development goal focused on sustainable production and consumption.

4. Ensure that proposals for a new institutional framework for sustainable development, and related global governance reforms, include a mandate of trusteeship for global common goods on behalf of all peoples, the greater community of life, and future generations.

5. Ensure that all have access to quality education for sustainable ways of living.

6. Make Climate Justice a guiding principle in efforts to address global climate change, ensuring that the benefits and burdens associated with climate change are distributed equitably, with special concern for the rights of the poor, indigenous peoples, and other vulnerable peoples.

7. Provide supportive mechanisms for a Just Transition – ensuring the right to sustainable Development.

(Clugston et al. 2011)

REFERENCES

Bosselmann K. and Engel R. Eds. 2010. *The Earth Charter: a Framework for Global Governance*. Amsterdam: Kit Publishers.

Clugston, R., R. Lubbers, B. Mackey, S. Rockefeller, A. Roerrink, and M. Vilela. 2011. "Earth Charter International Recommendations for the Zero Draft of the UNCSD "Rio+20 Outcome Document." UNCSD Website, Compilation Document, November 1, 2011, available at http//www.uncsd2012org/rio+20/index.php?

Earth Charter Commission . 2000. *The Earth Charter*. San Jose, Costa Rica. Earth Charter International available on line at http://www.earthcharter.org

Earth Charter History, N.D, http://www.earthcharterinaction.org/download/about_the_Initiative_history_2t.pdf

Earth Charter International Secretariat .2008. "EC-Assess: The Earth Charter ethics-based assessment tool. San Jose, Costa Rica, www.earthcharterinaction.org/invent/images/uploads/EC-Assess.pdf. Earth Negotiations Bulletin . 2012. June 25, pp.20-23.

Lubbers, R., W. van Genugten, T. Lambooy, and Marie-Ève Rancourt . 2008. *Inspiration for Global Governance*. Amsterdam: Kluwer Academic Publishers.

Rockefeller, S. 2010. "Challenges and Opportunities Facing the Earth Charter Initiative." Unpublished Keynote Address at "An Ethical Framework for a Sustainable World," 1-3 November 2010, Ahmedabad, India.

UN Sustainable Development Goals Report, 2014. https://sustainabledevelopment.un.org/sdgsproposal

World Commission on Environment and Development . 1987. *Our Common Future*. Oxford: Oxford University Press.

THE EARTH CHARTER
AS A NEW GLOBAL ETHIC[1]

ELISABETH M. FERRERO & JOE HOLLAND

During the many Spirituality and Sustainability Assisi conferences in which Tom Berry participated, the Earth Charter was a central focus of attention, and Tom was a great supporter of the Earth Charter. Therefore, in honor of Tom's relationship with the Earth Charter, this essay is included here.

Over the last three hundred years, ethics has tended to become the exclusive domain of religion, while the sciences, economics, law, and technology have dealt with the practical side of the 'business of living.' Furthermore, ethics has been referred almost exclusively to human beings. By contrast, the Earth Charter is proposing fundamental rights applicable to *all* forms of life, and is also arguing that this broader sense of ethics, rooted in an ecological vision, is indispensable for a sustainable human future. As Willis Guerra has stated, the Earth Charter needs to be understood as "a continuation to the declaration of human rights. We can conceive it as the next step in the history of human rights" (Guerra 1999, 2).

---

[1] This essay was originally published in Elisabeth M. Ferrero M. and Joe Holland, *The Earth Charter: A Study Book of Reflection for Action*. (Miami, FL: Redwoods Press, 2005).

The need for a Global Ethic & Global Spirituality

There is a great urgency for the Earth Charter, especially in light of the multiplicity and escalation of environmental, social, and spiritual problems that we confront today in our lives. This visionary document calls us to action, as a human family, to work together to solve the full range of problems before us all – with no longer a separation between faith and reason, spirit and matter. This is a moment of real opportunity that carries within it the transformative power of those events that can change the course of history and life on Earth.

One of the major tasks and responsibilities of our times is centered on halting the immeasurable harm caused by the faulty perception of the relationship of the human to the natural world. We need to speak of the essential Earth-human relationship, and to understand what exactly this relation means in order to determine what humans' responsibilities are.

The sacred nature of all creation has deep theological roots in all religions. For example, Saint Thomas Aquinas clearly states in his *Summa Theologiae* that, because the Divine could not express itself in one single being, it created the great multiplicity of beings so that the perfection lacking in one could be supplied by the others (Aquinas 1917).

The differentiation of all species -- human and non-human, the rivers and the stars -- expresses the Divine both within the interior of human consciousness and across the order of the universe. This divinely ordered integration of exterior and interior, personal and cosmic, is the inner law mentioned by Saint Paul in his Epistle to the Romans (Jerusalem Bible 1966).

The natural world is not simply a background for the human or a context into which humans are inserted. Humans are absolutely dependent upon the rest of creation not only for survival, but also for spiritual growth and identity. By experiencing nature the human experiences the divine as well. The Bible speaks again and again of the goodness and beauty of creation.

Moreover, all major religions seem to have several points of agreement in environmental ethics.

- The natural world has value in itself and does not exist solely to serve human needs.
- Non-human living beings are morally significant, in the eyes of God and/or in the cosmic order.
- Greed and destructiveness are condemned.
- Humans and non-human beings are morally significant, in the eyes of God or the cosmic order.
- Moral norms such as justice, compassion and reciprocity apply (in appropriate ways) both to human beings and to non-human beings. The well-being of humans and the well-being of non-human beings are inseparably connected.
- The dependence of human life on the natural world can and should be acknowledged in rituals and other expressions of appreciation and gratitude (Bassett and Bedrich 1999).

Although each part of creation exists for itself, for its own growth and development, primarily and above all, each part exists to bring life to a single integral community, to creation itself. The human cannot function independently from the rest of the universe; humans cannot exploit the natural world for their own good, because by seeking one's own well being at the expense of the wider community of life we diminish our own well-being *and* the well being of all creation, of the entire universe.

Bedrich Moldan speaks of the human dominance on the natural world as, *our magnificent contemporary feast without a price. The problem is that this price is not paid by we who enjoy the feast. It is paid by somebody else. It is paid by nature, by the global geosphere that provides us with all the essential services we need for our rich banquet.* (Bassett and Bedrich 1999, 1)

This domination on Earth is aggravated by the fact that the carrying capacity of the planet is limited. Therefore, a utilitarian approach (the dominant ethos guiding modern Western culture) to the environment of the non-human world can only increase the disorder of the universe, with the resulting spiritual and social degradation of humankind as well (Berry 1988, 33-35). Greed, selfishness, instant gratification, and over-consumer-ism (only to mention some of the great social problems of today) have disturbed the natural balance of the universe and in the process have impoverished our souls and hearts. What is needed is a fundamental shift as a global society to adopt a transformative global ethic.

The solutions to our problems today are acceptable only if they are sustainable in every way. A sustainable society satisfies its needs without diminishing the prospects for future generations. We should not work for efficiency but to preserve the whole network of relationships of the humans to the non-human world. The Earth Charter presents us with a blueprint to meet the challenges before us. We must pledge a strong commitment to its principles in our attitudes, our values, and in the way we live. Institutions and governments must shift drastically from their myopic human-centered values and services to embrace the universe.

As Robert Muller has expressed it so well, "we are entering a thrilling, transcending, new global, cosmic phase of evolution in the line indicated by Teilhard de Chardin, the anthropologist, if the human species understands its suddenly momentous, incredibly important evolutionary role and responsibility. Existing institutions must be reformed and/or created to perform this role" (Muller 1999, 6).

Creating Sustainable Communities

The Earth Charter heralds the vision of a transformative global ethic grounded in two fundamental principles: 1) environmental conservation; and 2) sustainable development. In this ethic, the human and the non-human live systemically in a mutually enhancing relationship. Interdependence is what the Earth Charter affirms in all its principles. Steven Rockefeller says that the Earth Charter,

is not just a document about the environment. It has been constructed with the understanding that humanity's environmental, economic, and social problems are interrelated and can only be effectively addressed with integrated global solutions. (Rockefeller 1999, 2)

The need, then, is for governments, institutions, and all members of civil society to work together. This is why the Earth Charter has been constructed not as an inter-governmental document, but as a people's treaty, with a bottom-up strategy, in order for dialogues and negotiations to involve *all* the peoples of Earth working toward sustainability.

The World Commission on Environment and Development's definition of sustainable development states clearly our goals as a global society in meeting,

the needs of the present without sacrificing the ability of future generations to meet their own needs ... Economics and ecology must be completely integrated in decision-making and law-making processes not just to protect the environment, but also to protect and promote development. (World Commission on Environment and Development, 1987)

Maximo Kalaw added that in order for sustainability to become a reality we must have,

> *changes in personal behavior. In other words, how do we relate to society and how do we govern ourselves? This question has a political dimension and, at bottom, it has a very deep spiritual dimension . . . (and how these values) reflect in terms of people's lives, in terms of their livelihood, in terms of the organizations they join, in terms of how they communicate, and in terms of the political advocacy they undertake for the public interest.* (Kalaw 1997, 28)

The issue of social justice is central to sustainability. The Earth Charter reiterates with its many "oughts" and moral imperatives the deeply felt sense of obligation that we all share towards the natural world <u>and</u> in providing an adequate quality of life for all humans. In the process of becoming sustainable, we must foster and pledge ourselves to service and specifically to the creation of effective outreach resources to assist especially the wider community of the poor, indigenous peoples, women and youth.

Is sustainability still possible when so many giant multinational corporations seem to dominate many aspects of our lives in a way that is unaccountable to the natural world? Thomas Berry strongly speaks against any giant corporations whose main goal is only,

> *to exploit the planet, with reference only to its economic value. Their products are delivered to the consumer public after convincing them that an economy based on the extraction and transformation of the components of Earth, thought of simply as 'natural resources,' is making for a better and infinitely more fulfilling life than a way of life lived within the organic ever renewing systems of the planet. The corporation has become the basis of survival of the human community. We now live in a world created by the industrial way of life with a vast number of technological controls over the natural world . . . (and) when we survey the extent to which corporations control our lives, their possession of*

legal rights to the use of property throughout the planet, their control over governments, the legal profession, the universities, their thought control through the public media; and when we consider their relative isolation from any political authority or cultural norms of action, we begin to realize the dimensions of the challenge before us. (Berry 1997, 32)

If we follow Berry's analysis, we conclude that wide ranges of modern Western economic systems are no longer sustainable, and, therefore, we *must* search for new solutions to meet the challenge of our times.

Supporting Berry's challenge, Robert Muller, the founder of the United Nations University for Peace says that, "the world corporate community should be asked to answer how they would provide for a well-preserved planet and the well-being of all humanity, full employment, the renewal of natural resources, the long-term evolution of the planet and continuation of life on it, the real democracy of the consumers in a corporate power and wealth economy" (Muller 1999, 2).

As Ashok Khosla has written, in order for an economy to be sustainable, it is imperative to look at how we deal with the use of our natural resources. Six billion people cannot rely on how we deal presently with our resources throughout the world (Khosla 1999, 2). New ways to use natural resources are needed. Besides solar, wind, microhydro, and biomass alternatives to the use of energy from petroleum, creative efforts must be employed in the search of alternatives in all aspects of our lives.

In India, Khosla continues, Development Alternatives have worked with a totally different kind of construction material in the building of houses. They use mud to make beautiful buildings and have developed an entire new series of roofing materials as well (Khosla 1999). It is essential that technology be used in a way that will, *"create jobs instead of destroying them, that regenerates the environment instead of destroying it and (creates) jobs that bring meaning and dignity into the lives of people, because the technologies underlying them are basically geared to our needs and not to their own* (Khosla 1999, 2).

The Earth Charter speaks for a sustainable life for all the peoples of Earth who must feel empowered and responsible for their own lives.

Women's rights are emphasized in the Earth Charter, especially in relation to the issues of their health and economic equality. The plight of women around the globe was globally recognized at the Beijing Women's Conference in 1995. The resulting *Platform for Action* for the first time defined women's rights as human rights. Consequently women have the right to health, development, equality and peace. The Earth Charter stands firmly for gender equality because women and girls presently around the globe still need to be protected from poverty, sexual abuse and lack of self-esteem. Susan Davis sums up the repercussions of the present condition of most women over the world today by stating that "gender equality is the prerequisite for sustainable development" (Davis 1997, 44).

Soon-Young Yoon illustrates this concept with the crisis of gender apartheid in Afghanistan. In some Taliban-controlled territories, including Kabul, women were prevented from attending schools and work. However, the result was that the education of boys was impaired because 70% of all elementary school teachers were women. The same problem was encountered in hospitals where women had formerly rendered most of the services (Yoon 1999). The Earth Charter emphasizes the need to open our hearts and minds and create sustainable ways of living also for women, the poor, the indigenous people and the youth.

One of most important solutions towards sustainability is the building of local communities. The concept of a global society is not contradictory to the development of local communities. On the contrary, sustainable living is only possible by promoting social and economic systems of a particular region thereby strengthening the self-reliance and responsibility of its local people who implement and maintain their systems.

Susan Darlington says that,

The full potential of the Earth Charter lies in how it is perceived, interpreted, and acted on by the people in local areas throughout the world" and on how the Earth Charter's *"abstract principles (will be) applied to concrete situations and begin to have an effect on the world's environment and well-being.* (Darlington 1997, 50-52)

Building local communities, then, with the respect for the diversity of cultures, spirituality, geography and so forth, is one of our present tasks. No global ethic, no global community can maintain itself without affirming the vastness of the diversity of the human and non-human that comprise the globe.

The principle of diversity is fundamental in the Earth Charter and needs to be translated at the local level not only in the development of social and economic systems of livelihood, but also in affirming and celebrating the many different experiences that previous generations have transmitted to us through the arts, rituals and stories. We are told that "stories, parables, and commentaries on the precepts carry forward the wisdom of those who have come before us. Their struggles with restraint have yielded priceless insight into the realm of human nature" (Kaza 1997, 73-75).

At times, the Earth Charter has been seen as a document consisting of principles that are too abstract and therefore do not inspire and move people to change. Donald Swearer reiterates the urgent need for the Earth Charter principles to be grounded in concrete examples of particular lives, and he emphasizes "the value of stories in our search for the principles of a universal environmental ethic, for stories are more compelling than principles no matter how praiseworthy they may be" (Swearer 1997, 90). We need to carry on the wisdom of our "living elders" so that their deep humanity may encourage others by example.

The transformation to which the Earth Charter calls each of us is a kind of inner work. It is the change of mind and heart that each one of us has to bring about. In the words of Consolación Alarsas, our main task is that "our conscience must catch up to our reason, otherwise we are lost" (Alaras 1999. 2).

With this personal transformation, Robert Muller sees the necessity for all the nations of the world to unite in creating a "World Union on the pattern of the European Union – reminding oneself of the incredible progress of the fifteen nations of the European Union, which have put an end to their antagonisms and wars and have embraced a common destiny and goals." He further states that "this example is so hopeful, so powerful, so novel and inspiring that I recommend it as an outstanding guide-light for more regional communities and for the entire globe" (Muller 1999, 6).

Muller's vision embraces not only humanity but all of creation when he reiterates the proposal by Barbara Gaughen-Muller,

> *To create a United Nature, a transformed United Nations to respond to the fundamental unity of nature of which humans are part. Humans would not dominate nature but cooperate with it and learn from it. It is probably the most advanced, timely and imaginative vision of the total, proper functioning of planet Earth.* (Muller 1999, 3-6).

We are truly at the dawn of a new era with tremendous possibilities. The Earth Charter calls each one of us to transformation and in the process save humankind and this wonderful planet Earth.

Thomas Berry speaks of our current crises as fundamentally spiritual in nature (Berry 1999, 61). Our sensitivities need to recognize fully the sacred dimension of Earth. Without the awareness that all forms of life are sacred in themselves, without experiencing this, all our clean-up efforts, all changes in our lifestyles are just another form of work; they do not transform us and are not healing us. We have to change the perception of who we are, and our role *vis a` vis* the rest of creation. We have to accept creation as "the communion of subjects (and) not a collection of objects" (Berry 1999, 103). Each part of creation is necessary and indispensable. If we diminish any part of this communion, we diminish our sense of the sacred.

Moreover, this transformation requires also that we experience the sense of the sacred in the history's unfolding of ideas, the arts, poetry and literature. We also have to recapture the sacred dimension by experiencing the planet and the history of the universe. In all our institutions we must judge what inhibits or fosters the mutually enhancing relationship that humans have with the rest of Earth.

Berry reminds us that there is not an isolated human community, but one earth community (Berry 1993). We need to gather hope and strength in order to endure the pains in the days to come that such transformation will bring about.

What can each of us really do? How and where do we start? Above all, we must bring about in our lives some kind of "voluntary simplicity" that supports ecological sustainability, social justice, and human peace (Elgin 1993). This requires a great deal of inner work, as well as outer work. We need to ask ourselves: How much do we need for our well-being? We must be gentle and patient with ourselves and with others, since this is a long and complex process. Yet we also need constantly to remind ourselves that some things are not negotiable.

REFERENCES

Alaras, Consolacion R. 1999. "The Absolute, Urgent Need for Proper Earth Government." *Global Ethics, Sustainable Development and the Earth Charter*. An on-line Conference. www.earthcharter.org/files/resources/bulletin20 June201999.doc

Aquinas, Thomas. 1917. *Summa Theologiae*. New York, NY: Benzinger Brothers Printers.

Berry, Thomas. 1988. *The Dream of the Earth*. San Francisco: CA: Sierra Club Books.

--- 1997. "The Challenge of Our Times." *Earth Ethics*, 32. Washington DC: Center for Respect of Life and Environment.

--- 1999. The *Great Work: Our Way into The Future*. New York: Bell Tower.

Darlington, Susan M. 1997. "The Earth Charter and Ecology Monks in Thailand." *Buddhist Perspectives on the Earth Charter*: 50-52. Cambridge, MA: Boston Research Center for the 21st century.

Davis, Susan. 1997. "Principle-Centered Evolution: A Feminist Enviromentalist." *Women's Views on the Earth Charter*: 44. Cambridge, MA: Boston Research Center for the 21st Century.

Elgin, See Duane. 1993. *Voluntary Simplicity: Toward a Way of Life that is Outwardly Simple, Inwardly Rich*. Revised Ed. Tempe, AZ: Dimension Books.

Ferrero, Elisabeth M., and Joe Holland. 2005. *The Earth Charter: A Study Book of Reflection for Action*. Miami, FL: Redwoods Press.

Guerra, Willis S. 1999. "Environmental Rights and the Earth Charter." Earth Forum, An on-line Conference. www.earthforum.org.

Jones, Alexander. 1966. *The Jerusalem Bible*, Garden City, N.Y.: Doubleday.

Kaza, Stephanie. 1997. "A Matter of Great Consequence." *Buddhist Perspectives on the Earth* Charter: 73-75. Cambridge, MA: Boston Research Center for the 21st Century.

Kalaw, Maximo. 1997. "Framework for the Earth Charter." *Women's Views on Earth Charter*: 28. Cambridge, MA: Boston Research Center for the 21st Century.

Khosla, Ashok. 1999. "Development Alternatives." *Global Ethics, Sustainable Development and the Earth* Charter: 2. New Delhi. An on-line Conference. www.earthforum.org.

Muller, Robert. 1999. "The Absolute, Urgent Need for Proper Earth Government." *Global Ethics, Sustainable Development and the Earth Charter*: 2-6. Earth Forum. An on-line Conference. www.earthforum.org.

Rockefeller, Steven. 1999. "An Introduction to the Text of the Earth Charter." *Global Ethics Sustainable Development and the Earth Charter*: 2. Earth Forum. An on-line Conference. www.earthforum.org.

Swearer, Donald. 1997. "'Rights' because of Intrinsic Nature or 'Responsibilities' because of Mutual Interdependence.?" *Buddhist Perspectives on the Earth Charter*: 90. Cambridge, MA: Boston Research Center for the 21st Century.

Yoon, Soon-Young. 1999. "A healthy Self, a Healthy Society, a Healthy Planet." *Global Ethics Sustainable Development and the Earth Charter*: 2. Earth Forum. An on-line Conference. www.earthforum.org.

31

TRIBAL LINK AND THE SACRED MAP

Pamela Kraft

Reflections on Father Thomas Berry and the power of indigenous wisdom in a global context

Destination Assisi

In 1996 I was invited to Assisi, Italy, to participate in the Conference on *Spirituality and Sustainability* sponsored by the Center for Respect of Life and Environment and St. Thomas University. Representing the Tribal Link Foundation, my key objective at this historic gathering in Assisi was to ensure that indigenous peoples were included in the dialogue on spirituality and sustainability. Indigenous peoples have much to contribute on these particular topics; both they and the faith movement can greatly benefit from meaningful collaboration. Discussions during this conference contributed to the drafting of the Earth Charter, an international people's declaration of fundamental values and ethical principles for building a just, sustainable, and peaceful global society. The Charter is seen by many as a vision of hope and a call to action; within its focus areas it promotes special attention to the rights of indigenous peoples. Assisi was a deeply significant encounter with the sacred for me at a personal level, as well as the first time I met Fr. Thomas Berry, and a first step for Tribal Link toward its work connecting members of the faith community to indigenous peoples.

The town of Assisi is best known as the birthplace of St. Francis of Assisi, the patron saint of animals and ecology. With the *Basilica di San Francesco* as its main attraction, along with other churches, Roman ruins, medieval streets, and sacred shrines, Assisi continues to be a major spiritual pilgrimage destination. The town sits majestically upon a hill asserting itself as a vantage point between the past and future. It was therefore only fitting that one of the most eminent cultural historians of our time, Fr. Thomas Berry, with his deep connection to St. Francis, became the bridge in design and by choice at Assisi. It is well known that Fr. Berry immersed himself not only in the wisdom of China and the East but also in the ancient wisdom of indigenous peoples. He was able to take the present into the past in order to inform the future. In his address to the Conference Fr. Berry said, "it is appropriate then for us to come here for a few days of thoughtful brooding over the decisions we must make in these terminal years of the twentieth century and the opening years of the twenty-first century; for the period of St. Francis, the opening years of the thirteenth century, was the period when our present world began to take shape" (Berry 1996).

My deepest memories of Assisi are not in words but in sensations of all being committed to the vision of a harmonious Earth. In my brief time there, I quickly came to realize that Assisi is filled with invisible doorways to other dimensions and consciousness. There is a sacred energy that lives there, and it led me to reflect on just how does a space or a place becomes designated as sacred? I now see it as the level of devotion of the soul to the higher purpose of selflessness entering another dimension. During his own life journey, Thomas Berry came to see things as indigenous elders around the world have always understood: life on our planet is connected in a delicate, intricate web. I cherish this understanding and also believe that each person's life path along this web is revealed through deep listening to follow a sacred map that is embedded deep within us. This map helps us get to the places we need to be at the physical and spiritual level.

Looking back on my own map, I see places such as the United Nations, Rio, Assisi, South Africa, and back to Rio twenty years later. These are all physical and spiritual destinations on my map, which is a knowledge map, a map to invisible doorways, and encounters with the sacred. Indigenous peoples create many of these doorways traveling back and forth between worlds for generations. Likewise, St. Francis was an ecologist and a kindred spirit to indigenous peoples. He created doorways in Assisi through his devotion to God and all of nature. It is important to view Assisi within this context in order to see that this special place played a part in promoting the recognition of the rights of indigenous peoples in a global context. Assisi is a part of my journey encountering the power of the sacred and indigenous wisdom, but not the starting point, so I will continue to tell this tale from where it began.

The Journey Begins

The 1990s held special spiritual significance for many of the indigenous peoples from the Americas. In the Andes Mountains of South America there are ancestral prophecies that say that starting about 1490 a time of extreme sorrow for the "people of the land" would begin. During the next age, however, which begins 500 years later (the 1990s), there would be a time of coming together, of partnership and union, when the Eagle of the North will fly with the Condor of the South and their combined efforts will bring healing to this Earth. Indigenous peoples throughout the Americas have similar prophecies about a time of sorrow and imbalance followed by a time of healing and re-balancing.

In 1991, I was at the United Nations for the first time attending a preparatory meeting for the U.N. Conference on Environment and Development (UNCED). Inside the building, there in the hall, were representatives of indigenous peoples from the Amazon. I was able to ask, through a translator, "What can I do to help?" They said, "You can document our conference in Brazil." I said, "Yes." I say yes to all that touches me deeply. It is my personal navigating system, my compass for my sacred map. I immediately began gathering a team of videographers, photographers and journalists.

In June 1992, off to Brazil we went to document the convergence of seven hundred tribal leaders gathered in response to the United Nations Conference on Environment and Development (UNCED). Also known as the Earth Summit, this global conference brought together about forty thousand people including policy makers, diplomats, scientists, media, and representatives of non-governmental organizations (NGOs) from 179 countries and indigenous peoples from around the globe. Their goal was to formally recognize and address the impact that human socio-economic activities have on the environment.

Prior to the Earth Summit, indigenous peoples gathered outside of Rio at their own conference, the *World Conference of Indigenous Peoples on Territories, Environment and Development*, also known as the *Kari Oca Conference*. It was at this gathering that the indigenous peoples' representatives expressed their desire to fully participate in the UN global environmental conference at every level, and expressed a desire to bring the healing powers of their traditions and ceremonies to bear on the crises of the Earth, to speak in their own voices, and to communicate for themselves. Marcos Terena, an indigenous leader from Brazil and founder of the *Union of Indigenous Nations (UNIND)*, was chosen to present the Kari Oca Declaration to the Earth Summit. He began by saying, "we, the Indigenous Peoples, walk to the future in the footprints of our ancestors. From the smallest to the largest living being, from the four directions, from the air, the land and the mountains. The creator has placed us. The Indigenous peoples upon our Mother the earth" (Terena 1992).

The United Nations

I kept my promise to be an ally of indigenous peoples and do my part to be of assistance to them from that point forward. Coming back from Rio transformed, yet alone, I began to seek out others in the circle of which I had just become a part. The United Nations was a destination on my map. Having funded the Tribal Link Foundation, I placed significant focus on the UN system and to this day continue to help bridge indigenous communities and this international community. As my sacred map continues to unfold, I have had the great honor to meet and work with many other indigenous leaders at the United Nations.

Chief Arvol Looking Horse, the Nineteenth Generation Keeper of the Sacred White Buffalo Calf Pipe of the Lakota, Dakota and Nakota Sioux Nations, for example, is from a tradition which has a deep belief system that, at its core, is infused with the idea that we are responsible for our actions and interactions with every element of our surroundings. Nothing, and no one, is separate from nature. It remains one of my greatest honors to have assisted in organizing several opportunities for Chief Looking Horse to conduct sacred pipe ceremonies for peace at United Nations Headquarters. He and others continue to speak out at the United Nations and international forums, and sharing the portent of their prophecies that say the time has come to act, to protect and to heal the earth.

I also had the great opportunity to escort a Hopi Elder, Thomas Banyacya, into the UN, which the Hopi people refer to it as the House of Mica. The Hopi people have an ancient prophecy that says some day world leaders would gather in a Great House of Mica with rules and regulations to solve the world's problems without war. As I walked with him, I felt myself pass through another invisible doorway with the understanding that Indigenous peoples have a common awareness of a common past, a vision of a common future, and the determination to preserve that common future. Fr. Thomas Berry was keenly aware of this long-term vision and commented on this often. He understood that in partnership with indigenous peoples we have an opportunity now, amidst all of these crises, at the beginning of the millennium, to help change consciousness in a real way.

The Journey Continues

Tribal Link's work is founded on the principle that indigenous peoples should speak for themselves. Our core mission -- linking indigenous peoples to relevant networks and organizations -- provides an expanded forum for the expression of indigenous cultural perspectives and issues. This is not simply a matter of promoting human rights for indigenous peoples. Tribal Link's work also includes finding ways to publicize the unique contribution these societies can make to the preservation of the very basic human values of community, spirituality, ethics and culture, all of which are disappearing at an alarming rate as marketing and commoditization become the ruling principles globally.

At a spiritual level, I feel Tribal Link's assistance to indigenous peoples helps provide encouragement toward humanity's ability to recapture the unity of a global tribal consciousness and see itself as a single inter-connective entity. This is the type of encouragement Thomas Berry promoted in his works; helping to guide humanity's transition to sustainable ways of living and sustainable human development. Fortunately, many are now beginning to realize that the survival of indigenous and tribal peoples is intrinsically linked to the survival of all of humanity.

Whether coordinating capacity building programs to better prepare indigenous peoples at relevant United Nations meetings; supporting Maasai girls education in east Africa; organizing or participating in urgent action campaigns; facilitating opportunities for dialogue between indigenous and business or religious leaders, Tribal

Link Foundation remains deeply committed to the indigenous philosophy of introducing the dimension of the sacred into the process of global sustainability. When something is held as sacred there is a deep understanding that it must not be destroyed. It is about joining the Circle of Humanity, that sacred circle of light, and saying "yes" to the unity that exists. It is interesting that once one understands and joins the circle, one no longer has to be convinced; you just keep following your sacred map. Building caring, supportive partnerships and personal connections that assist indigenous communities and individuals meet their most pressing needs and goals are, in essence, Tribal Link's goals. From what I recall during our time together at Assisi, I feel Fr. Berry would agree that working in meaningful and respectful partnership with indigenous peoples, as well as incorporating indigenous values within the realms of ethics, politics, economics, and education, is critical if both we humans and the planet are to survive.

REFERENCES

Berry, Thomas. 1996. *"Minding the Spirit, an Ecologically Sensitive Spirituality."* Lecture at Spirituality and Sustainability Conference, Assisi, IT, June 14.

Marcos Terena presents the Kari-Oca Declaration to the United Nations Conference on Environment and Development, (UNCED) Rio, 1992". Last modified 1999. http://www.dialoguebetweennations.com/ir/english/kariocakimberley/Terena_translation.html.

32

"A UNIQUE COMMUNITY OF LIFE"
THE EARTH CHARTER IN ASSISI
A GERMAN VIEW IN A GLOBAL CONTEXT

FRANK MEYBERG

This essay will reflect on Thomas Berry's thinking and my experience of the Assisi conferences (1997-1999). It will summarize some aspects of the sustainability process in Germany since the 1970s; it will then discuss the concept of "Humanity as Part of a Vast Evolving Universe," which is Thomas Berry's visionary view of the universe. It will conclude by describing the Earth Charter drafting sessions with Steven Rockefeller and other highlights of the Assisi conferences with some reflections on other speakers and participants in the wonderful atmosphere of Assisi.

Introduction

Sustainability as a guiding principle in environmental and development policies started with the UN Brundtland Commission in the 1980s and with the Conference on Environment and Development (UNCED), the famous "Rio conference" or "Earth Summit," in June 1992 in Rio de Janeiro. "Sustainability" and "Agenda 21" have been widely used in regional and global discussions from then on.

The German equivalent of sustainability is "*Nachhaltigkeit*," and it is found already in the 18th century in the forest economy, demanding long-term cultivation of trees. Before "sustainability" became a global key word (and later on a "buzz" word), the underlying idea of temporal and spatial justice between people living all over the world, now and in the future, arose in the context of environmental problems and development goals. It is important to consider the ecumenical background in the preceding decades. Within the framework of plenary assemblies of the WCC -- the World Council of Churches -- many activities began and many NGOs were established. "The Ecumenical One World Initiative (OeIEW)" was founded in 1975/76 as a network of local groups and concerned citizens aiming at a change of personal life-style in small, realistic steps, with religious and political perspectives for the "One World." Development goals for the then so-called Third-World countries were combined with environmental goals. In the 1980s and 1990s the Conciliar Process of Justice, Peace and Integrity of Creation (JPIC) arose as a grass-roots movement as well as an official WCC programme, influencing discussions beyond the churches.

After Rio 1992, manifold dimensions of sustainability came about. INES – The International Network of Engineers and Scientists for Global Responsibility -- contributed to the public discussion with a congress in Amsterdam 1995 (Smith and Tenner 1997). Besides the scientific and technical dimensions the ethical, philosophical and spiritual dimensions of sustainability were included. The INES project "Spiritual Dimensions of Sustainability" was founded, preparing a number of events in Protestant Academies in Mülheim/Ruhr, Hamburg and Bad Segeberg, as well as a workshop during the international INES conference in Stockholm (2000).

What it means to implement principles of sustainability and justice into the German society and economy was formulated in a study called "*Zukunftsfaehiges Deutschland,*" "Sustainable Germany." The

"Wuppertal Institute for Climate, Environment and Energy" did a study on behalf of Bund (Friends of the Earth Germany) an NGO for nature conservation and environmental protection -- and of MISEREOR -- the German Catholic Bishops' Organisation for Development Cooperation. The book was an impressive combination of "Zaehlen und Erzaehlen" – a play on German words meaning "Counting, calculating, balancing of figures and index numbers" on the one hand, as well as "Telling stories/epics of empowering guiding principles for a sustainable, better world" on the other (Bund/Misereor 1996).

These are some aspects of Germany's societal and my personal history during the last decades. They have revealed problems, challenges and hopes for sustainability in a global world. They are important for us, decisive for parts of our life. But they are only a small moment in the long history of human culture and incredibly tiny in the much longer history of our Earth and the universe -- but they are connected with this long history in a special, mysterious way.

"Humanity is Part of a Vast Evolving Universe"
Thomas Berry's Vision of the Universe

Dealing with the meaning of science and religion for decades, I already knew and worked with the ideas of Teilhard de Chardin. He may not be accepted by all Christian theologians, but his combination of Christian and evolutionary thinking seems to be absolutely essential for all who are involved in the dialogue between science and religion. His mystical view of the cosmos may be strange for some people, but it is at least stimulating and inspiring. Moreover, I feel that mysticism points at important truths about our cosmos.

With Teilhard I already knew one of the sources of Berry's thinking, but unfortunately I did not know his books. In Germany they are not as well-known as they are in the United States. Only a few of them are published in German (e.g., *Das Wilde und das Heilige* in 2011). Nevertheless, in Germany and Europe "Deep Ecology" is present. Many authors, who are analysing the roots of the ecological crises, are searching very deeply in the foundation of our philosophical, scientific, psychological and spiritual thinking and actions. For me, some German philosophical and theological thinkers with a scientific background were most stimulating, e.g., Guenter Altner (Altner 1987, 1991), A.M Klaus Mueller (Mueller 1987), or Carl Friedrich von Weizsaecker (cf. Huebner 1987). My first impressions in Assisi concerning Berry were that he was highly esteemed by many participants, speakers and the organizers of the conferences. They were full of praise for his clear, far-sighted, deeply-grounded and comprehensive thinking. I was impressed by his calm and associative but determined thoughts and reflections.

What have I learned in Assisi from Berry's thoughts? Which questions were raised in me during my first attempts of understanding him? Some of his thoughts either confirmed my views or supplemented and challenged them. I took many notes at the Assisi conferences (1997) which I reviewed for this essay along with a paper I received with gratitude from Lisa Bardack, another participant at the *Spirituality and Sustainability* conference of 1997.

Berry's thoughts are at the foundation of the Earth Charter process, both in the preamble and other parts of this visionary text. The chapter "Earth, Our Home" starts with the insight that "Humanity is part of a vast Evolving Universe" (Earth Charter 2000, Preamble). For Berry, the Earth community has to look for the deeper meaning and connection between the human community and the Earth process. Most often people think of the natural world as an economic resource or as a place of recreation, giving us a moment of joy which is quite legitimate; yet this fosters a certain trivializing attitude. If we were truly moved by the beauty of the world about us, we would honour the Earth in a profound way, especially as we would recognize ourselves not simply as a human community but as genetically related to the entire community of living beings, since all species are descended from a single origin. Within the context of a very long history of the universe and the Earth, human beings can only play a rather modest, humble role in the world. We should act as stewards of the wilderness with "Respect and Care for the Wilderness of Life" (Earth Charter 2000, Chapter I).

The ecological age means living in profound communion with one another in the universe and also in economics and politics. Any particular activity must find its place within the larger pattern. In contrast to the power of the industrial companies, of politics and media, Berry sketches the idea of an organic, vivid society and economy. It is to overcome the "myth of companies" by a new myth of peace, justice, no hunger, having plenty of life. Culture and education should refer and point to the natural frame of our existence. First we should learn "nature," then reading (Meyberg 1997).

Since our sense of the divine is so extensively derived from verbal sources, mostly through biblical scriptures, we seldom notice how extensively we have lost contact with the revelation of the divine in nature. Returning to our native place may be promoted by bearing in mind indigenous people: indeed their traditional mystique of the Earth might be a guide into a viable future.

Berry is skeptical about our modern religions. He does not see them as very helpful in the crisis, because their traditions developed rather late in history. It might be better to deal with the history of the universe as we know it today from science and with the basic experiences expressed in the myths of indigenous people. When humans relate to the cosmic order, we learn participation in the universe as a mythical process. Thus, scientific and shamanic faculties could be combined. The whole world belongs together. There are no separations, but only distinctions.

Mysticism is thought to give us the creative energy we need. Berry's evocation of a mystique of the Earth is not an old-fashioned attitude, simply replaced by rational thinking. In a Ph.D. study, Caspar Soeling identifies mysticism (beside myths, rituals and ethics) as one of four fundamental elements of every religion (Soeling, 2002).

Berry's vote for the "spirituality of the shaman" (relating human and nature) is understandable (Berry 1996, 1). But does it really mean that the "spirituality of the prophet," relating God and human, is no longer helpful? Altner, who also states "Naturvergessenheit," i.e. forgetting/ignoring nature as our basis in modern thinking probably would not agree (Altner 1987).

The universe is a communion of subjects, the celebration of our existence (Berry 1996). These are true and heart-warming thoughts, giving direction to our hopes for sustainability. Or are they too harmonious? Klaus Mueller, physicist and one of the most profound, radical thinkers of the ecological crisis, carves out nature as a case of conflict "Konflikt-Fall Natur," which should not be easily harmonized (Mueller 1987). By these exemplary comments we may guess the variety of responses to Berry's thoughts, flowing into discussions and implications on the Earth Charter and its process.

Earth Charter Drafting Sessions with Steven Rockefeller & Other Highlights of the Assisi Conferences 1997-1999

In the 1998 conference the participants were dealing specifically with the Earth Charter drafts. Members of the Earth Council, the Earth Charter Committee and the Drafting Committee hosted workshops on diverse topics. Moreover, participants especially from Latin America presented a variety of vitally practical projects. One of the outstanding personalities in the discussions was Steven Rockefeller, chairperson of the Earth Charter Drafting Committee. His unassuming nature, his attitude of esteem towards everyone, his clear mind and his power of judgement were indeed impressive. All who know him will understand my words of respect for a man of high merits. I remember a participant giving a somehow polarizing comment on an Earth Charter principle. Rockefeller listened upright and with keen awareness; he thought for some time and then asked if what he meant could be expressed in a sentence that he gave -- followed by a well-worded, integrating, consensual suggestion, ready for press! This anecdote may underline that the wonderful words and the ingenious structure of the Earth Charter cannot be understood without seeing all those wonderful people participating in the drafting process with intelligence and good will, based on various experiences of life and much wisdom.

Assisi of course is the town of St. Francis, the Christian monk who treated all nature, even its wildest species, as his brother and sister. Francis became a symbol for a simple life style and material poverty, a patron saint for the environmental movement and by this a guide to sustainability. Uncounted pilgrims and tourists visit the Franciscan town every year, admiring the works of art and experiencing the spirit of this place. In 1997 when Assisi was hit by a series of heavy earthquakes destroying life and buildings, it also became a symbol for the power of nature and the vulnerability of human beings and their work.

As mentioned above, projects of INES and some Protestant Academies had started in the 1990s exploring "Spiritual Dimensions of Sustainability." In Assisi, we found ourselves not only embedded in activities similar to those all around the world, but also in the wonderful Franciscan spirit of that town. "You can become aware of St. Francis in every part of Assisi," we were informed by a resident monk. During walks and excursions as well as in lectures and talks, the necessary and promising transformations to sustainability in religion, ethics, economics, science, politics, education and the arts were discussed and became a distinct possibility. The "celebration of life" as a whole during these days really could change one's heart and life in some way, going back home differently than you had arrived! Inspiring words, vital projects and encouraging visions all occurred in what was really "A Community of Life" (Earth Charter 2000, Preamble). Even now, fifteen years later, I am deeply touched by the memories and very grateful for having been there. And during the weeks writing this essay I have booked a trip to re-visit Assisi !

Thus, sustained by a flow of enthusiastic, visionary insights and feelings, some skeptical attitudes towards ethics might be neglected. It is one of the benefits of the Earth Charter process, however, that questions and conflicts are not to be ignored, but can be picked up actively. Life and ethics, law and love can all be understood as deeply interconnected and not necessarily in contradiction.

Some Aspects of Power, Meaning & the Limits of Ethics

In a skeptical view ethics might be disapproved and rejected. Indeed, ethics may be boring, formalistic, abstract, too general, harsh etc. People often do not like ethics, and they do not like other people who are moralizing. But, general ethical principles may be so fruitful because of their integrative power! People dealing with more special topics of sustainability often say that it is helpful to see, by means of the Earth Charter, how other people all over the world may deal with different topics; but all are included into the overriding meaning of main principles like the "Respect and Care for the Community of Life" (Earth Charter 2000, Principle I).

Furthermore, ethics can be an important step for establishing law. From environmental lawyers like Klaus Bosselmann we can learn about the interaction between personal and public opinions the so-called "soft law," plus the possible expansion to "hard law" (Bosselmann 2003). And obviously we do need national and international laws for creating a sustainable world. Therefore, it was very encouraging for me to see for example the connections between the Earth Charter movement and the World Conservation Movement (IUCN -- International Union for Conservation of Nature). This institution started endorsing the Earth Charter as a guide to IUCN policy, programme and international law (IUCN 2014).

As far as ethics uses academic methods and generalized concepts, it may become estranged from real life, so-called "Lebenswelt" (life-world), as Mueller criticizes in his book (Mueller 1987). He emphasises a strong difference between ethics (allowing or banning this or that) and love, which is alive. We cannot discuss here in detail (although it would be worthwhile), how Mueller explains his position and why he is so resolute. But we may understand him when he refers to Augustine of Hippo's famous aphorism "Love and then what you will, do" ("Liebe und tu, was du dann wollen kannst"). This reminds me of a vivid discussion in Assisi (1998) about the question as to whether "love" should explicitly be named in the Earth Charter text, or if it is enough to imply a spirit of love in all of its principles. Today we know that "love" is indeed included in Principle 2, "Care for the community of Life with understanding, compassion and Love" (Earth Charter 2000, Principle 2).

Mueller's position or other objections against ethics, therefore, do not really come into conflict with the Earth Charter concept, which is more than pure ethics. The Earth Charter was subtitled and characterized as "Vision, Ethics and Action for a Just, Sustainable, and Peaceful World." Vision gives the power to the Earth Charter; ethics gives it the structure, and the action gives the confirmation. May our struggle for sustainability, justice and peace be blessed and successful!

In an essay about the Earth Charter and humanity's challenges Guenter Altner (2004) speaks highly of the special function of this document, as it combines with circumspection different dimensions of sustainability and moreover empowers people to act in an immobilized world: a world that knows a lot of alarming facts, but does not act adequately. This ethical stagnancy may be overcome by a positive outlook on life, a "Yes for Life" ("Lebensbejahung"), empowered by the attitude of "Reverence, Gratitude and Humility" (Earth Charter 2000, Preamble). With this, Altner refers to Albert Schweitzer, who stresses such a "Yes for Life and World" as a prerequisite for ethics. Ethics and "Lebensbejahung" do not form a mutual alliance with each other but rather are said to stand in such a relation that ethics arises from the basic ground of a "Yes for Life and World" (Altner 2004). This "Yes" already exists in simple plants and animals. To the same extent as beings during the process of evolution start to think this "Yes," it becomes ethical in a natural process! For Schweitzer (and Altner) the essence of ethics is a full and deep "Yes." The special situation of humans is that they realize the "Yes for Life and World" in a physical way within their bodies but they can also express it with their thinking. In an act of awareness humans can express "Yes" with their words and can creatively shape it by means of their responsibility. By this we can be released from ethical stagnancy and make up our minds to reflected actions.

In the context of the "Ecumenical One World Initiative (OeIEW)" we have been working on the process as Earth Charter Affiliate in Germany for over fifteen years [OeIEW 2014]. The UN Decade of Education for Sustainable Development (DESD, 2005-2014) gave us a good framework and further support during the past years. The OeIEW is a founding member of the "National Learning Sustainability Alliance," the UNESCO-led DESD roundtable that brings together over 100 educational institutions. Our Earth Charter education project has been recognized as an official German contribution to the Decade. We have developed Earth Charter teacher trainings that are part of required training modules for teachers in several federal states of Germany; we created a vibrant Earth Charter Youth Network, and we offer training for "Earth Charter ambassadors" who are spreading the word about the Earth Charter in diverse contexts. In this way, we are not only giving information about the Earth Charter principles but also encouraging creative ideas, methods and projects on how to put these principles into practice.

Conclusion

We started with sustainability as a global guiding principle, following Berry's visionary view of humanity as part of a vast evolving universe. We then revisited Assisi with its unique community of life, while becoming enriched by sophisticated drafting work on the Earth Charter and we were empowered by deep academic and existential insights into our human life and thinking. How to express all of this in a few pages! This is not the place for a detailed comparison of the surveyed authors with Thomas Berry. In all their attitudes towards nature and humanity I feel they share common spiritual sources. I'm very grateful for all these Assisi experiences, based on Thomas Berry's work, in an unimaginable way.

REFERENCES

Altner, Guenter. 1987. *Die Ueberlebenskrise in der Gegenwart. Ansaetze zum Dialog mit der Aatur in Naturwissens chaft und Theologie.* Darmstadt: Wissenschaftlich Buchgesellschaft.

---.1991. *Naturvergessenheit–Grundlagen einer umfassenden Bioethik.* Darmstadt: Wissenschaftliche Buchgesellschaft.

---. 2004, "Die Erd-Charta und die Aufgaben von morgen." *ECHT - Erd-Charta-Themen* Nr. 09:2-6. (Ecumenical One World Initiative, http://erdcharta.de/materialien/hintergrund/).

Bardack, Lisa. 1997. (Unpublished essay).

Berry, Thomas. 1996. "An ecologically sensitive spirituality." *Earth Ethics*, vol.8, Fall: 1-3.

Bosselmann, Klaus. 2003. "Auf dem Weg zu globalem Recht - Die Erd-Charta aus juristischer Sicht." *Initiativ Rundbrief* Nr. 104: 20-33.

Bund, Misereor, ed. 1996. *Zukunftsfaehiges Deutschland, Ein Beitrag zu einer global nachhaltigen Entwicklung; Studie des Wuppertal Instituts fuer Klima-Umwelt-Energie.* Basel, Boston, Berlin: Birkhaeuser.

Earth Charter 2000. http://www.earthcharterinaction.org/content/ Accessed February 24, 2014.

Huebner, Juergen. 1987. *Der Dialog zwischen Theologie und Naturwissenschaft. Ein bibliographischer Bericht.* Muenchen: Chr. Kaiser.

Meyberg, Frank. 1997. (Unpublished notes).

Mueller, Adolf M. Klaus. 1987. *Das unbekannte Land. Konflikt-Fall Natur. Erfahrungen und Visionen im Horizont der offenen Zeit.* Stuttgart: Radius.

OeIEW. 2014. "Ecumenical One World Initiative (OeIEW)," *Earth Charter Affiliate in Germany.* www.oeiew.de or www.erd-charta.de.

Schmitthenner, Ulrich. 1998. *Der konziliare Prozess: gemeinsam fuer Gerechtigkeit, Frieden und Bewahrung der Schoepfung.* (Pax Christi, deutsches Sekretariat, Schriftenreihe "Probleme des Friedens"). Idstein: Meinhardt.

Smith, Philip, and Armin Tenner. 1997. "Dimensions of Sustainability," *Proceedings of the Congress, Challenges of Sustainable Development.* Amsterdam 22-25 August 1996. Baden-Baden: Nomos.

Soeling, Caspar. 2002. "Der Gottesinstinkt. Bausteine fuer eine Evolutionaere Religionstheorie." PhD diss., University of Giessen.

CONCLUDING POEM

33

CAROLINA PROPHET:
POEM FOR THOMAS BERRY

DREW DELLINGER

we were dreamed
in the cores
of the stars.
like the stars,
we were meant to unfold

we were dreamed in the depths
of the undulating ocean.
like the waves,
we were meant to unfold

like bursting supernovas, birthing elements,
which crucibles give rise to creativity?

the world makes us
its instrument.

Father Thomas,
speaking for stars, in a voice
old as wind: 'origin moments
are supremely important'

what are the origins
of a prophet?

found in syllables of Sanskrit,
or Chinese characters?
in a decade of midnight prayer?

in childhood epiphanies
rising like heat?

blue Carolina sky;
dark pines;
crickets;
birds;
sunlight
on the lilies,
in the meadow,
across the creek.

born in Carolina
on the eve of the Great War,
Saturn conjoining Pluto in the sky.
raised in a world of wires and wheels,
watching dirt roads turn to pavement.

brooding intensity,
measuring loss
when others could see only progress.

white hair communing with angels of Earth

Father Thomas, reminding us
we are constantly bathed in shimmering memories
of originating radiance

we are constantly bathed in shimmering memories
of originating radiance

the psychic stars:
the conscious soil:

this thin film of atmosphere;

and only gravity
holding the sea from the stars.

when a vision of the universe takes hold
in your mind, your soul becomes vast as the cosmos.

when the mind is silent,
everything is sacred.

like the spiral
like the lotus
like the waves
like the trees
like the stars,

we were meant to unfold.

APPENDIXES

CONTRIBUTORS

Monsignor Franklyn M. Casale became President of St. Thomas University in Miami Gardens, Florida in 1994. He is a renowned scholar and lecturer on issues ranging from human trafficking to minority student education and opportunity. Monsignor Casale is active – and plays leadership roles – in numerous local, state and national associations focused on higher education, as well as various organizations dedicated to addressing social and community issues, such as homelessness, human rights, economic development and health care.

Richard Clugston, Ph.D., directs the Ethics and Spirituality Initiative for Sustainable Development of Forum 21. He is also the Co-Director of the Association of University Leaders for a Sustainable Future (ULSF). Rick was Project Coordinator for the Earth Charter Scholarship Project at the Center for Environmental and Sustainability Education at Florida Gulf Coast University from 2009-2012. He served as Executive Director of the Center for Respect of Life and Environment in Washington, DC, from 1989 to 2009.

Béatrice Colastin Skokan is the Manuscripts Librarian at the University of Miami Libraries Special Collections. Ms. Skokan received her MLIS from Florida State University. She holds an M.A. in International Studies from the University of Miami. Ms. Skokan is Sr. co-chair of the Society of American Archivists Human Rights Archives Roundtable. Her research interests include the documentation of oral, immigrant and peripheral cultures.

James Conley, Ph.D. is Professor of English and Humanities at St. Thomas University (Miami Gardens, FL) where he has taught since

1976 and where he served as Associate Dean of the Biscayne College for Liberal Arts and Social Sciences. He holds the Ph.D. in Comparative Literature from the University of Wisconsin, an MA in Italian from Middlebury College, and a BA in English from Georgetown University. He has published several articles on Petrarch, Tasso and Milton.

Anthony D. Cortese, Ph.D., is a principal of the Intentional Endowments Network to foster sustainable investing and was the founder of Second Nature, the Boston-based advocacy organization committed to creating a healthy, just and sustainable society through higher education. He was the organizer of the American College & University Presidents Climate Commitment. He is a graduate of Tufts University and the Harvard School of Public Health. He was the first Dean of Environmental Programs at Tufts University. He has written numerous articles and essays on transforming higher education.

Drew Dellinger, Ph.D., is an internationally known speaker, poet, writer and teacher who was mentored by Thomas Berry for twenty years. He is author of the poetry collection, *Love Letter to the Milky Way*, and the upcoming book, *The Mountaintop Vision: Martin Luther King's Cosmology of Connection*. Dellinger's work has appeared in books, magazines, anthologies, and films, and has been quoted in venues ranging from prison workshops, to classrooms, to climate change hearings before the US Congress.

Eugenia P. Ferrero, received her J.D. from The University of Georgia School of Law. Her publications have focused on the law, ethics and environmental issues. She is presently completing a Ph.D. in Communication. Ms. Ferrero's research interests focus on environmental communication and ethics. She participated in all of the Study

Abroad for Earth programs and the *Spirituality* and *Sustainability* conferences with Fr. Berry in Assisi.

John Grim, Ph.D. is a Senior Lecturer and Research Scholar at Yale University, where he has appointments in the School of Forestry and Environmental Studies as well as the Divinity School and the Department of Religious Studies. He teaches courses in Native American and Indigenous religions and World religions and ecology. He has undertaken field work with the Crow/Apsaalooke people of Montana and Salish people of Washington State. He has numerous published works. He is co-founder and co-director of the Forum on Religion and Ecology at Yale with Mary Evelyn Tucker.

Joe Holland, author of many books and articles, holds a Ph.D. from the University of Chicago in Social Ethics and is Professor of Philosophy & Religion at St. Thomas University in Miami Gardens, Florida, as well as Adjunct Professor in its School of Law and its School of Theology & Ministry. He serves as President of Pax Romana / Catholic Movement for Intellectual & Cultural Affairs, as Editor of Pacem in Terris Press, as Vice-Chairperson of Catholic Scholars for Worker Justice, and as a member of the International Association for Catholic Social Thought based at the University of Leuven, in Leuven, Belgium.

Hildur Jackson is trained in law and cultural sociology, permaculture design and spiritual development. She is a long-time grass roots activist and initiator with her husband of 48 years, Ross Jackson, of one of the first Danish co-housings (1972). She is a co-founder of Gaia Trust in 1987, Denmark and GEN -- The Global Ecovillage Network in 1996 and Gaia Education in 2004. She lives on the Farm Duemosegård. She has three grown sons and seven grandchildren. One of her latest books is *Hildur's Saga, Lighed, Forskellighed, Kærlighed* (2013).

Martin Kaplan, J.D., is a retired partner of the international law firm Wilmer Cutler Pickering Hale and Dorr. Kaplan received the 2009 Thomas Berry Award in recognition of his role in developing the field of religion and ecology. He has been an active leader in interreligious affairs with the American Jewish Committee, chair of the Massachusetts Board of Education, and a leader in many nonprofit organizations and foundations relating to the environment, education, the arts, and human rights.

Pamela Kraft is the founder and executive director of Tribal Link, an organization dedicated to supporting and sustaining the culture of the world's traditional peoples. Tribal Link works extensively with indigenous communities worldwide, offering innovative programs that address education, entrepreneurship, and capacity building. In 2012, Pamela was awarded the Spirit of the UN award in honor of her dedication to advocate for indigenous peoples.

Miriam MacGillis, OP is the Founder/Director of Genesis Farm, an ecological learning center in northwest New Jersey. She is a member of the Dominican Sisters of Caldwell, NJ and with her congregation has rooted the mission of Genesis Farm on the cosmological insights of Thomas Berry. For thirty-three years, Genesis Farm has been involved in the bioregion of the area, offering efforts in catalyzing its communities toward more ecologically-based agriculture, economics, education, energy, spirituality and ethics.

Peter Damian Massengill, OFM Conv was elected in 2013 as the Major Superior of the Conventual Franciscan Friars in Great Britain and Ireland. Prior to that he was elected Minister Provincial of the Province of Our Lady of Consolation until 2007 when he was elected Guardian of the Friary of the Twelve Holy Apostles, the General Headquarters in Rome. In 1990 the Minister General appointed him

General Delegate for the International Commission for Justice, Peace and the Safeguarding of Creation in Assisi, where he served until 2007.

Rashni Mayur, Ph.D. was the director of IISF, International Institute for Sustainable Future, Mumbai, India. He has written thousands of articles and in 2000-2001 he had his own very successful radio program: "A voice from the South," reaching all over the US. He was a strong and passionate advocate for a global environment and for the less privileged people of the South. Dr. Mayur was also a poet and his poetry has been compared to the work of Rumi expressing a new paradigm with eternal truths through a passionate and archetypal language.

Gary N. McCloskey, O.S.A., Ph.D. is the former Vice President of Academic Affairs and Professor of Education at Saint Thomas University, Miami, FL. He is a multigenerational and intercultural educator with specializations in Augustinian pedagogy, instructional technology, social justice and geriatric care. He currently serves as the Executive Director of the Federation of Augustinians of North America (FANA) co-ordinating the inter-provincial work of the North American provinces of the Roman Catholic Religious Order of Saint Augustine (O.S.A.).

Frank Meyberg holds a Ph.D. in Environmental Trace Element Analysis with theology as a minor. He is a Lecturer at the University of Hamburg (Analytical Chemistry, Teacher Training) and at the Lutheran University of Applied Sciences in Nuernberg. As a member of the board of OeIEW -- Ecumenical One World Initiative -- he introduced the Earth Charter project for Germany. Special fields of interest are: dialogue between science and religion ("Nature and Spirit"), and sustainable life-styles.

Rodney Petersen, Ph.D. serves as executive director of The Lord's Day Alliance, and as interim executive director of Cooperative Metropolitan Ministries in Boston. He was executive director of the Boston Theological Institute (BTI), the consortium of theological schools, seminaries, and university divinity schools in the Greater Boston area. He has taught in BTI member schools and overseas; has facilitated workshops on restorative justice; was co-founder of the Religion and Conflict Transformation program centered at Boston University School of Theology.

Lauren Ross was Urban Conservation Director of Field Museum (2004 -2013); and presently is the Museum Research Associate. Since 2010 she has been on Illinois Endangered Species Protection Board. She was Director of the Conservation Programs at The Nature Conservancy, Illinois chapter (1992 – 2004); prior to that she was Director of North Park Village Nature Center, Chicago (1983 -1992). Since 1990 she has been a Volunteer Steward, at the North Branch Restoration Project. Ross was ordained as a Soto Zen Buddhist priest in 2014.

Fred vom Saal received a Ph.D. in neuroscience from Rutgers University. He served on the National Academy of Sciences Committee on Hormonally Active Agents in the Environment; is an elected fellow of the American Association for the Advancement of Science; a recipient of the Heinz Foundation Award in environmental science; the Environmental Health Hero Award from the Clean Med Association, and the Upstream Award from the Jenifer Altman Foundation. He has published over 200 articles. He is Curators' Professor at the University of Missouri-Columbia.

Karl-Ludwig Schibel, sociologist, has taught for twenty years social ecology at the University of Frankfurt. He was a co-founder of the Climate Alliance of European Cities and coordinates Alleanza per il Clima Italia. He coordinates since 1988 the Fair of Practical Utopias -

- a small think-tank for territorial self-sustainable in Città di Castello, Italy. He is the president of an agricultural cooperative, writes columns in two journals on ecological life style; elaborates with Wolfgang Sachs the yearly colloquium of Toblach.

Steve Snider was born and raised in North Carolina, but has called Oakland, California, home since 1997. He received a Bachelor of Arts degree in Contemporary Religious Studies from Prescott College in 1994 and his Master of Arts degree in Humanities and Leadership from New College of California in 1999. He is the co-owner of Oakland Venue Management, Inc. and works as the District Manager for the Downtown Oakland and Lake Merritt-Uptown District Associations. He has been a student of Thomas Berry's work for over 25 years.

Brian Thomas Swimme is a professor at the California Institute of Integral Studies in San Francisco where he teaches courses on the evolutionary cosmology to graduate students in the humanities. He received his Ph.D. from the Department of Mathematics at the University of Oregon in 1978 for work in gravitational dynamics. Swimme is the author of numerous books and videos. He hosted and co-wrote the Emmy award winning film "Journey of the Universe" (http://www.storyoftheuniverse.org/products page/dvd/ journey-of-the-universe/), broadcast on PBS television stations nation-wide. The *Journey of the Universe* book, eBook and educational series are published by Yale University Press.

Roberto Tagliaferri, Ph.D., teaches theology at the Istituto di Liturgia Pastorale di Santa Giustina in Padova, Italy. He specializes in the aesthetic language of rites and epistemological problems. His research deals with the various areas of cultural debates focusing on their "scientific" aspect. He has written extensive books on theology, aesthetics, architecture, and the arts. His last book is *'Pagan' Christianity in Popular Religion* (2014).

Mary Evelyn Tucker, Ph.D., is a Senior Lecturer and Senior Research Scholar at Yale University where she teaches in a joint master's program between the School of Forestry & Environmental Studies and the Divinity School where she directs the Forum on Religion and Ecology with John Grim. In 2011 Tucker completed the "Journey of the Universe" with Brian Swimme, which includes a book from Yale University Press, an Emmy award winning film on PBS and Netflix, and an educational series of 20 interviews.

Jacqueline Wagner, born in Austria, studied export, economics and civil engineering. As a global entrepreneur she enhances the need for renewable energies. As former chairperson of the *International Institute for Global Ethics* she promoted the Earth Charter. She was guest lecturer at the International University of Vienna. She is the author of seven books on emotional education and one novel. She is the founder and director of the International Academy for Emotional Education.

LETTER FROM THOMAS BERRY

July 22, 93

Dear Elizabeth,

Such a joy to be with you in Assisi. Each year the experience has been more exhilarating! This time with Brian and the exciting group of students it was a more grand experience than ever. It requires an infinite amount of concern and energy on your part, I am sure. Yet it has achieved so much for the students. The experience has awakened them to thoughts, experiences and possibilities in their lives that they would never have discovered otherwise. For me it has been a learning as well as a teaching experience. The overall significance of what you are doing can be seen, I think, especially in Drew & Steve and Richard and so many others.

Perhaps I am more indebted to you than anyone else. You have enabled me to present my thoughts to some of the more significant of the younger generation in an unforgettable setting. I often think of yourself and your work at St. Thomas University. Your experience at creative relations with the next generation and providing them with both the knowledge and the discipline of thought that they will need, is not entirely different from my own experience. Even when we succeed in some limited way, we find it difficult to accept the limits; it seems inadequate in relation to the effort.

I look forward to reading your translations of the poet you mention. Then too perhaps you will publish some of your own poetry. Meanwhile it would be a great source of jubilation for myself to know that you are finishing your own academic work, while this sometimes seems aimless, it serves some minimum purposes and it provides a way into future possibilities that would be less available otherwise. Somehow we must go through the pathologies of the late Cenozoic before we emerge into the Ecozoic. In this regard I am recommending these days the reading of the book by Clarissa P. Estés, Women who Run with the Wolves (Ballentine Books 1992). You have no doubt heard of it, possibly have read it already. It complements much of my own thinking concerning wilderness and the wild — that I tried to present in Ecuador.

I could write forever on these thoughts of mine and my appreciation of your own work. Hopefully I will be able to put some of these thoughts of mine into my other writing on the 20th century, and my thoughts with the 21st century, for the younger generation. If perchance these experiences and these thoughts would assist somewhat in the activities task assigned to them in the larger purposes of the universe.

I am much interested in your thoughts concerning 1994 — what I might be able to contribute — — I would be especially concerned not to enfuse my duties so much as I did for this year.

My best to yourself and Eugenia and all your students this at C.I. Thomas.

Norm Berry

PHOTOGRAPHS

THOMAS BERRY IN ITALY

Thomas Berry walking to S.A.F.E
with music composer Maia Aprahamian, Assisi, 1991

Brian Swimme teaching physics
in the fields of San Damiano, Assisi, 1993

S.A.F.E. students in Thomas Berry's Dante course in Sacro Convento, Basilica di San Francesco, Assisi, 1993

Thomas Berry teaching in Assisi's park, 1993

*Thomas Berry with Rashmi Mayur and Hilda Jackson
during a break of the Spirituality and Sustainability Conference, Assisi, 1997*

*Special sweet treats for Thomas Berry
by the chef of Hotel Posta, Assisi, 1996*

*Reception for Spirituality and Sustainability Conference
by the Franciscan Friars Commission for Justice, Peace, and the
Safeguarding of Creation, Assisi, 1997*

*Thomas Berry as main speaker at Spirituality and Sustainability Conference
With Mary Evelyn Tucker and Colonel Caldari at City Hall, Assisi, 1997*

Thomas Berry with the Mayor of Bari, 2003

*A moment of humor with Stefano Parmigiani and the Mayor of Bari
On the occasion of Thomas Berry receiving the 2003 Federico II Award for Peace
From the City of Andria, Bari, 2003*

Thomas Berry with Elisabeth Ferrero, Roberto Tagliaferri, Joe Holland, the Ambassador of Japan, the Japanese artisti Yumiko, and the Italian artist Sabino Ventura at the official presentation of the book La Carta dell Terra: Manuale di Riflessione per l'Azione, *by Elisabeth Ferrrero and Joe Holland, translated by Giovanni Principato and Paolo Diotallevi, Rome, 2003*

Elisabeth Ferrero translating Thomas Berry's presentation at the Federico II Award for Peace, the Coppa della Fraternitá, given to Thomas for his life-long dedication to a holistic paradigm respecting all forms of Creation.
Castel del Monte, City of Andria, Bari, 15 March 2003

*First Occasional Seminar: The Earth Charter,
with plenary address by Thomas Berry, flanked by Elisabeth Ferrero,
Roberto Tagliaferri, Sr. Cathy Arrata, SSND, and Joe Holland.
Generalate of the School Sisters of Notre Dame, Rome, 2003*

Thomas Berry with the Japanese artist, Yumiko. Rome, 2003

Thomas Berry with the Ambassador of Japan and the artist Sabino Ventura who created the Murano glass Coppa della Fraternita' given to Thomas Berry. Rome, 2003

Spirituality and Sustainability Conference participants, Assisi, 1996

*S.A.F.E. in the arms of Thomas Berry,
Assisi, 1993*

www.ingramcontent.com/pod-product-compliance
Lightning Source LLC
Chambersburg PA
CBHW070933230426
43666CB00011B/2425